EUROPEAN HANDI

FREN
RAILWAYS
LOCOMOTIVES & MULTIPLE UNITS

THIRD EDITION

The complete guide to all Locomotives
and Multiple Units of the Railways of France

David Haydock and Peter Fox

Published by Platform 5 Publishing Ltd., Wyvern House, Sark Road, Sheffield S2 4HG, England.
Printed in England by Hubbard Print, Dronfield, Sheffield.
ISBN 1 872524 87 7

▲ BB 6527 in Grand Confort livery passes Marseillan Plage with the 08.02 Narbonne–Marseille on 3rd June 1994. **Chris Wilson**

Front Cover Photograph: BB 9318 near Béziers with the 12.05 Nice–Bordeaux on 6th June 1995. **Chris Wilson**

Rear Cover Photograph: RGP X 2738/7738 at Morez on 3rd June 1996 forming the 09.23 Dole Ville–St. Claude. This set is the only member of the class in red livery. **Peter Fox**

CONTENTS

INTRODUCTION TO THIRD EDITION

Welcome to the long awaited third edition of French Railways, which contains full details of all locomotives and multiple units of the Société Nationale des Chemins de Fer Français, hereafter referred to as the SNCF. In this edition, we have fully updated the SNCF section and sought to expand the section on minor railways. We have therefore included more extensive details of CFTA, CFD's Class 20 diesels, the fleets of four track maintenance companies, the Lorraine coal field network and RATP's fleet for Paris RER lines. We have also vastly expanded the section on ex SNCF locos in industrial service. Data is updated to April 1999.

The main changes since the 1991 edition are the expanding TGV fleet – now running to six main types with increasingly complex sub-series. In the last eight years, in contrast, the locomotive fleet has evolved very slowly. SNCF slowed down the introduction of new Class BB 26000 electrics, meaning many types to be replaced have continued in service. The delivery of new shunters has now finished and there are still no new diesels on the horizon! In contrast, delivery of new double-deck EMUs to the Paris region has continued apace, leading to a cascade of stock and slow withdrawal of older types. The biggest trend is towards the involvement of the 22 regional councils in transport planning and financing new stock or refurbishment. The regions are very much behind the designs of a new single railcar, two-car DMU and two-car double-deck EMU. Recent years have also been marked by increasing specialisation of locos and stock. Although SNCF has not been fully "sectorised" like British Railways, new modifications for specific duties now tend to be limited to smaller numbers of locos.

Since the last edition, the following types have become extinct:

BB 300, BB 4200, BB 4730, BB 9400, BB 10000, BB 13000, CC 14100, BB 20011/12, CC 21000, CC 40100, A1AA1A 62000, BB 66600, T 1000, XR 7800, X 94750, Y BL, Z 5100, Z 6000.

The following new types have been introduced:

TGV Duplex, Thalys, BB 80000, BB 88500, BB 9600, BB 9700, BB 36000, X 72500, X 73500, Z 22500, Z 23500, Z 92050.

The next five years will see the introduction of several new types:

- 90 BB 27000 dual-voltage electric locos for freight.
- 30 BB 37000 tri-voltage electric locos for freight.
- 139 X 73500 single, lightweight railcars.
- 2 X 74500 two-car, metre-gauge panoramic DMUs for the Blanc-Argent line.
- 32 Z 20500 four-car double-deck EMUs for Paris RER line C.
- 22 Z 24500 three-car 200 km/h EMUs for regional services.

New electrics are expected to replace Classes CC 7100, BB 8100 and BB 12000 within 2 years.

As usual, the author welcomes sightings and other fresh information, particularly on locos sold to industry.

To keep this book up to date, subscribe to **Today's Railways**, a monthly magazine produced by Platform 5 which gives updates of SNCF allocations plus details of usage and some loco diagrams.

ABBREVIATIONS

Standard abbreviations used in this book are:

km/h	kilometres per hour
kN	kilonewtons
kW	kilowatts
DB	Deutsche Bahn AG (German Railway)
EU	Eurostar (UK) Ltd
NS	Nederlandse Spoorwegen (Netherlands Railways)
RRR	Rames Réversibles Régionales (regional push-pull hauled sets)
RATP	Regie Autonome des Transports Parisiens (Paris Transport Authority)
SNCB	Société Nationale des Chemins de Fer Belgesi (Belgian Railways)
Length	Length over couplings or buffers
Power	One hour rating
T.E.	Tractive Effort

PASSENGER VEHICLE TYPE CODES

The vehicle type codes used in France are as follows:

T	Turbotrain driving motor.
TGV	TGV driving motor.
TGVZ	TGV vehicle with one power bogie.
X	Diesel railcar or multiple unit driving motor.
Z	Electric multiple unit driving motor.
R	indicates a trailer vehicle. (French=remorque).
A	1st Class.
B	2nd Class.
D	Luggage, i.e., vehicle with luggage space and guard's compartment.
r	Catering vehicle.
P	Post, i.e., vehicle with compartment(s) for mail (and guard).
x	indicates a driving trailer.

Examples:

XBD	Second class DMU driving motor with luggage/guard's compartment.
ZRABx	Composite EMU driving trailer.

Note – The continental system does not differentiate between open and compartment stock, but all railcars and multiple unit vehicles are open.

Under 'accommodation' are shown the number of 1st and 2nd class seats, followed by the number of toilets, e.g. 24/49 1T indicates 24 first class seats, 49 second class seats and one toilet.

ACKNOWLEDGEMENTS

We would like to thank all who helped prepare this book, especially Bernard Collardey, Eric Dunkling and Brian Garvin.

INTRODUCTION (FRANÇAIS)

Bienvenue à la troisième édition du livre "French Railways" qui contient des détails de tout le matériel moteur des chemins de fer de l'État français (SNCF) ainsi que plusieurs autres réseaux en France.

FORMAT DU LIVRE

Malgré l'utilisation de la langue de Shakespeare, ce livre est assez facile d'utilisation pour quelqu'un avec quelques notions d'anglais. Chaque série de locomotives, d'autorails ou d'automotrices est décrite par biais d'une fiche technique. Ensuite, chaque machine est répertoriée avec son numéro de série et un code de deux lettres qui indique son dépôt d'affectation. Les codes ne sont pas officiels et sont expliqués sous le titre SNCF DEPOTS.

Eventuellement, d'autres lettres ou symboles indiquent la livrée (les codes sont indiqués au sous le titre SNCF LIVERY CODES) ou un aménagement spécial – par exemple, la reversabilité – dont le code est indiqué dans la fiche technique. La plupart des séries SNCF sont illustrées en couleurs.

Après la première partie du livre sur la SNCF vient celle sur les autres réseaux et exploitants (PRIVATE RAILWAYS). Vers la fin du livre nous incluons un listing de locomotives SNCF en service industriel (ex SNCF LOCOMOTIVES IN INDUSTRIAL USE) ou préservées (PRESERVED LOCOMOTIVES AND MULTIPLE UNITS) et une section sur les lignes musées (MUSEUMS AND MUSEUM LINES).

Vous pourrez garder ce livre à jour en vous abonnant au magazine mensuel Today's Railways; produit par l'éditeur de ce livre. Voir la publicité à l'arrière de ce livre.

Bienvenue à la troisième Édition du livre "French Railways" qui contient des détails de tout le matériel moteur des chemins de fer de l'État français (SNCF) ainsi que plusieurs autres réseaux en France.

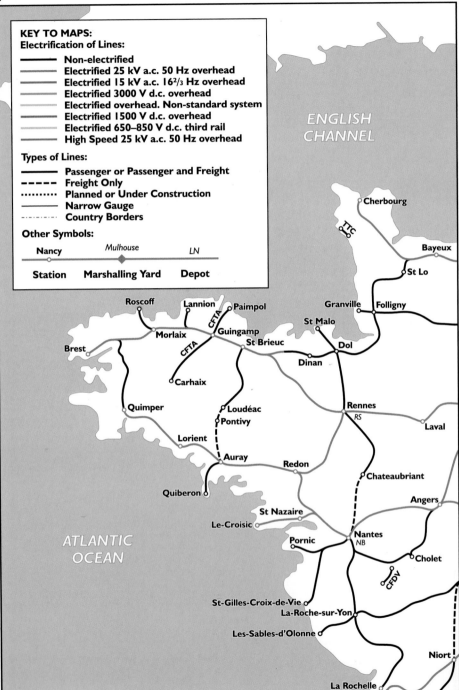

KEY TO MAPS:
Electrification of Lines:

- ─────── Non-electrified
- ─────── Electrified 25 kV a.c. 50 Hz overhead
- ─────── Electrified 15 kV a.c. 16²/₃ Hz overhead
- ─────── Electrified 3000 V d.c. overhead
- ─────── Electrified overhead. Non-standard system
- ─────── Electrified 1500 V d.c. overhead
- ─────── Electrified 650–850 V d.c. third rail
- ─────── High Speed 25 kV a.c. 50 Hz overhead

Types of Lines:

- ─────── Passenger or Passenger and Freight
- ─ ─ ─ ─ Freight Only
- ·········· Planned or Under Construction
- ─────── Narrow Gauge
- ·─··─··─·· Country Borders

Other Symbols:

Nancy —— *Mulhouse* ◆ *LN* ——

Station   Marshalling Yard   Depot

ENGLISH CHANNEL

ATLANTIC OCEAN

Cherbourg
TTC
Bayeux
St Lo
Granville Folligny
Roscoff Lannion Paimpol
CFTA
St Malo
Morlaix Guingamp
Brest CFTA St Brieuc Dol
Dinan
Carhaix
Quimper Loudéac Rennes
Pontivy RS
Laval
Lorient
Auray Redon
Chateaubriant
Quiberon Angers
St Nazaire
Le-Croisic Nantes
Pornic NB Cholet
CFDV
St-Gilles-Croix-de-Vie
La-Roche-sur-Yon
Les-Sables-d'Olonne
Niort
La Rochelle

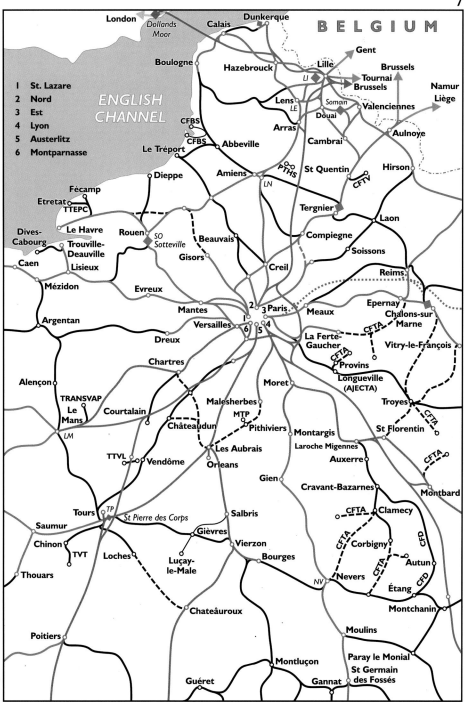

1 St. Lazare
2 Nord
3 Est
4 Lyon
5 Austerlitz
6 Montparnasse

BELGIUM

LUXEMBOURG

GERMANY

SWITZERLAND

Givet
Gouvy
Koblenz
Charleville-Mézières
Brussels
Trier
Luxembourg
Longwy
Longuyon
Apach
Thionville *TV*
Saarbrücken
Mannheim
Verdun
Woippy *HBL*
Winden
Conflans-Jarny
Metz
Béning
Sarreguemines
MZ
Bitche
Wissembourg
Niederbronn
Lauterbourg
Bar-le-Duc
Reding
Toul
Nancy
Hausbergen *SB*
Karlsruhe
CFBD
St Dizier
Strasbourg
Offenburg
St Dié
Selestat
Epinal
CFTR
Chaumont
Merrey
Metzeral
Colmar
Remiremont
Freiburg-im-Breisgau
Mulhouse
Kruth
Mülheim
CY
Culmont-Chalindrey
Mulhouse
Belfort
Vesoul
Basel
CFTA
Biel
Olten
Dijon
Dijon
DP
Gray
Besançon
Gevrey
Dole
Biel/Bienne
Mouchard
Chagny
Frasne
Pontarlier
Le Locle
CFTPV
Vallorbe
Morez
Lausanne
St Amour
Mâcon
Bourg-en-Bresse
Genève
Evian
Annemasse

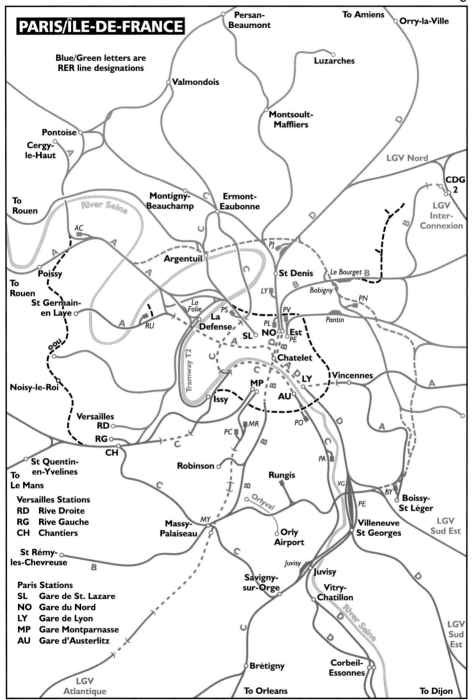

PARIS/ÎLE-DE-FRANCE

Blue/Green letters are
RER line designations

Persan-Beaumont

To Amiens

Orry-la-Ville

Luzarches

Valmondois

Montsoult-Maffliers

Pontoise

Cergy-le-Haut

LGV Nord

CDG 2

LGV Inter-Connexion

To Rouen

AC

River Seine

Montigny-Beauchamp

Ermont-Eaubonne

PJ

Argentuil

St Denis

Le Bourget B

Poissy

To Rouen

LY

Bobigny

PN

St Germain-en Laye

La Folie

PS

La Défense

PV

Pantin

RU

PL

SL NO

Est

PE

Chatelet

Noisy-le-Roi

Tramway T2

Issy

MP

AU

LY

Vincennes

Versailles RD

MR

PO

RG

PC

CH

PA

St Quentin-en-Yvelines

Robinson

Rungis

To Le Mans

Orlyval

VG

BY

Boissy-St Léger

Versailles Stations
RD   Rive Droite
RG   Rive Gauche
CH   Chantiers

Massy-Palaiseau

MY

PE

Villeneuve St Georges

LGV Sud Est

St Rémy-les-Chevreuse

B

Orly Airport

Juvisy

Juvisy

Paris Stations
SL   Gare de St. Lazare
NO   Gare du Nord
LY   Gare de Lyon
MP   Gare Montparnasse
AU   Gare d'Austerlitz

Savigny-sur-Orge

Vitry-Chatillon

River Seine

LGV Sud Est

LGV Atlantique

Brétigny

To Orleans

Corbeil-Essonnes

To Dijon

Ruffec

Rochefort

Saintes

CFTS

Royan

Pointe-de-Grave

Angoulême

LG Limoges

Felletin

Meymac

Ussel

Tulle

ATLANTIC
OCEAN

TTGM

Coutras

Périgueux

Brive

Libourne Bergerac

Sarlat

Bordeaux

BD

Hourcade

Le Buisson

Aurillac

Arcachon

Facture

Marmande

Cahors

Figeac
QUERCY
RAIL

Capdenac

Rodez

CFLG

Agen

Morcenx

Roquefort

Mont-de-Marsan

Montauban

Albi

Tessonières

Dax

Hagetmau

Auch

St Jory

Toulouse
TL

Castres

Bayonne
Biarritz

Puyôo

Mazamet

HE
Hendaye
Irun CF DE LA RHUNE

Oloron
Sainte
Marie

Pau

Tarbes

Carcassonne

St Jean-Pied-
de-Port

Lourdes

Montréjeau

Foix

Quillan

Luchon

Ax-les-Thermes

L' Hospitalet

Villefranche-
Vernet-
le-Bains

Le
Boulou-
Perthus

La Tour-de-Carol

Puigcerda

SPAIN

Barcelona

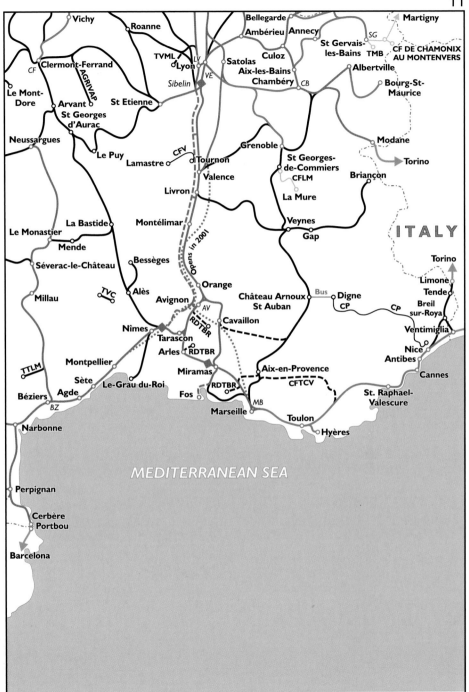

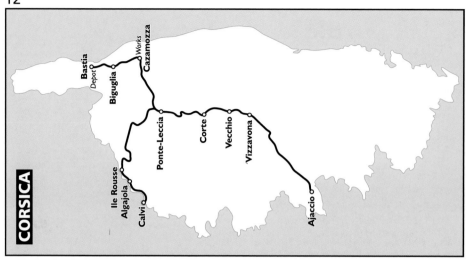

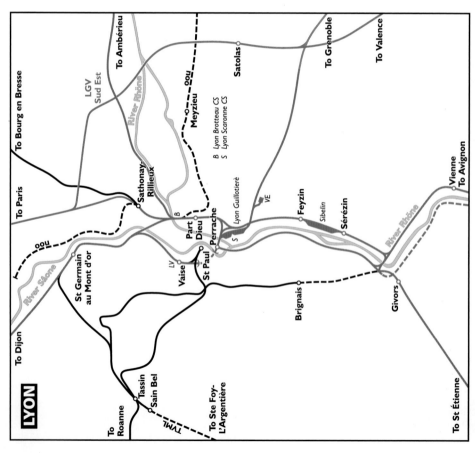

1. SOCIÉTÉ NATIONALE DES CHEMINS DE FER FRANÇAIS (SNCF)

SNCF (French National Railways) was formed in 1937 when several private companies were nationalised. These formed the basis of the SNCF "Réseaux" or systems/networks. They were:

1. Est (East)–former CF de l'Est.
2. Nord (North)–former CF du Nord.
3. Ouest (West)–former CF d'État.
4. Sud Ouest (South West)–former PO-Midi.
5. Sud Est (South East)–former CF PLM.

These areas remained stable for many years but réseaux 1 and 2 have been combined into a new region "Nord-Est" and 3 and 4 are now combined to form the "Atlantique" region.

NUMBERING SYSTEM

The SNCF numbering system for steam locomotives was based on axle grouping so that a 4–6–2 became a 231 etc. Class letters then followed the axle details and then came the running number. eg 231 E 22. For tank locomotives an additional T followed the axle arrangement eg 141 TC 8.

No electric locomotives were renumbered on the formation of SNCF. Most locos came from the PO-Midi system with just a few others from the État and PLM. Those delivered to SNCF between 1938–50 continued the PO-Midi series. However from 1950 a new system was introduced bringing the locomotives somewhat into line with the steam system, but here the axle arrangement was shown by letters so that a BoBo became a BB.

Diesel locomotives were originally given a steam type number with an additional D in the number after the axle arrangement e.g. 040 DA 1 but in 1960 the whole fleet was renumbered into the present system.

SNCF traction is numbered in several different ways. eg BB 7250, CC 6505, A1AA1A 68001, T 2001, X 2101, Y 8101, Z 6101.

In this book locomotive numbers are listed without their prefix letters, but letter prefixes are used for multiple unit power cars or shunting tractors. (NB: not all locomotives carry their prefixes).

Electric locomotives:

Electric Locomotives are numbered in the following ranges:

```
   1– 9999   d.c. locomotives.
10000–19999   a.c. locomotives.
20000–29999   Dual voltage locomotives.
30000–39999   Triple voltage locomotives.
40000–49999   Quadruple voltage locomotives.
```

Examples: BB 8500, DC locomotive with BB axle arrangement; BB 17000, AC locomotive with BB axle arrangement; BB 25500 dual voltage locomotive of same type. (8500+17000=25500).

Diesel locomotives:

Diesel Locomotives are numbered in the following ranges:

```
50000–51999   Diesel locomoteurs (No longer in stock).
60000–79999   Diesel locomotives.
```

Shunting locos ("locotracteurs") are prefixed Y and numbered between 2201–9999.

Multiple units:

"T" denotes a turbotrain, power car numbers ranging between 1001 and 2082.
"X" denotes a DMU, power car numbers ranging between 2101 and 4999.
"Z" denotes an EMU, power car numbers ranging between 3711 and 9636.

Diesel and electric units owned or subsidised by local authorities or other "third parties" have their numbers prefixed by "9". e.g. EMUs. Z 97381–97384 belong to the local regions and are the same as Class Z 7300.

Trains à Grande Vitesse:

TGV power cars are numbered as 2, 3 or 4-voltage locomotives but they also carry a set number, e.g. TGV power cars 23001/2 are set 01 and can be referred to as TGV 01.

There can be some confusion with the present numbering system. 7301 can be a BB electric locomotive, an EMU, or a tractor. SNCF have recognised this problem and a new numbering system has been devised to eliminate duplicate numbers. In future locomotives will be numbered up to 499 in a series and 500 upwards will be an m.u. of some description. e.g. 11001–499 would be a.c. electric locomotives, 11500–999 would be a.c. EMUs. It is not at present intended to renumber any existing stock.

Activity or Sector Prefixes:

In 1999, SNCF introduced prefixes to existing locomotive numbers to designate the activity to which the unit belongs. Prefixes are 1 for "Grandes Lignes" or long distance passenger, 4 for "Fret SNCF" or freight, 5 for "Action Régionale" or regional passenger, 6 for "Infrastructure" and 8 for "Île-de-France" or the Paris region. Other prefixes are not used. These prefixes will, in principle, be applied only in front of the transfer number on the side of the loco, not on the front end, and not at all to locos which have cast numbers. As we completed this book in May 1999, application of the prefixes was still patchy. In the case of the BB 63000 group of diesel locos, used mainly for shunting, a final decision on prefixes had not been made.

SNCF DEPOTS

The following unofficial depot codes are used in this book. SNCF's traction and operating departments have different codes for depots ranging from one to three letters. Those used by the traction department are not widely known or used:

AC	Achères		NV	Nevers
AV	Avignon		PA	Paris Vitry (les Ardoines)*
BD	Bordeaux		PC	Paris Châtillon
BZ	Béziers		PE	Paris Sud Est
CB	Chambéry		PJ	Paris Les Jonchérolles§
CF	Clermont Ferrand		PL	Paris La Chapelle
CY	Chalindrey		PN	Paris Noisy-le-Sec†
DP	Dijon Perrigny		PO	Paris Sud Ouest
DV	Dijon Ville		PS	Paris St. Lazare
HE	Hendaye		PV	Paris La Villette
LE	Lens		RS	Rennes
LG	Limoges		SB	Strasbourg
LI	Lille Champ-de-Mars		SG	St. Gervais les Bains
LM	Le Mans		SO	Sotteville
LN	Longueau		TL	Toulouse
LV	Lyon Vaise		TP	Tours St. Pierre
LY	Le Landy (Paris)		TV	Thionville
MB	Marseille Blancarde		VE	Vénissieux
MR	Montrouge		VF	Villefranche de Conflent
MZ	Metz		VG	Villeneuve St. Georges
NB	Nantes Blottereau			

* sub-shed of Paris Sud Ouest.
§ sub-shed of Paris La Chapelle.
† sub-shed of Paris La Villette.

The following depot codes of other railway companies are also used:

BY	Boissy St. Leger (RATP)		NP	London North Pole (Eurostar)
FF	Brussels Forest (SNCB/NMBS)		RU	Rueil-Malmaison (RATP)
MY	Massy (RATP)			

The following abbreviations are used after the depot code:

(D) Departmental use.
(S) Stored servicable.
(U) Stored unservicable.

STABLING POINTS

The main depots and the codes used for them are listed for convenience on page 176 at the end of this book. Generally speaking, depots have large allocations but many locomotives and units are stabled at other places. A list of the most important stabling points is shown below with an approximate number of how many locomotives might be found there on an average Sunday.

Réseau Nord-Est (North-East Area):

Stabling Point	Locos	Stabling Point	Locos
Amiens	20	Le Bourget (Paris)	40
Aulnoye	25	Longwy	10
Belfort	15	Mohon	20
Blainville	20	Mulhouse Ville	15
Châlons-sur-Marne	25	Nancy	15
Conflans-Jarny	15	Petit Thérain (Creil)	15
Forbach	15	Reims	25
Fives (Lille)	20	Somain	25
Fréthun (Calais)	35	Tergnier	20
Grande Synthe (Dunkerque)	30	Troyes	10
Hausbergen (Strasbourg)	40	Vaires (Paris)	15
La Délivrance (Lille)	20	Woippy	25
La Plaine (Paris)	15		

Réseau Atlantique (Western Area):

Stabling Point	Locos	Stabling Point	Locos
Batignolles (Paris)	10	Poitiers	10
Bourges	10	Sotteville yard (Rouen)	20
Brive	10	St. Jory (Toulouse)	20
Caen	25	Tarbes	10
La Rochelle Ville	10	Thouars	10
Le Havre	20	Trappes	25
Le Mans Ville	20	Vaugirard (Paris)	10
Les Aubrais (Orléans)	25	Vierzon	25

Réseau Sud-Est (South-East Area):

Stabling Point	Locos	Stabling Point	Locos
Ambérieu	25	Modane	20
Besançon	10	Narbonne	10
Cerbère	25	Nîmes	30
Dole	10	Nice St. Roch	20
Grenoble	25	Portes-les-Valence	10
Laroche-Migennes	25	Paris Charolais	25
Lyon Mouche	25	St. Étienne	15
Marseille St. Charles	25	St. Jean-de-Maurienne	15
Miramas	60	Sibelin	25

WORKSHOPS

The SNCF has no really large locomotive works, but has kept open many pre-nationalisation workshops. Each of these deals with specific classes for major overhauls. Rationalisation is continuing and Béziers works is under particular threat. Bordeaux and La Folie works have closed since the last edition, whilst Tours is doing much more work. Increasing amounts of work are being farmed out to depots.

Workshop	Types overhauled
Béziers	CC 1100, BB 8100/80000, BB 8500/88500, BB 9600, Z 100.
Bischheim (Strasbourg)	TGV Sud-Est.
Epernay	BB 12000, BB 16500, BB 17000, CC 65500.

Hellemmes (Lille)	TGV Sud-Est, TGV Postal, TGV Duplex, TGV Atlantique, TGV Réseau, Thalys, Eurostar. Hellemmes also "manages" SNCF-owned Class 92 locos.
Le Mans	X 4300, X 4500, X 4630, X 4750, X 4790, X 4900, T 1500.
Nevers	BB 62400, BB 63400, BB 63500, BB 64700, BB 66000, BB 66400, BB 66700, X 2100, X 2200, X 2400, X 2720, X 2800, X 3800, X 72500, X 73500, XR 6000, XR 6200, Y 7100, Y 7400, Y 8000, Y 8400.
Oullins (Lyon)	CC 6500, CC 7100, BB 7200, BB 9200, BB 9300, BB 9700, BB 15000, BB 16000, BB 16100, BB 20200, BB 22200, BB 25100, BB 25150, BB 25200, BB 26000, BB 36000, Z 600, Z 800, Z 7100, Z 7300, Z 7500, Z 9500, Z 9600, Z 11500.
Quatres Mares (Rouen)	BB 25500, BB 63000, BB 64800, BB 67000, BB 67200, BB 67300, BB 67400, A1AA1A 68000, A1AA1A 68500, CC 72000.
Tours	Z 5300, Z 5600, Z 6100, Z 6300, Z 6400, Z 8800, Z 20500, Z 22500, Z 23500.
Massy (RATP)	Z 8100.

SNCF LIVERY CODES

The following codes for liveries are either used in number lists or in class introductory notes:

A TGV Atlantique livery. Metallic grey with blue window band.

B White with a blue window band. Adopted by the regions Centre, Basse Normandie, Champagne-Ardennes, Pays de la Loire, Midi-Pyrenées, Franche-Comté and Provence-Alpes-Côte d'Azur.

C Cement grey with orange bands. Standard 1980s/90s electric loco livery.

D Blue and grey with white lining. Standard main-line diesel livery.

E Blue-green with white lining or aluminium trim. The old standard livery for passenger or mixed traffic electrics.

F Fret SNCF livery. Two-tone grey with green ends. To be applied to Class BB 27000.

G White with green window band. Adopted by the regions Auvergne, Bretagne and Haute Normandie.

I Île-de-France livery for greater Paris region. White with blue window bands plus red doors and front ends on EMUs. White with blue and red panels on Class BB 8500, BB 17000 and BB 25500 locos.

J Orange with brown lining. Now the standard shunting loco livery.

K Pale grey with red band lined in orange. Grand Confort livery. CC 6500 and BB 15000.

M "Massif Central". Blue with a white window band. This was the standard multiple unit/railcar livery in the 1970s/80s.

N Non-standard. Refer to text.

O Orange with white bands. Turbotrains.

P Corail Plus Livery. Metallic grey with red flash on side and front end. Adopted in 1997 as standard livery for both diesel and electric passenger locomotives matching Corail Plus refurbished coaches.

Q TGV Sud Est livery. Orange with dark grey window band and white lining.

R White with red window band. Standard mid-80s DMU livery. Also adopted by the regions Alsace, Aquitaine, Limousin, Rhone-Alpes.

S Class specific livery. Refer to text.

T TER livery. Metallic grey with blue ends and large light grey TER logo on bodyside.

U Unpainted stainless steel.

V Dark green with yellow panels or lines.

W All over white. Old Pays de la Loire livery.

X Red and cream with dark grey around windows. Classic DMU livery.

Y White with yellow window band. Adopted by the regions Bourgogne, Languedoc-Rousillon, Lorraine, Nord-Pas-de-Calais.

Z Dark blue with red front end and doors. The original livery of Z2 EMUs.

1.1. ELECTRIC LOCOMOTIVES

Many SNCF locos have monomotor bogies which can be regeared when the loco is at rest. An arrow on the bogie will be found pointing to the letter 'M' or 'V' denoting "marchandises" or "voyageurs" (freight/passenger) and this indicator is one of the items a driver must check when preparing a locomotive. In this publication, where two sets of figures are shown for max. speed, tractive effort, power etc., the first refers to the low gear ratio and the second to the high gear ratio.

All electric locomotives are livery **E** (blue-green with white lining or aluminium trim) unless otherwise shown.

CLASS CC 1100   C-C

This class was ordered by the PO–Midi with the first two being delivered in December 1937 as E 1001/2. Put into stock in 1938 they do not appear to have entered traffic until 1943. The remainder of the class was delivered in 1943–48 as E 1003–12. The whole class was renumbered in 1950 to CC 1101–12. They were built for heavy shunting duties, a task they still perform today. All locos have recently been refurbished, equipped with new cabs, a modern electronic control package and were repainted in the new orange/brown livery. The class shunt in Villeneuve, St. Pierre-de-Corps and Toulouse St. Jory yards.

Built: 1938–48.
Builder-Mech. Parts: CGC.
Traction Motors: Four Oerlikon 6FM 640Z.
Continuous Rating: 400 kW.
Max. T.E.: 183 kN.
Wheel Dia.: 1400 mm.

System: 1500 V d.c.
Builder-Elec. Parts: Oerlikon.

Weight: 91 tonnes.
Length: 17.19 m.
Max. Speed: 30 km/h.

401101	J	VG	401104	J	TL	401107	J	TL	401111	J	TL
401102	J	VG	401105	J	TP	401108	J	TL	401112	J	VG
401103	J	VG	401106	J	VG	401110	J	TL			

CLASS CC 6500   C-C

This class is the most powerful on the SNCF. There are three sub series: 6501–38, 6539–59 and 6560–74. with different body side grills. The second batch is of particular interest as these locos were originally fitted out for working off third-rail supply on the Chambéry–Modane "Maurienne" route. They were all converted to standard some years ago but some still carry their original light green livery. Some have been repainted in the standard red and grey livery which was designed to blend with TEE and "Grand Confort" liveries. The class is fitted with monomotor bogies with two gear ratios. SNCF is now taking advantage of the class's pulling power by modifying gear ratios for a 160 km/h maximum with a higher tractive effort. The converted locos are transferred to Vénissieux but operate all over the Sud-Est region. The class was joined in 1995/6 by the four Class CC 21000 locos, a non-standard dual-voltage version from which 25 kV a.c. equipment was removed. These were renumbered 6575–6578 (ex 21001–4 respectively). 6519 and 6541 were withdrawn after accidents. The class has now been designated for freight and passenger work is extremely limited.

Built: 1969–75.
Builders: Alsthom/MTE.
Traction Motors: Two Alsthom TTB 665 A1 frame-mounted monomotors.
Continuous Rating: 5900 kW.
Max. T.E.: 288/131 (416/258†) kN.
Wheel Dia.: 1140 mm.
Non-Standard Livery: N Maurienne green.

System: 1500 V d.c.

Weight: 115–118 tonnes.
Length: 20.19 m.
Max. Speed: 200 (160†) km/h.

Fitted with rheostatic braking, electro-pneumatic braking and driver-guard communication.

e Fitted with snowploughs.

406501	K		VE		406506	K †	VE	VIERZON
406502	K †	VE	IVRY-SUR-SEINE		406507	K †	VE	SAINTE-FOY-LA-GRANDE
406503	K †	VE			406508	K †	VE	MONTAUBAN
406504	K †	VE	VITRY-SUR-SEINE		406509	K †	VE	AGEN
406505	K †	VE	CASTELNAUDARY		406510	K †	VE	CARCASSONNE

406511	**K** †	VE	PAMIERS		406546	**K** e	VE		
406512	**K** †	VE	NARBONNE		406547	**K** e	VE		
406513	**K** †	VE	COGNAC		406548	**K** e	VE		
406514	**K**	VE	POITIERS		406549	**N** e	VE		
406515	**K** †	VE	BLOIS		406550	**N** e	VE		
406516	**K** †	VE	CHÂTELLERAULT		406551	**K** e	VE		
406517	**K** †	VE	ARCACHON		406552	**K**	VE		
406518	**K** †	VE	ORLÉANS		406553	**K** e	VE		
406520	**K** †	VE	RUFFEC		406554	**K** e	VE		
406521	**K**	VE	SAINTES		406555	**K** e	VE		
406522	**K**	VE	LIMOGES		406556	**K** e	VE		
406523	**K**	VE	BRIVE		406557	**K** e	VE		
406524	**K**	VE	TOULOUSE		406558	**K** e	VE		
406525	**K**	VE	CHÂTEAUROUX		406559	**K** e	VE		
406526	**K**	VE	CHOISY-LE-ROI		406560	**K**	VE	OULLINS	
406527	**K**	VE	AMBOISE		406561	**K**	VE		
406528	**K**	VE	LUCHON		406562	**K**	VE		
406529	**K**	VE	ISSOUDUN		406563	**K**	VE	LAVAL	
406530	**K**	VE	CAHORS		406564	**K**	VE	BEAUNE	
406531	**K**	VE	SAINT-PIERRE-DES-CORPS		406565	**K**	VE		
406532	**K**	VE			406566	**K**	VE	MAUBEUGE	
406533	**K**	VE	BEAUTIRAN		406567	**K**	VE	BREST	
406534	**K**	VE	BÉZIERS		406568	**K**	VE		
406535	**K**	VE	SAINT-CHAMOND		406569	**K**	VE	LA MULATIÈRE	
406536	**K**	VE	ANNECY		406570	**K**	VE	ARMENTIÈRES	
406537	**K**	VE	SALON-DE-PROVENCE		406571	**K**	VE	JEUMONT	
406538	**K**	VE			406572	**K**	VE	RÉSISTANCE-FER	
406539	**K**	VE			406573	**K**	VE	LIBOURNE	
406540	**K**	VE			406574	**K**	VE	DOLE	
406542	**K**	VE			406575	**K** †	VE		
406543	**K**	VE			406576	**K** †	VE		
406544	**K** e	VE			406577	**K** †	VE		
406545	**K** e	VE			406578	**K** †	VE		

CLASSES CC 7000/7100   Co-Co

The outline of these locomotives will be familiar to visitors to The Netherlands and Spain where examples exist as Class 1300 and Class 276 respectively. The two prototypes 7001/2 were the first big Co-Co locomotives on the SNCF that were designed for express passenger use, previous ones being 2D2s. The class has moved around somewhat over the years but is now seeing out its days based at Avignon but still operating over a large area. from Dijon to Marseille and Port Bou. The class is still popular for fill-in passenger turns especially on the Nîmes-Narbonne line. 7121 set up a world record of 243 km/h in 1953 and 7107 is joint holder of the standing world record for electric traction – 331 km/h attained in 1955. This loco is a favourite for open days. 7002 is approaching the 10 million km mark. The class are being withdrawn very slowly and should just see the century out.

Built: 1949*/1952–55.
Builder-Mech. Parts: Alsthom/Fives-Lille.
Traction Motors: Six TA621B (TA628C†) fully suspended.
Continuous Rating: 3490 (3240†) kW.
Max. T.E.: 260 kN.
Wheel Dia.: 1250 mm.
Class Specific Livery: **S** As **E** but with turquoise band.

System: 1500 V d.c.
Builder-Elec. Parts: Alsthom/CEM.
Weight: 107 (104*, 106†) tonnes.
Length: 18.92 (18.83*) m.
Max. Speed: 140 km/h.

7002	**S**	*	AV	7110	**S**	AV	7123	**S**	AV	7139	**S**	AV
7101	**S**		AV	7112	**S**	AV	7126	**S**	AV	7140	**S**	AV
7102	**S**		AV	7115	**S**	AV	7128	**S**	AV	7145	**S** †	AV
7105	**S**		AV	7122	**S**	AV	7134	**S**	AV	7152	**S** †	AV
7107	**S**		AV								

CLASS BB 7200   B-B

This mixed traffic class is part of a large family of locomotives, Class BB 7200 is the d.c. version, Class BB 15000 the a.c. version and Class BB 22200 the dual-voltage version. (7200 + 15000 = 22200). Unlike most monomotor-bogied locomotives Class BB 7200 has fixed gearing for freight or passenger use, certain locos being limited to 100 km/h with the remainder having the higher rating of 160 km/h. 407411–40 also have modern microprocessor controls regenerative braking. The Standard members of the class have moved around depots in recent years but duties have not changed. The class dominates on passenger services on the Sud-Est region and also hauls most express freight services. Less dominant on the Sud-Ouest region but very common on both freight and passenger. 7209 and 7308 were destroyed in accidents.

Built: 1976–85.   **System:** 1500 V d.c.
Builders: Alsthom/MTE.
Traction Motors: Two TAB 674 frame-mounted monomotors.
Continuous Rating: 4040 kW.   **Weight:** 84 tonnes.
Max. T.E.: 288 (3xx*†) kN.   **Length:** 17.48 m.
Wheel Dia.: 1250 mm.   **Max. Speed:** 160 (100*†, 200) km/h.

Fitted with cowcatchers, rheostatic brakes, electro-pneumatic brakes and driver-guard communication.

c Modified for working the 'Catalan Talgo'.
† Fitted with self-ventilated motors and multiple working for use on the Maurienne line. 7411–40 also have regenerative braking.
§ Fitted with "préannonce" cab signalling.

No.				No.				No.				No.		
407201	C	*	BD	407240	C		PO	407278	C		MB	407317	C	BD
407202	C	*	BD	407241	C		PO	407279	C		MB	407318	C	BD
407203	C	*	BD	407242	C		PO	407280	C		MB	407319	C	BD
407204	C	*	BD	407243	C		PO	407281	C	c	PO	407320	C	BD
407205	C	*	BD	407244	C		PO	407282	C	c	PO	407321	C	BD
407206	C	*	BD	407245	C		PO	407283	C	c	PO	407322	C	BD
407207	C	*	BD	407246	C		PO	407284	C	c	PO	407323	C	BD
407208	C	*	BD	407247	C		PO	407285	C	c	PO	407324	C	BD
407210	C	*	BD	407248	C		PO	407286	C	c	PO	407325	C	BD
407211	C	*	BD	407249	C		PO	407287	C	c	PO	407326	C	BD
407212	C	*	BD	407250	C		PO	407288	C	c	PO	407327	C	BD
407213	C	*	BD	407251	C		PO	107289	C	c	VG	407328	C	BD
407214	C	*	BD	407252	C		PO	107290	C	c	VG	407329	C	BD
407215	C	*	BD	407253	C		PO	107291	C	c	VG	407330	C	BD
407216	C	*	BD	407254	C		PO	107292	C	c	VG	407331	C	BD
407217	C	*	BD	407255	C		PO	107293	C	c	VG	407332	C	BD
407218	C	*	BD	407256	C		PO	107294	C	c	VG	407333	C	BD
407219	C	*	BD	407257	C		PO	107295	C	c	VG	407334	C	BD
407220	C	*	BD	407258	C		PO	107296	C	c	VG	407335	C	MB
407221	P	*	BD	407259	C		PO	107297	C		VG	407336	C	MB
407222	C	*	BD	407260	C		PO	107298	C		VG	407337	C	MB
407223	C	*	BD	407261	C	§	PO	107299	C		VG	407338	C	MB
407224	C	*	BD	407262	C	§	PO	107300	C		VG	407339	C	MB
407225	C	*	BD	407263	C	§	PO	107301	C		VG	407340	C	MB
407226	C	*	BD	407264	C		PO	107302	C		VG	407341	C	MB
407227	C	*	BD	407265	C		PO	107303	C		VG	407342	C	MB
407228	C	*	BD	407266	C		PO	107304	C		VG	407343	C	† CB
407229	C	*	BD	407267	C		PO	107305	C		VG	407344	C	† CB
407230	C	*	BD	407268	C		PO	107306	C		VG	407345	C	† CB
407231	C	*	BD	407269	C		MB	107307	C		VG	407346	C	† CB
407232	C	*	BD	407270	C		MB	107309	C		VG	407347	C	† CB
407233	C	*	BD	407271	C		MB	107310	C		VG	407348	C	† CB
407234	C	*	BD	407272	C		MB	107311	C		VG	407349	C	† CB
407235	C	*	BD	407273	C		MB	107312	C		VG	407350	C	† CB
407236	C		PO	407274	C		MB	107313	C		VG	407351	C	† CB
407237	C		PO	407275	C		MB	107314	C		VG	407352	C	† CB
407238	C		PO	407276	C		MB	407315	C		BD	407353	C	† CB
407239	C		PO	407277	C		MB	407316	C		BD	407354	C	† CB

407355	C	†	CB	407377	C	†	CB	107399	C	VG
407356	C	†	CB	407378	C	†	CB	107400	C	VG
407357	C	†	CB	407379	C	†	CB	107401	C	VG
407358	C	†	CB	407380	C	†	CB	107402	C	VG
407359	C	†	CB	407381	C		BD	107403	C	VG
407360	C	†	CB	407382	C		BD	107404	C	VG
407361	C	†	CB	407383	C		BD	107405	C	VG
407362	C	†	CB	407384	C		BD	107406	C	VG
407363	C	†	CB	407385	C		BD	107407	C	VG
407364	C	†	CB	407386	C		BD	107408	C	VG
407365	C	†	CB	407387	C		BD	107409	C	VG
407366	C	†	CB	407388	C		BD	107410	C	VG
407367	C	†	CB	407389	C		BD	407411	C	†	CB
407368	C	†	CB	407390	C		BD	407412	C	†	CB
407369	C	†	CB	107391	C		VG	407413	C	†	CB
407370	C	†	CB	107392	C		VG	407414	C	†	CB
407371	C	†	CB	107393	C		VG	407415	C	†	CB
407372	C	†	CB	107394	C		VG	407416	C	†	CB
407373	C	†	CB	107395	C		VG	407417	C	†	CB
407374	C	†	CB	107396	C		VG	407418	C	†	CB
407375	C	†	CB	107397	C		VG	407419	C	†	CB
407376	C	†	CB	107398	C		VG				

407420	C	†	CB
407421	C	†	CB
407422	C	†	CB
407423	C	†	CB
407424	C	†	CB
407425	C	†	CB
407426	C	†	CB
407427	C	†	CB
407428	C	†	CB
407429	C	†	CB
407430	C	†	CB
407431	C	†	CB
407432	C	†	CB
407433	C	†	CB
407434	C	†	CB
407435	C	†	CB
407436	C	†	CB
407437	C	†	CB
407438	C	†	CB
407439	C	†	CB
407440	C	†	CB

Names:

407203	SAINT-FLOUR
407221	SAINT-AMAND-MONTROND
407223	LA SOUTERRAINE
407232	SOUILLAC
407236	CHAMBÉRY
407237	PIERRELATTE
407238	THONON-LES-BAINS
407239	SAINT-PIERRE-D'ALBIGNY
407240	SAINT-ETIENNE
407241	VILLEURBANNE
407242	VIENNE
407243	VILLENEUVE-SAINT-GEORGES
407244	VERNOU-LA CELLE-SUR-SEINE
407253	MONTRÉJEAU
407256	VALENTON
107410	FONTENAY-SOUS-BOIS
407411	LAMURE-SUR-AZERGUES

CLASS BB 8100   Bo-Bo

A post-war development of Class BB 300 which was also exported to other countries, e.g. the Netherlands (Class 1100). Although only based at two depots the class sees general use on freight trains all over the Sud Est region but also as far as Toulouse and, occasionally, Bordeaux. Locos from the 8240–8271 batch have unmodified suspension which limits their speed. Most have therefore been withdrawn or limited to empty stock duties out of Paris Austerlitz.

Built: 1947–55.   **System:** 1500 V d.c.
Builder-Mech. Parts: Alsthom/Schneider-Jeumont/CGC.
Builder-Elec. Parts: Alsthom/Siemens/Jeumont/Oerlikon.
Traction Motors: Four Alsthom M1 TC.
Continuous Rating: 2100 kW.   **Weight:** 92 tonnes.
Max. T.E.: 152 kN.   **Length:** 12.93 m.
Wheel Dia.: 1400 mm.   **Max. Speed:** 105 km/h.

Multiple working fitted, except 8240–8271.

408101	C	AV	408131	C	DP	408163	C	AV	408194	C	DP
408103	C	AV	408132	C	DP	408164	C	DP	408196	C	DP
408105	C	AV	408134	C	DP	408171	C	DP	408197	C	DP
408106	C	AV	408135	C	DP	408172	C	DP	408198	C	DP
408107	C	AV	408137	C	DP	408173	C	DP	408199	C	DP
408110	C	AV	408138	C	DP	408174	C	DP	408206	C	DP
408117	C	AV	408142	C	DP	408177	V	AV	408207	C	DP
408120	C	AV	408143	C	AV	408180	C	DP	408210	C	AV
408122	C	DP	408145	C	AV	408186	C	DP	408212	C	DP
408123	C	AV	408148	C	DP	408187	C	DP	408214	C	DP
408127	C	DP	408152	C	AV	408190	C	DP	408216	C	AV
408129	C	AV	408153	C	DP	408191	C	DP	408219	C	AV
408130	C	DP	408159	C	DP	408192	C	DP	408223	C	DP

408224	C	AV	408228	C	AV	408233	C	DP	108252	C	PO
408225	C	DP	408229	C	AV	408234	C	AV	108257	V	PO
408226	C	DP	408231	C	DP	408235	C	DP	108266	C	PO
408227	C	DP	408232	C	DP	108240	C	PO	108271	V	PO

CLASS BB 8500 B-B

A mixed traffic loco being a d.c. version of Class BB 17000. Monomotor bogies with two gear ratios. Being such a large class there are detail variations between batches. They are often used in multiple for freight on the difficult Paris–Toulouse line and on push-pull suburban trains out of Toulouse and Paris Montparnasse. Many have been replaced on push-pull passenger services by Class BB 9600 in recent years as they are more valuable on freight. The tendency of the class to sway from side to side led to them being blacked by several depots in 1995. SNCF is now modifying most of the class but most of the first batch, which are not equipped for push-pull operation, are being downgraded for empty stock workings and renumbered in the 88500 series.

Built: 1964–74. **System:** 1500 V d.c.
Builder: Alsthom.
Traction Motors: Two TAB 660B1 frame-mounted monomotors.
Continuous Rating: 2940 kW except 8501–36 which are 2610 kW.
Max. T.E.: 323 /197 kN.
Weight: 78 tonnes (8501–36), 79 tonnes (8537–87), 80 tonnes (8588–8646).
Length: 14.70 m (8501–36), 14.94 m (8537–87), 15.57 m (8588–8646).
Wheel Dia.: 1100 mm. **Max. Speed:** 100/140 km/h.

Multiple working fitted. Rheostatic braking. Push-pull fitted (120 km/h) except 8501–36.

p Equipped for push-pull at 140 km/h.
§ Downgraded to 100 km/h for e.c.s. working and renumbered with an '8' prefix.

188501	C §	VE	408537	C p	PO	188574	C §	VE	508610	C p	TL
408502	C	PO	408538	C p	PO	408575		PO	508611	C p	TL
408503	C	PO	408539	C p	PO	408576	C	TL	508612	C p	TL
188504	C §	PO	408540	C	PO	408577	C	AV	508613	C p	TL
188505	C §	PO	408541	C p	PO	408578	C	AV	508614	C p	TL
188506	C §	PO	408542	C p	PO	408579	C	AV	508615	C p	TL
188507	C §	VE	408543	C p	PO	408580		PO	508616	C p	TL
188508	C §	VE	408544	C p	PO	508581	C	MR	508617	C p	TL
188509	C §	AV	408545	C p	PO	408582	C	AV	508618	C p	TL
188510	C §	AV	408546	C	TL	408583	C	TL	508619	C p	TL
188511	C §	AV	408547	C	TL	408584	C	AV	508620	C p	TL
188512	C §	VE	408548	C	AV	508585	C	MR	508621	C p	TL
408513	C	PO	408549	C	TL	408586	C	AV	508622	C p	TL
188514	C §	PO	408551	C	PO	408587	C	AV	508623	C p	TL
188515	C §	PO	408552	C	AV	508588	C	MR	508624	C p	TL
188516	C §	PO	608553	C s	TL	508589	C	MR	508625	C p	TL
188517	C §	PO	408554	C	TL	508590	C	MR	508626	C p	TL
188518	C §	VE	408555	C p	PO	508591	I	MR	408627	C p	TL
188519	C §	PO	408556	C	TL	508592	I	MR	508628	p	TL
188520	C §	VE	408557	C	TL	508593	I	MR	508629	C p	TL
188521	C §	VE	508558	C	MR	508594	I	MR	408630	C	TL
188522	C §	VE	408559	C	TL	508595	I	MR	408631	C	TL
188523	C §	PO	408560	C p	PO	508596	I	MR	408632	C	TL
188524	C §	VE	408561	C p	PO	508597	I	MR	408633	C	TL
188525	C §	PO	408562	C	AV	508598	I	MR	408634	C	TL
188526	C §	PO	408563	p	PO	408599		TL	408635	C	TL
188527	C §	PO	408564	p	PO	508600	C p	TL	408636	C	TL
188528	C §	VE	408565	C	AV	408601	p	TL	408637	C	TL
188529	C §	PO	408566	C p	PO	408602	C p	TL	408638	C	TL
408530	C	PO	408567	C	AV	408603	C p	TL	408639	C	TL
188531	C §	PO	508568	C	MR	408604	p	TL	408640	C	TL
408532	C	PO	508569	C	MR	408605	C p	TL	408641	C	TL
188533	C §	VE	408570	C	AV	408606	C p	TL	408642	C	TL
188534	C §	VE	408571	C	AV	408607	C p	TL	808643	C	MR
188535	C §	PO	408572	C	PO	408608	C p	TL	408644	C	TL
408536	C	AV	408573	C	AV	408609	C p	TL	408645	C	TL

808646 **C** MR |

Names:

508600	FLEURY-LES-AUBRAIS	508603	LANNEMEZAN
508601	AX-LES-THERMES	508604	CERDAGNE
508602	FOIX	508605	SAINT-GAUDENS

CLASS BB 9200 Bo-Bo

This class was the first of the SNCF standard types of the late 1950s. The same styling is also found on Classes BB 9300, 9600, 16000, 25100, 25150 and 25200. Class BB 9200 was originally scattered over the d.c. network south of Paris but now they are concentrated at Bordeaux and Paris Sud Ouest and are used on mixed traffic all over the Sud–Ouest network and on the line from Toulouse to Marseille. A small number operate passenger services between Paris Montparnasse and Le Mans.

Built: 1957–64.
Builders: Schneider-Jeumont/CEM/MTE.
Traction Motors: Four Alsthom GLM 931B.
Continuous Rating: 3850 kW.
Max. T.E.: 260 kN.
Wheel Dia.: 1250 mm.
Non-Standard Livery: N Special Arzens livery.

System: 1500 V d.c.

Weight: 82 tonnes.
Length: 16.20 m.
Max. Speed: 160 km/h.

109263–109292 are fitted with rheostatic braking.

p Modified for push-pull operation with Corail stock.
t TDM push-pull fitted.
v 200 km/h gear ratio.

409201		BD	409223		BD	409245		BD	109268	**C** t	PO
409202	**C**	BD	409224		BD	409246		BD	109269	**C**	PO
409203	**C**	BD	409225	**C**	BD	109247		PO	109270	**C**	PO
409204	**C**	BD	409226		BD	109248	**C**	PO	109272	**C**	PO
409205		BD	409227		BD	109250	**C**	PO	109273	**C** t	PO
409206	**C**	BD	409228		BD	109251	**C**	PO	109274	**C** t	PO
409207	**C**	BD	409229		BD	109252	**C**	PO	109275	**C** t	PO
409208		BD	409230		BD	109253	**C**	PO	109276	**C** t	PO
409209		BD	409231	**N**	BD	109254	**C**	PO	109277	**C** t	PO
409210		BD	409232	**C**	BD	109255	**C**	PO	109278	**C** t	PO
409211		BD	409233		BD	109256		PO	109279	**C** t	PO
409212		BD	409234		BD	109257	**C**	PO	109280	**C** p	PO
409213		BD	409235	**C**	BD	109258		PO	109282	**C** p	PO
409214		BD	409236	**C**	BD	109259	**C**	PO	109283	**C**	PO
409215		BD	409237	**C**	BD	109260	**C**	PO	109284	**C**	PO
409216		BD	409238		BD	109261	**C**	PO	109287	tv	PO
409217		BD	409239	**C**	BD	109262	**C**	PO	109288	**N** p	PO
409218	**C**	BD	409240	**C**	BD	109263	**C** t	PO	109289	**C** t	PO
409219		BD	409241	**C**	BD	109264	**C** t	PO	109290	**C** tv	PO
409220		BD	409242		BD	109265	t	PO	109291	**C** p	PO
409221		BD	409243		BD	109266	**C**	PO	109292	**C** p	PO
409222		BD	409244	**C**	BD	109267	**C** t	PO			

Names:

109248 LA-TESTE-DE-BUCH | 109280 ARPAJON

CLASS BB 9300 Bo-Bo

An updated version of Class BB 9200. All are now grouped at Toulouse but see widespread use on the Paris–Sud Ouest main lines and the Toulouse–Marseille route. 9302 was cannibalised at Oullins after a serious accident.

Built: 1967–69.
Builders: Schneider-Jeumont/MTE/CEM.
Traction Motors: Four Alsthom GLM 931B.
Continuous Rating: 3850 kW.

System: 1500 V d.c.

Weight: 84 tonnes.

Max. T.E.: 260 kN.
Wheel Dia.: 1250 mm.
Length: 16.20 m.
Max. Speed: 160 km/h.
Fitted with rheostatic braking, electro-pneumatic brakes and driver-guard communication.

109301	C	TL	109312	C	TL	109322	C	TL	109332	C	TL
109303	C	TL	109313	C	TL	109323	C	TL	109333	C	TL
109304	C	TL	109314	C	TL	109324	C	TL	109334	C	TL
109305	C	TL	109315	C	TL	109325	P	TL	109335	C	TL
109306	C	TL	109316	C	TL	109326	C	TL	109336	C	TL
109307	C	TL	109317	C	TL	109327	C	TL	109337	C	TL
109308	C	TL	109318	C	TL	109328	C	TL	109338	C	TL
109309	C	TL	109319	C	TL	109329	C	TL	109339	C	TL
109310	C	TL	109320	C	TL	109330	C	TL	109340	C	TL
109311	C	TL	109321	C	TL	109331	C	TL			

Names:

109326 MONTRABÉ | 109329 CASTRES

CLASS BB 9600 B-B

Of the 135 light Class BB 9400 electrics, built in 1959–64, most were withdrawn in the early 1990s due to their low power but 42 were retained and modified for push-pull passenger working at 140 km/h by Béziers works in 1991–95. The class now carry out these duties in the Lyon, Marseille, Montpellier and Toulouse areas, filling in with the odd freight. Class BB 9600 are also the only locos to haul long distance trains on the Béziers–Neussargues line. 9641/2 are dedicated to the Tours–St. Pierre-des-Corps shuttles and carry a similar livery to TGV Atlantique sets.

Built: 1967–69.
Builder-Mech. Parts: Fives-Lille/MTE.
Traction Motors: Four SW 408.
Continuous Rating: 2210 kW.
Max. T.E.: 270 kN.
Wheel Dia.: 1020 mm.
Non-Standard Livery: N Similar livery to TGVs.
System: 1500 V d.c.
Builder-Elec. Parts: CEM/MTE.
Weight: 59 tonnes.
Length: 14.93 m.
Max. Speed: 140 km/h.

Multiple working fitted and push-pull fitted.

509601	(9477)	C	AV	509615	(9450)	C	AV	509629	(9438)	C	AV
509602	(9489)	C	AV	509616	(9440)	C	AV	509630	(9503)	C	AV
509603	(9454)	C	AV	509617	(9429)	C	AV	509631	(9490)	C	AV
509604	(9426)	C	AV	509618	(9447)	C	AV	509632	(9514)	C	AV
509605	(9487)	C	AV	509619	(9508)	C	AV	509633	(9474)	C	AV
509606	(9464)	C	AV	509620	(9505)	C	AV	509634	(9478)	C	AV
509607	(9444)	C	AV	509621	(9436)	C	AV	509635	(9504)	C	AV
509608	(9434)	C	AV	509622	(9480)	C	AV	509636	(9506)	C	AV
509609	(9416)	C	AV	509623	(9468)	C	AV	509637	(9497)	C	AV
509610	(9442)	C	AV	509624	(9507)	C	AV	509638	(9520)	C	AV
509611	(9403)	C	AV	509625	(9471)	C	AV	509639	(9485)	C	AV
509612	(9437)	C	AV	509626	(9439)	C	AV	509640	(9496)	C	AV
509613	(9451)	C	AV	509627	(9500)	C	AV	509641	(9452)	N	TP
509614	(9498)	C	AV	509628	(9513)	C	AV	509642	(9470)	N	TP

Names:

509641 TOURS | 509642 TOURS

CLASS BB 9700 Bo-Bo

As Class BB 9200 but equipped with time division multiplex equipment for use with double-deck outer suburban stock on the Paris gare de Lyon–Laroche-Migennes service.

Class Specific Livery: S Pale grey with dark grey and orange bands.

509701	(9271)	S	PO	509703	(9285)	S	PO	509704	(9286)	S	PO
509702	(9281)	S	PO								

CLASS BB 12000   Bo-Bo

Called "Monocabines" or "flat irons" this class was built for the newly electrified Valenciennes–Thionville line and was the first 25 kV ac type to go into series production. Previously mixed traffic locos, the class are now restricted to freight and are slowly being withdrawn. The class now operates mainly in the area around Lille, Dunkerque and Somain and around Thionville, Metz, Forbach and Nancy. Most are fitted with e.t.h.

Built: 1954–61.
Builders-Mech. Parts: Alsthom/Schneider.
Traction Motors: Four SW 435.
Continuous Rating: 2470 kW.
Max. T.E.: 353 kN.
Wheel Dia.: 1250 mm.

System: 25 kV a.c.
Builders-Elec. Parts: MTE/Alsthom.

Weight: 82–86 tonnes.
Length: 15.20 m.
Max. Speed: 120 km/h.

12003	V	LE	12035	V	LE	12063	V	LE	12098	V	LE
12004	V	LE	12040	V	LE	12065	V	LE	12099	V	LE
12007	V	LE	12041	V	LE	12067	V	LE	12100	V	LE
12011	V	LE	12045	V	LE	12068	V	LE	12101	V	LE
12013	V	LE	12046	V	LE	12069	V	LE	12103	V	LE
12016	V	LE	12048	V	LE	12070	V	LE	12111	V	LE
12021	V	LE	12051	V	LE	12083	V	LE	12124	V	LE
12027	V	LE	12059	V	LE	12086	V	LE	12125	V	LE
12029	V	LE	12060	V	LE	12096	V	LE	12143	V	LE

CLASS BB 15000   B-B

The first of the 1970 generation of locomotives. They work passenger from Paris Est to Basel, Luxembourg and Longwy as well as from Mulhouse to Besançon. 15007 became prototype 7003 later becoming 10003 and 15055 became prototype 10004, but both have since reverted to their previous identities. 15015 was destroyed in an accident near Basel in 1995. The class is also now used on passenger services over the Paris Nord to Amiens and Maubeuge lines.

Built: 1971–78.
Builders: Alsthom/MTE.
Traction Motors: Two TAB 674 frame-mounted monomotors.
Continuous Rating: 4400 kW.
Max. T.E.: 294 kN.
Wheel Dia.: 1250 mm.

System: 25 kV a.c.

Weight: 90 tonnes.
Length: 17.48 m.
Max. Speed: 160 km/h.

Rheostatic braking.
f Equipped with forced air ventilation for traction motors.

115001	K f	SB	GRETZ-ARMAINVILLIERS	115023	P	SB	MEAUX
115002	K f	SB	LONGWY	115024	K	SB	LUNÉVILLE
115003	K f	SB	SARREGUEMINES	115025	K	SB	TOUL
115004	K f	SB	SEDAN	115026	P	SB	ÉPERNAY
115005	K f	SB	SAINT-LOUIS	115027	P	SB	CREUTZWALD
115006	K f	SB	METZ	115028	P	SB	VILLIERS-LE-BEL
115007	P f	SB		115029	K	SB	AURILLAC
115008	K f	SB	NANCY	115030	K f	SB	FORBACH
115009	K f	SB	REIMS	115031	P f	SB	MOYEUVRE-GRANDE
115010	K f	SB	STRASBOURG	115032	P f	SB	CHAMBLY
115012	K f	SB	CHÂLONS SUR MARNE	115033	P f	SB	GAGNY
115013	K f	SB	LONGUYON	115034	P f	SB	SÈTE
115014	K f	SB	THIONVILLE	115035	P f	SB	NOGENT-SUR-MARNE
115016	P	SB	CHARLEVILLE-MÉZIÈRES	115036	P f	SB	LE PERREUX-SUR-MARNE
115017	K	SB	SAINT-AVOLD	115037	P f	SB	LA FERTÉ-SOUS-JOUARRE
115018	K	SB	BONDY	115038	P f	SB	ARS SUR MOSELLE
115019	P	SB	MONTIGNY-LÈS-METZ	115039	P f	SB	ROSNY-SOUS-BOIS
115020	P	SB	PAU	115040	P f	SB	LIVRY GARGAN
115021	P	SB	CHÂTEAU-THIERRY	115041	P f	SB	SAINTE MENEHOULD
115022	K	SB	PANTIN	115042	P f	SB	ETIVAL-CLAIREFONTAINE

115043	K f	SB	MAIZIÈRES LES METZ	115054	K	SB	
115044	P f	SB	SUIPPES	115055	K	SB	
115045	K f	SB	RAON L'ÉTAPE	115056	K	SB	VANNES
115046	P f	SB		115058	K	SB	ÉPINAL
115047	P f	SB	CHELLES	115059	K	SB	TOURCOING
115048	P f	SB	HAGUENAU	115060	K	SB	CREIL
115049	K f	SB		115061	K	SB	SARREBOURG
115050	K	SB	VITRY-LE-FRANÇOIS	115062	K	SB	MONTMÉDY
115051	K	SB	AULNOYE-AYMÉRIES	115063	K	SB	VERDUN
115052	K	SB	CAMBRAI	115064	K	SB	SAVERNE
115053	K	SB	TROUVILLE-SUR-MER	115065	K	SB	VAIRES-SUR-MARNE

CLASSES BB 16000 & BB16100   Bo-Bo

Class BB16000 is is an a.c. version of Class BB 9200. At one time split between La Chapel and le Strasbourg the delivery of new Class BB 15000 allowed all Class BB 16000 to be concentrated at La Chapelle. The class have virtually no freight work. Since 1996, a number of the class have started operating on the Paris St. Lazare to Cherbourg line and the whole class has been reallocated to Achères as La Chapelle is due to close.

Built: 1958–63.
Builder: MTE.
Traction Motors: Four Jeumont TO 136-8.
Continuous Rating: 4130 kW.
Max. T.E.: 309 kN.
Wheel Dia.: 1250 mm.

System: 25 kV a.c.

Weight: 88 tonnes.
Length: 16.68 m.
Max. Speed: 160 km/h.

p Push-pull fitted.

116001	C		AC	116018	C p	AC	116033	P	AC	116051	C		AC
116002	C		AC	116019	P	AC	116036	P	AC	116052	P		AC
116003	C p	AC	116020	C	AC	116037	P	AC	116053	C p	AC		
116005	C		AC	116021	C	AC	116039	C p	AC	116054	C		AC
116006	C p	AC	116022	C	AC	116041	C	AC	116055	C		AC	
116007	C p	AC	116024	C	AC	116042	P	AC	116056	P p	AC		
116008	C p	AC	116027	P p	AC	116043	C	AC	116057	C		AC	
116011	P		AC	116028	C	AC	116044	C p	AC	116058	C		AC
116012	C		AC	116029	C	AC	116047	C p	AC	116059	C		AC
116013	C		AC	116031	C	AC	116049	C	AC	116061	C		AC
116015	C		AC	116032	C p	AC	116050	C p	AC				

The following locos were equipped with time division multiplex equipment in 1991–94 for use with double-deck outer suburban stock on the Paris Nord–St. Quentin/Amiens and Paris St. Lazare–Rouen lines.

Class Specific Livery: S Pale grey with dark grey and orange bands.

516101	(16004) S	PL	516106	(16009) S	PL	516111	(16016) S	PL
516102	(16017) S	PL	516107	(16048) S	PL	516112	(16010) S	PL
516103	(16046) S	PL	516108	(16026) S	PL	516113	(16030) S	PL
516104	(16040) S	PL	516109	(16023) S	PL	516114	(16062) S	PL
516105	(16014) S	PL	516110	(16035) S	PL	516115	(16060) S	PL

Names:

16001	NEUILLY-SUR-MARNE		16008	DRANCY
16007	MANTES-LA-JOLIE		16114	DOL-DE-BRETAGNE

CLASS BB 16500   B-B

The monomotor bogie originated with this class and with it the idea of providing alternative gear ratios to create true mixed traffic locomotives. With such a large class there are many detail variations. The most interesting is 16700 which has modified cab front end panels. 16540 became the prototype of the Class BB 25500s and was numbered 20004 in the 1960s. Batches of the class are increasingly specialised in use. Most of 16501–16598 were not modified for 100 km/h operation in freight mode and are dedicated to push-pull suburban trains in the Lille (LE) and Paris Est (PV) areas. 20 locos at TV have been modified for operation in push mode at 140 km/h and work mainly on Nancy–Metz–Thionville services. Finally, batches at TV and LE are in a dedicated fleet for block freight trains as part of the TENOR experiment. The remaining locos work mainly freight with a little passenger work over an area covering the Nord-Est region plus the Paris–Rouen–Le Havre line. In 1998 a small number were reallocated to Achères for the Paris–Caen–Cherbourg line. The experiment with t.d.m. working of ultra-heavy freights has now ceased.

Built: 1958–64.   **System:** 25 kV a.c.
Builder: Alsthom.
Traction Motors: Two Alsthom TAO 646A1 frame-mounted monomotors.
Continuous Rating: 2580 kW.   **Weight:** 71–74 (81*) tonnes.
Max. T.E.: 324/192 kN.   **Length:** 14.40 (15.27*) m.
Wheel Dia.: 1100 mm.   **Max. Speed:** 100 (90†)/140 km/h.

Multiple working and push-pull fitted (120 km/h).
t t.d.m. fitted for push-pull.
g Equipped with g.p.s. satellite tracking.
p Equipped for push-pull at 140 km/h.

No.				No.				No.				No.			
516501	C	†	LE	516550	C	†	LE	516598	C	†	LE	416646			AC
516502	C	†	LE	516551	C	†	LE	416599	C		AC	416647	C		AC
516503	C	†	LE	516552	C	†	LE	416600	C		AC	416648			AC
516504	C	†	LE	516553	C	†	LE	416601	C	g	TV	416649			AC
516505	C	†	LE	516554	C	†	LE	416602	C	g	TV	416650	C		AC
516506		†	LE	516555	C	†	LE	416603		g	TV	416651	C		AC
516507	C	†	LE	516556	C	†	PV	416604	C	g	TV	416652	C		AC
516508	C	†	LE	516557		†	PV	416605	C	g	TV	416653			AC
516509	C	†	LE	516558	C	†	PV	416606	C	g	TV	416654	C		TV
516510	C	†	LE	516559	C	p†	PV	416607	C	g	TV	416655	C		PV
516511	C	†	LE	516560	C	†	PV	416608	C	g	TV	416656	C		SB
516512	C	†	LE	516561	C	†	PV	416609	C	g	TV	416657	C		SB
516513	C	†	LE	516562	C	†	PV	416610	C	g	TV	416658	C		SB
516514	C	†	LE	516563	C	†	PV	416611	C	g	TV	416659		p	SB
516515	C	†	LE	516564		†	PV	416612	C	g	TV	416660			SB
516516	C	†	LE	516565	C	†	PV	416613	C	g	TV	416661	C		SB
516518	C	†	LE	516566	C	†	PV	416614		g	TV	416662			SB
516519	C	†	LE	516567	C	†	PV	416615	C	g	TV	416663			SB
516520	C	†	LE	516568		†	PV	416616	C	g	TV	416664	C		SB
516521	C	†	LE	516569	C	†	PV	416617		g	TV	416665	C		SB
516522	C	†	LE	516570	C	†	PV	416618		g	TV	416666			SB
516523	C	†	LE	516571		†	PV	416619	C	g	TV	416667	C		SB
516524	C	†	LE	516572	C	†	PV	416620	C	g	TV	416668	C		SB
516525	C	†	LE	516573	C	†	PV	416621			LE	416669	C		SB
516526	C	†	LE	516574	C	†	PV	416622	C		LE	416670			SB
516527	C	†	LE	516575		†	PV	416623			LE	416671	C		SB
516528	C	†	LE	516576	C	†	PV	416624	C		LE	416672	C		SB
516529	C	†	LE	516577	C	†	PV	416625			LE	416673			SB
416530	C		LE	516578	C	†	PV	416626	C		LE	416674	C		SB
516531	C	†	LE	516579	C	†	PV	416627	C		LE	416675	C		SB
516532	C	†	LE	516580	C	†	PV	416628			LE	416676			SB
416533	C		LE	516581	C	†	PV	416629	C		LE	416677	C		SB
516534	C	†	LE	516582	C	†	PV	416630			LE	416678	C		SB
416535	C		PV	516583		†	PV	416631	C		LE	416679			SB
416536	C		PV	516584	C	†	PV	416632			LE	416680			SB
416537	C		PV	516585	C	†	PV	416633	C		LE	516681		p	TV
516538	C	†	LE	516586	C	†	PV	416634	C		LE	516682	C	p	TV
516539	C	†	LE	516587	C	†	PV	416635	C		LE	516683	C	p	TV
516540	C	†	LE	516588	C	†	PV	416636			LE	516684	C	p	TV
516541	C	†	LE	516589	C	†	PV	416637			LE	516685	C	p	TV
516542	C	†	LE	516590	C	†	PV	416638	C		LE	516686	C	p	TV
516543	C	†	LE	516591	C	†	PV	416639	C		LE	516687	C	p	TV
516544	C	†	LE	516592		†	PV	416640	C		LE	516688	C	p	TV
516545	C	†	LE	516593	C	†	PV	416641			LE	516689	C	p	TV
416546	C		PV	516594	C	†	PV	416642	C		LE	516690	C	p	TV
516547	C	†	LE	516595		†	LE	416643			LE	516691		p	TV
516548	C	†	LE	516596	C	†	LE	416644	C		LE	516692		p	TV
516549	C	†	LE	516597	C	†	LE	416645			LE	516693	C	p	TV

516694	C	p	TV	416720	C		SB	416745	C		LE	416770	C	g	LE
516695	C	p	TV	416721	C		SB	416746	C		LE	416771	C	g	LE
516696	C	p	TV	416722			SB	416747	C		LE	416772	C	g	LE
516697	C	p	AC	416723	C		SB	416748	C		LE	416773	C	g	LE
516698	C	p	AC	416724	C		SB	416749	C		LE	416774	C	g	LE
516699	C	p	AC	416725	C		SB	416750	C		LE	416775	C	g	LE
516700	C	p*	AC	416726	C		SB	416751		g	TV	416776	C	g	LE
516701		p	AC	416727	C		SB	416752	C	g	TV	416777	C	g	LE
516702	C	p	AC	416728	C		SB	416753	C	g	TV	416778	C		LE
516703	C	p	AC	416729	C		SB	416754	C	g	TV	416779	C		LE
516704	C	p	AC	416730	C		SB	416755	C	g	TV	416780	C	t	PV
416705	C		SB	416731	C		SB	416756	C	g	TV	416781	C	t	PV
416706	C		SB	416732	C		SB	416757		g	TV	416782	C	t	PV
416707			SB	416733	C		SB	416758		g	TV	416783	C	t	PV
416708	C		SB	416734	C		SB	416759	C	g	TV	416784	C	t	PV
416709	C		SB	416735			SB	416760	C	g	TV	416785	C	t	LE
416710	C		SB	416736	C		SB	416761	C	g	TV	416786	C	t	LE
416711	C		SB	416737	C		SB	416762	C	g	TV	416787	C		LE
416712	C		SB	416738	C		SB	416763	C	g	TV	416788	C		LE
416713	C		SB	416739	C		SB	416764	C	g	TV	416789	C		LE
416714	C		SB	416740	C		SB	416765	C	g	LE	416790	C		LE
416715	C		SB	416741			SB	416766	C	g	LE	416791	C		LE
416716	C		SB	416742	C		SB	416767	C	g	LE	416792	C		LE
416717	C		SB	416743	C		SB	416768	C	g	LE	416793	C		LE
416718	C		SB	416744	C		SB	416769	C	g	LE	416794	C		LE
416719	C		SB												

CLASS BB 17000   B-B

Similar in outline to Class BB 16500, their main use is on suburban trains from Paris Nord, Est and St. Lazare. They now do not work freight. 17005 has a similar outline to 16700.

Built: 1965–68.   **System:** 25 kV a.c.
Builder: Alsthom.
Traction Motors: Two Alsthom TAB 660B1 frame-mounted monomotors.
Continuous Rating: 2940 kW.   **Weight:** 78 tonnes.
Max. T.E.: 323/197 kN.
Length: 14.70 (15.57*) m. (17001–17037), 14.94 m (17038–17105).
Wheel Dia.: 1100 mm.   **Max. Speed:** 90/140 km/h.

Multiple working and push-pull fitted (120 km/h).

p Equipped for push-pull at 140 km/h.
t VDU in cab for one-person operation. These locos have their numbers between two blue lines.

817001	C	pt AC	817022	I	pt AC	817043	I	pt AC	817064	I	pt AC
817002	C	pt AC	817023	C	pt AC	817044	C	pt AC	817065	I	pt AC
817003	C	pt AC	817024	I	pt AC	817045	I	pt AC	817066	I	PV
817004	C	pt AC	817025	I	pt AC	817046	I	pt AC	817067	C	PV
817005	I	p* AC	817026	I	pt AC	817047	C	pt AC	817068	I	PV
817006	I	pt AC	817027	C	pt AC	817048	I	pt AC	817069	C	PV
817007	C	pt AC	817028	I	pt AC	817049	I	pt AC	817070	C	PV
817008	I	pt AC	817029	C	pt AC	817050	I	pt AC	817071	I	PV
817009	I	pt AC	817030	I	pt AC	817051	C	pt PV	817072	C	PV
817010	I	pt AC	817031	I	pt AC	817052	C	pt PV	817073	I	PV
817011	C	pt AC	817032	I	pt AC	817053	C	pt PV	817074	I	PV
817012	C	pt AC	817033	I	pt AC	817054	C	pt PV	817075	I	PV
817013	I	pt AC	817034	C	pt AC	817055	C	pt PV	817076	C	PV
817014	C	pt AC	817035	C	pt AC	817056	C	pt PV	817077	I	PL
817015	I	pt AC	817036	C	pt AC	817057	I	pt AC	817078	C	p AC
817016	I	pt AC	817037	C	pt AC	817058	C	pt AC	817079	I	p AC
817017	C	pt AC	817038	C	pt AC	817059	I	pt PV	817080	C	pt AC
817018	I	pt AC	817039	C	pt AC	817060	I	pt PV	817081	I	PL
817019	I	pt AC	817040	I	pt AC	817061	C	p PV	817082	I	PL
817020	I	pt AC	817041	C	pt AC	817062	I	p PV	817083	I	PL
817021	I	pt AC	817042	I	pt AC	817063	I	p PV	817084	I	PL

817085	C	PL	817091	I	p PL	817096	C	PL	817101	I	PL
817086	C	PL	817092	I	PL	817097	C	PL	817102	C	PL
817087	C	PL	817093	I	PL	817098	C	PL	817103	C	PL
817088	C	PL	817094	I	PL	817099	C	PL	817104	C	PL
817089	I	PL	817095	I	PL	817100	I	PL	817105	I	PL
817090	I	PL									

Names:

817011 COLOMBES

817042 CHAUMONT-EN-VEXIN

817051 CORMEILLES-EN-PARISIS

CLASS BB 20200 B-B

This small class which is a dual-voltage version of Class BB 17000 is allocated to Strasbourg for working into the West German (Neuenberg) and Swiss (Basel Muttenz) systems which use 15 kV a.c. They are highly concentrated on the Mulhouse–Basel line. They rarely stray from these duties.

Built: 1969.   **Systems:** 25 kV 50 Hz/15 kV $16^2/_3$ Hz.a.c.

Builder: Alsthom.

Traction Motors: Two Alsthom TAB 660B1 frame-mounted monomotors.

Continuous Rating: 1660 kW (15 kV)/2940 kW (25 kV).

Weight: 80 tonnes.

Max. T.E.: 324/197 kN.   **Length:** 14.94 m.

Wheel Dia.: 1100 mm.   **Max. Speed:** 100/140 km/h.

420201	C	SB	420205	C	SB	420208	C	SB	420211	C	SB
420202	C	SB	420206	C	SB	420209	C	SB	420212	C	SB
420203	C	SB	420207	C	SB	420210	C	SB	420213	C	SB
420204	C	SB								

CLASS BB 22200 B-B

This dual-voltage version of Classes BB 7200/15000 started off working in the Marseille are a but can found virtually over the whole electrified network on through trains from or over routes with different voltages. The class now work passenger and freight throughout France, except for south of a line from Toulouse to Bordeaux. Although each depot has its own diagrams, MB locos being concentrated on the Marseille-Ventimiglia line and RS locos in Brittany and the west, the locos are organised in a pool and can turn up anywhere. Rennes locos have been noted in Metz and Ventimiglia. Nine of the class were modified for operation in the Channel Tunnel – 22379/80, 22399–22405, but have now gone back to normal service. 22379/80/99 are equipped for testing high-speed lines.

Built: 1976–1986.   **Systems:** 1500 V d.c./25 kV a.c.

Builders: Alsthom/MTE.

Traction Motors: Two Alsthom TAB 674 frame-mounted monomotors.

Continuous Rating: 4360 kW.   **Weight:** 90 tonnes.

Max. T.E.: 294 kN.   **Length:** 17.48 m.

Wheel Dia.: 1250 mm.   **Max. Speed:** 160 (200 t) km/h.

Fitted with rheostatic braking, electro-pneumatic brakes, cowcatchers and driver-guard communication.

t 200 km/h locos equipped with TVM430 cab signalling for working parcels trains over high speed lines.

422201	C	DP	422213	C	DP	422226	C	DP	422238	C	DP
422202	C	DP	422214	C	DP	422227	C	DP	422239	C	DP
422203	C	DP	422215	C	DP	422228	C	DP	422240	C	DP
422204	C	DP	422216	C	DP	422229	C	DP	422241	C	DP
422205	C	DP	422217	C	DP	422230	C	DP	422242	C	DP
422206	C	DP	422218	C	DP	422231	C	DP	422243	C	DP
422207	C	DP	422219	C	DP	422232	C	DP	422244	C	DP
422208	C	DP	422221	C	DP	422233	C	DP	422245	C	MB
422209	C	DP	422222	C	DP	422234	C	DP	422246	C	MB
422210	C	DP	422223	C	DP	422235	C	DP	422247	C	MB
422211	C	DP	422224	C	DP	422236	C	DP	422248	C	MB
422212	C	DP	422225	C	DP	422237	C	DP	422249	C	MB

422250	C	MB	422257	C	MB	422264	C	MB	422270	C	MB
422251	C	MB	422258	C	MB	422265	C	MB	422271	C	MB
422252	C	MB	422259	C	MB	422266	C	MB	422272	C	MB
422253	C	MB	422260	C	MB	422267	C	MB	422273	C	MB
422254	C	MB	422261	C	MB	422268	C	MB	422274	C	MB
422255	C	MB	422262	C	MB	422269	C	MB	422275	C	MB
422256	C	MB	422263	C	MB						

Names:

422202	OYONNAX		422239	LONS LE SAUNIER
422216	LAGNY-SUR-MARNE		422249	VELAUX
422218	FOURMIES		422256	ROGNAC
422219	ALBERTVILLE		422267	LA CIOTAT

422276	C	MB	DIJON		122327	C	MB	
422277	C	MB	IS-SUR TILLE		122328	C	MB	
422278	C	MB			122329	C	MB	QUIMPER
422280	C	MB	HAZEBROUCK		122330	C	MB	
422281	C	MB			122331	C	MB	
422282	C	MB			122332	C	MB	
422283	C	MB			122333	C	MB	
422284	C	MB	GEVREY-CHAMBERTIN		122334	C	MB	
422285	C	DP	CHANTILLY		122335	C	MB	
422286	C	DP	BÉTHUNE		122337	C	MB	
422287	C	DP	SAINT-JEAN-DE-MAURIENNE		122338	C	MB	
422288	C	DP	LOUHANS		122339	C	MB	
422289	C	DP			122340	C	MB	CAVAILLON
422290	C	DP			122341	C	MB	
422291	C	DP	LA FERTÉ-ALAIS		122342	C	MB	CARNOULES
422292	C	DP			122343	C	MB	
422293	C	DP			122344	C	MB	
422294	C	DP			122345	C	MB	
422295	C	DP			122346	P	RS	AUBAGNE
422296	C	DP			122347	C	RS	
422297	C	DP			122348	C	RS	SAINT-MARTIN-DE-CRAU
422298	C	DP			122349	C	RS	
422299	C	DP			122350	C	RS	
422300	C	DP	CHALON-SUR-SAÔNE		122351	C	RS	VALOGNES
422301	C	DP	VILLENEUVE-D'ASCQ		122352	C	RS	SABLÉ-SUR-SARTHE
422302	C	DP	RIVE-DE-GIER		122353	C	RS	PLAISIR
422303	C	DP	CROIX		122354	C	RS	ANCENIS
422304	P	DP			122355	C	RS	SÈVRES
422305	C	DP	ST-RAMBERT-D'ALBON		122356	C	RS	LORIENT
422306	C	DP			122357	C	RS	
122307	C	MB	LE TEIL		122358	C	RS	
122308	C	MB	GISORS		122359	C	RS	
122309	C	MB			122360	C	RS	
122310	C	MB			122361	C	RS	
122311	C	MB	PIERREFITTE		122362	C	RS	
122312	C	MB	ANTIBES JUAN-LES-PINS		122363	C	RS	
122313	C	MB	DIGNE-LES-BAINS		122364	C	RS	
122314	C	MB	TAIN-L'HERMITAGE		122365	C	RS	
122315	C	MB	MIRAMAS		122366	C	RS	MALAKOFF
122316	C	MB	LOMME		122367	C	RS	5ème Regiment Du Génie
122317	C	MB	LA-TOUR-DU-PIN		122368	C	RS	
122318	C	MB	CARPENTRAS		122369	C	RS	
122319	C	MB	SORGUES-SUR-OUVÈZE		122370	C	RS	THOUARS
122320	C	MB	ISTRES		122371	C	RS	LADOIX-SERRIGNY
122321	C	MB	BELLEVILE		122372	C	RS	MAURIAC
122322	C	MB	BOLLÈNE		122373	C	RS	AULNAY-SOUS-BOIS
122323	C	MB	CAGNES-SUR-MER		122374	C	RS	NOYON
122324	C	MB	LANNION		422375	C	RS	MÉRICOURT
122325	C	MB	CHAMPIGNY-SUR-MARNE		122376	C	RS	DOUAI
122326	C	MB			122377	C	RS	ROUBAIX

622378	C t	VG	LE QUESNOY	122392	C	RS	CHARLES TELLIER
622379	C t	VG		122393	C	RS	PONT-À-VENDIN
622380	C t	VG		122394	C	RS	JOINVILLE-LE-PONT
122381	C	RS	LE BOURGET	122395	C	RS	NEUILLY-PLAISANCE
122382	C	RS	CLERMONT DE L'OISE	122396	C	RS	BAIE-DE-SOMME
122383	C	RS	BULLY-LES-MINES	122397	C	RS	PAGNY-SUR-MEUSE
122384	C	RS	SAINT-ANDRÉ-LÈS-LILLE	122398	C	RS	COUDERKERQUE-BRANCHE
122385	C	RS	LONGUEAU	622399	C t	VG	MORMANT
422386	C t	RS	BAILLEUL	122400	C	RS	MONTIGNY-EN-OSTREVENT
122387	P	RS	LIÉVIN	422401	C t	VG	MOULINS
122388	C	RS	SOMAIN	122402	C	RS	SAINT-DIÉ-DES-VOSGES
122389	C	RS	COMINES	422403	C t	VG	NEUVES-MAISONS
122390	C	RS	LESQUIN	122404	C	RS	LES PAVILLONS-SOUS-BOIS
122391	C	RS	HIRSON	422405	C t	VG	

CLASS BB 25100   Bo-Bo

An early dual-voltage design. Until 1988, the class rarely strayed from the Dijon–Thionville route but now they share a diagram with Thionville's Class BB 25150s and on freight work to Dunkerque via Charleville and to Paris via Châlons-sur-Marne. The class performs poorly under 1500 V d.c. and so is used largely as straight 25 kV a.c. locos apart from frequent operation to Dijon. The class is now managed in a pool with Class BB 25150 at TV and Class BB 25200 at RS. They are therefore increasingly turning up in the west of France.

Built: 1964–1965.   **Systems:** 1500 V d.c./25 kV a.c.
Builder: MTE.
Traction Motors: Four Jeumont TO 136-8.
Continuous Rating: 3400 kW (1500 V)/4130 kW (25 kV).
Weight: 85 tonnes.
Max. T.E.: 367 kN.
Wheel Dia.: 1250 mm.   **Length:** 16.20 m.
     Max. Speed: 130 km/h.

425101	C	TV	425108	C	TV	425114	C	TV	425120	C	TV
425102	C	TV	425109	C	TV	425115	C	TV	425121	C	TV
425103	C	TV	425110	C	TV	425116	C	TV	425122	C	TV
425104	C	TV	425111	C	TV	425117	C	TV	425123	C	TV
425105	C	TV	425112	C	TV	425118	C	TV	425124	C	TV
425106	C	TV	425113	C	TV	425119	C	TV	425125	C	TV
425107	C	TV									

CLASS BB 25150   Bo-Bo

Similar to Class BB 25100 from which it was developed. Thionville locos share a diagram with Class BB 25100 whilst Chambéry engines work over all the Alpine lines. The class has three different designs of lateral grilles.

Built: 1967–69/1974*/1976–77†.   **Systems:** 1500 V d.c./25 kV a.c.
Builder: MTE.
Traction Motors: Four Jeumont TO 136-8.
Continuous Rating: 3400 kW (1500 V)/4130 kW (25 kV).
Weight: 85 (89*†) tonnes.
Max. T.E.: 367 kN.
Wheel Dia.: 1250 mm.   **Length:** 16.20 (16.68*,16.73†) m.
     Max. Speed: 130 km/h.

Fitted with rheostatic braking. 425186–95 are fitted with snowploughs.

425151	C	TV	425161	C	TV	425171	C *	CB	425181	C †	TV
425152	C	TV	425162	C	TV	425172	C *	CB	425182	C †	TV
425153	C	TV	425163	C	TV	425173	C *	CB	425183	C †	TV
425154	C	TV	425164	C	TV	425174	C *	CB	425184	C †	TV
425155	C	TV	425165	C	TV	425175	C *	CB	425185	C †	TV
425156	C	TV	425166	C	TV	425176	C †	TV	425186	C †	CB
425157	C	TV	425167	C	TV	425177	C †	TV	425187	C †	CB
425158	C	TV	425168	C	TV	425178	C †	TV	425188	C †	CB
425159	C	TV	425169	C	TV	425179	C †	TV	425189	C †	TV
425160	P	TV	425170	C	TV	425180	C †	TV	425190	C †	CB

| 425191 **C** † CB | 425193 **C** † CB | 425194 **C** † CB | 425195 **C** † CB |
| 425192 **C** † CB | | | |

Name: 425175 LE CREUSOT

CLASS BB 25200   Bo-Bo

A faster version of the preceding two classes, being a dual voltage version of Classes BB 9200 and BB 16000. The class was completely displaced from passenger duties in Brittany by TGV A sets and Class BB 22200 and SNCF decided to downgrade 25203–25235 to freight work. This involved a change to their gear ratios which reduced maximum speed to 130 km/h. Although they have not been renumbered, Rennes diagrams refer to them as Class BB 25150! On the other hand, Vénissieux locos retain their push-pull passenger services from Lyon to the Alps. 25201/2 were renumbered 25252/3 to keep t.d.m.-equipped locos in the same batch. 25236 has been intentonally retained in livery **E**.

Built: 1965–67/1974*.   **Systems:** 1500 V d.c./25 kV a.c.
Builder: MTE.
Traction Motors: Four Jeumont TO 136-8.
Continuous Rating: 3400 kW (1500 V)/4130 kW (25 kV).
Weight: 85 (89*) tonnes.
Max. T.E.: 304 kN.   **Length:** 16.20 (16.68*) m.
Wheel Dia.: 1250 mm.   **Max. Speed:** 130 (160 t) km/h.

t TDM push-pull fitted.

425203 **C** TV	425216 **C** RS	425229 **C** RS	525242 **P** t VE
425204 **C** TV	425217 **C** RS	425230 **C** RS	525243 **P** t VE
425205 **C** TV	425218 **C** RS	425231 **C** RS	525244 **C** t VE
425206 **C** TV	425219 **C** RS	425232 **C** RS	525245 **C** t VE
425207 **C** TV	425220 **C** RS	425233 **C** RS	525246 **C** t VE
425208 **P** TV	425221 **C** RS	425234 **P** RS	525247 **P** *t VE
425209 **C** TV	425222 **C** RS	425235 **C** RS	525248 **P** *t VE
425210 **C** RS	425223 **C** RS	525236 t VE	525249 **C** *t VE
425211 **C** RS	425224 **C** RS	525237 **C** t VE	525250 **P** *t VE
425212 **P** RS	425225 **C** RS	525238 **C** t VE	525251 **C** *t VE
425213 **C** RS	425226 **C** RS	525239 **C** t VE	525252 **C** t VE
425214 **C** RS	425227 **C** RS	525240 **C** t VE	525253 **C** t VE
425215 **C** RS	425228 **C** RS	525241 **C** t VE	

Names:

| 525247 COMBOURG | 525251 VERSAILLES |
| 525250 VITRÉ | 525252 LE MANS |

CLASS BB 25500   B-B

A dual voltage version of Classes BB 8500 and BB 17000 and built in three batches with detail variations in styling and cabs. AC and TP locos are largely used on freight, particularly around the Grande Ceinture Paris freight orbital route. A number of locos have been modified for push-pull operation at 140 km/h and are more likely to be found on passenger work around Rennes (AC), Lyon (VE), on the Marseille–Ventimiglia line (MB) and Dijon (DP). 25539 was destroyed in an accident.

Built: 1964–76.   **Systems:** 1500 V d.c./25 kV a.c.
Builder: Alsthom.
Traction Motors: Two Alsthom TAB 660B1 frame-mounted monomotors.
Continuous Rating: 2940 kW.   **Max. T.E.:** 330/197 kN.
Weight: 79 tonnes (25501–44), 80 tonnes (25545–55), 77 tonnes (25556–87), 81 tonnes (25588–694).
Length: 14.70 m (25501–44), 14.94 m (25545–87), 15.57 m (25588–694).
Wheel Dia.: 1100 mm.   **Max. Speed:** 100/140 km/h.

Rheostatic braking. Multiple working fitted. Push-pull fitted (120 km/h) except 25501–11/32–46.
e Fitted with snowploughs.
p Equipped for push-pull at 140 km/h.

| 425501 **C** TP | 425503 **C** TP | 425505 **C** TP | 425507 **C** TP |
| 425502 **C** TP | 425504 **P** TP | 425506 **C** TP | 425508 **C** TP |

No.				No.				No.				No.			
425509	C		TP	425557	C	p	AC	825603	I		MR	525649	C		VE
425510	C		TP	425558	C		AC	825604	I		MR	425650	C	p	AC
425511	C		TP	425559	C		AC	825605	I		MR	525651			MB
425512	C		AC	425560	C		AC	825606	I	p	MR	525652			MB
425513	C		AC	425561	C		AC	825607	I		MR	525653			VE
425514	C		AC	425562	C	p	AC	825608	I		MR	525654	C		VE
425515	C		AC	425563	C		AC	825609	I		MR	425655	C	p	DP
425516	C		AC	425564	C		AC	825610	I		MR	525656	C		VE
425517	C		AC	425565	C		AC	825611	I	p	MR	525657			VE
425518	C		AC	425566	C		AC	825612	I		MR	525658			MB
425519	C		AC	425567	C		AC	825613	I	p	MR	525659			VE
425520	C		AC	425568	C	p	AC	425614	C		AC	425660	C	p	AC
425521	C		AC	425569	P		AC	425615	C		AC	425661	C	p	AC
425522	C		AC	425570	C	p	AC	425616	C	p	AC	425662	C		AC
425523	C		AC	425571	C		AC	425617	C		AC	425663	C		AC
425524	C		AC	425572	C		AC	425618	C	p	AC	525664			VE
425525	P		AC	425573	C	p	AC	425619	C		AC	525665	C	e	MB
425526	C		AC	425574	C		AC	525620			MB	525666			MB
425527	C		AC	425575	C		AC	525621			MB	525667			MB
425528	C		AC	425576	P		AC	525622	C		MB	525668	C		MB
425529	C		AC	425577	C		AC	525623			MB	525669			MB
425530	C		AC	425578	C		AC	525624	C		MB	525670	C		MB
425531	C		AC	425579	C		AC	525625	C		MB	425671		pe	DP
425532	P		TP	425580	P	p	AC	525626			MB	425672		pe	DP
425533	C		TP	425581	C		AC	525627			VE	525673		e	VE
425534	P		TP	425582	C		AC	525628			MB	425674	C	pe	DP
425535	C		TP	425583	C		AC	525629			MB	425675	C	e	AC
425536	C		TP	425584	C	p	AC	525630	C		MB	525676	C	e	MB
425537	P		TP	425585	C	p	AC	425631	C		AC	525677	C	e	MB
425538	C		TP	425586	C		AC	525632			VE	425678	C	p	DP
425540	C		TP	425587	C		AC	525633			MB	425679		p	DP
425541	C		TP	425588	C	p	AC	525634	C		VE	425680		p	DP
425542	C		TP	425589	C	p	AC	525635			MB	525681	C		VE
425543	C		TP	425590	C		AC	425636	C		AC	525682	C		VE
425544	C		TP	425591	C	p	AC	525637	C		VE	425683		p	DP
425545	C		TP	425592	C		AC	525638			VE	425684	C	p	DP
425546	C		TP	425593	C		AC	425639		p	DP	425685	C	p	DP
425547	C	p	TP	425594			AC	525640			VE	425686	C	p	DP
425548	C	p	TP	425595	P	p	AC	525641			VE	425687	C	p	DP
425549	C	p	TP	825596	I		MR	525642	C		VE	425688	C	p	DP
425550	C	p	TP	825597	I		MR	525643			VE	425689		p	DP
425551	C	p	TP	825598	I		MR	525644	C		MB	425690	C	p	DP
425552	C	p	TP	825599	I		MR	525645			MB	425691	C	p	DP
425553	C	p	TP	825600	I		MR	525646			MB	425692	C	p	DP
425554	C	p	TP	825601	I		MR	525647	C		MB	425693		p	DP
425555	C	p	TP	825602	C		MR	525648			MB	425694	C	e	DP
425556	C	p	AC												

Name: 425544 PARTHENAY

CLASS BB 26000   B-B

These new dual voltage locomotives feature synchronous motors and are known as "Sybics" (**Sy**nchronous-**bic**ourant). The original order was cut by 30 and replaced by 30 Class BB 36000 locos. Although the class is split between three depots, locos are managed in a pool and can be found over most of France although not yet in Brittany. Use is limited east of Marseille, west of Nîmes and in the Alps. Locos work 200 km/h services on Paris–Cherbourg, Paris–Toulouse (VG locos), Orléans–Nantes and Strasbourg–Mulhouse lines. Lens locos specialise in Channel Tunnel–Modane freights. 26129–42 have recently been dedicated to the TENOR block trains fleet. Locos fron 26188 onwards have a third, central headlight.

Built: 1988–98.   **Systems:** 1500 V d.c./25 kV a.c.
Builder: Alsthom.
Traction Motors: Two Jeumont-Schneider STS 105-37-8 frame-mounted three-phase synchronous monomotors.

Continuous Rating: 5600 kW. **Weight:** 91 tonnes.
Max. T.E.: 320 kN. **Length:** 17.48 m.
Wheel Dia.: 1250 mm. **Max. Speed:** 200 km/h.
Class Specific Livery: S Two-tone grey with orange front ends.
Non-Standard Livery: N Alsace Region livery.

† Equipped with multiplex equipment for multiple tests.

426001	S	VG	126058	S	VG	426115	S	LE	426172	S	DP
426002	S	VG	126059	S	VG	426116	S	LE	426173	S	DP
426003	S	VG	126060	S	VG	426117	S	LE	426174	S	DP
426004	S	VG	426061	S	LE	426118	S	LE	426175	S	DP
426005	S	VG	426062	S	LE	426119	S	LE	426176	S	DP
426006	S	VG	426063	S	LE	426120	S	LE	426177	S	DP
426007	S	VG	426064	S	LE	426121	S	LE	426178	S	DP
426008	S	VG	426065	S	LE	426122	S	LE	426179	S	DP
426009	S	VG	426066	S	LE	426123	S	LE	426180	S	DP
426010	S	VG	426067	S	LE	426124	S	LE	426181	S	DP
426011	S	VG	426068	S	LE	426125	S	LE	426182	S	DP
426012	S	VG	426069	S	LE	426126	S	LE	426183	S	DP
426013	S	VG	426070	N	LE	426127	S	LE	426184	S	DP
426014	N	VG	426071	S	LE	426128	S	LE	426185	S	DP
426015	S	VG	426072	S	LE	426129	S	LE	426186	S	DP
426016	S	VG	426073	S	LE	426130	S	LE	426187	S	DP
426017	S	VG	426074	S	LE	426131	S	LE	426188	S	DP
426018	S	VG	426075	S	LE	426132	S	LE	426189	S	DP
426019	S	VG	426076	S	LE	426133	S	LE	426190	S	DP
426020	S	VG	426077	S	LE	426134	S	LE	426191	S	DP
426021	S	VG	426078	S	LE	426135	S	LE	426192	S	DP
426022	S	VG	426079	S	LE	426136	S	LE	426193	S	DP
426023	S	VG	426080	S	LE	426137	S	LE	426194	S	DP
426024	S	VG	426081	S	LE	426138	S	LE	426195	S	DP
126025	S	VG	426082	S	LE	426139	S	LE	426196	S	DP
126026	S	VG	426083	S	LE	426140	S	LE	426197	S	DP
126027	S	VG	426084	S	LE	426141	S	LE	426198	S	DP
126028	S	VG	426085	S	LE	426142	S	LE	426199	S	DP
126029	S	VG	426086	S †	DP	426143	S	LE	426200	S	DP
126030	S	VG	426087	S †	DP	426144	S	LE	426201	S	DP
126031	S	VG	426088	S †	DP	426145	S	LE	426202	S	DP
126032	S	VG	426089	S	LE	426146	S	LE	426203	S	DP
126033	S	VG	426090	S	LE	426147	S	LE	426204	S	DP
126034	S	VG	426091	S	LE	426148	S	LE	426205	S	DP
126035	S	VG	426092	S	LE	426149	S	LE	426206	S	DP
126036	S	VG	426093	S	LE	426150	S	LE	426207	S	DP
126037	S	VG	426094	S	LE	426151	S	LE	426208	S	DP
126038	S	VG	426095	S	LE	426152	S	LE	426209	S	DP
126039	S	VG	426096	S	LE	426153	S	LE	426210	S	DP
126040	S	VG	426097	S	LE	426154	S	DP	426211	S	DP
126041	S	VG	426098	S	LE	426155	S	DP	426212	S	DP
126042	S	VG	426099	S	LE	426156	S	DP	426213	S	DP
126043	S	VG	426100	S	LE	426157	S	DP	426214	S	DP
126044	S	VG	426101	S	LE	426158	S	DP	426215	S	DP
126045	S	VG	426102	S	LE	426159	S	DP	426216	S	DP
126046	S	VG	426103	S	LE	426160	P	DP	426217	S	DP
126047	S	VG	426104	S	LE	426161	S	DP	426218	S	DP
126048	P	VG	426105	S	LE	426162	S	DP	426219	S	DP
126049	S	VG	426106	S	LE	426163	S	DP	426220	S	DP
126050	S	VG	426107	S	LE	426164	S	DP	426221	S	DP
126051	S	VG	426108	S	LE	426165	S	DP	426222	S	DP
126052	S	VG	426109	S	LE	426166	S	DP	426223	S	DP
126053	S	VG	426110	S	LE	426167	S	DP	426224	S	DP
126054	S	VG	426111	S	LE	426168	S	DP	426225	S	DP
126055	S	VG	426112	S	LE	426169	S	DP	426226	S	DP
126056	S	VG	426113	S	LE	426170	S	DP	426227	P	DP
126057	S	VG	426114	S	LE	426171	S	DP	426228	S	DP

426229	**S**	DP	426231	**S**	DP	426233	**S**	DP	426234	**S**	DP
426230	**S**	DP	426232	**S**	DP						

Names:

426001	GIEN
426002	SOUFFELWEYERSHEIM
426003	FONTVIELLE
426004	CERNAY
426006	MUSÉE FRANÇAIS DU CHEMIN DE FER
426007	BÉNING-LÈS-SAINT-AVOLD
426009	LONGVIC-EN-BOURGOGNE
426010	VALLORBE
426011	LE PIENNOIS
426012	HAGONDANGE
426013	MIRAMAS
426014	DOLE
426015	FLORANGE
426016	CAUSSADE TARN ET GARONNE
426020	MENTON
126043	EMERAINVILLE
126044	PONTAULT-COMBAULT
126046	SELESTAT
126047	JARVILLE
126052	SAINT DIZIER
126054	JARNY
426088	REMIREMONT
426100	POMPEY
426121	COMPIÈGNE/MARNY-LES-COMPIÈGNE

CLASS BB 36000   Bo-Bo

After ordering 264 Class BB 26000 "Sybic" locos from GEC Alsthom, SNCF decided to ask for a change to the contract and the last 30 locos became three-voltage, asynchronous motored locos. In order to accommodate two traction motors per bogie, the locos are slightly longer than Sybics. The class is nicknamed "Astride" by SNCF, the previous named "Asytrit" having been dropped. The two pre-series locos, 36001/2, were still being tested in late 1997. Production locos started being delivered from mid 1997. The whole class will be maintained at Lens depot. Originally designed as a "universal" locomotive, the class will only operate only freight services, particularly from the Channel Tunnel and from Belgium to Italy where SNCF hopes to arrange through working.

Built: 1996– .   **Systems**: 1500 V d.c./3000 V d.c./25 kV a.c.
Builder: GEC-Alsthom.
Traction Motors: Four FXA 4559 three-phase asynchronous.
Continuous rating: 5600 kW.   **Weight**: 89 tonnes.
Maximum Tractive Effort: 320 kN.   **Length**: 19.30 m.
Continuous Tractive Effort: 250 kN.
Wheel Dia.: 1250 mm.   **Max. Speed**: 140 km/h.
Class Specific Livery: S Grey with red front ends and dark grey side band.

Regenerative and rheostatic braking.

436001	**S**	LE	436014	**S**	LE	436027	**S**		436040	**S**
436002	**S**	LE	436015	**S**	LE	436028	**S**		436041	**S**
436003	**S**	LE	436016	**S**	LE	436029	**S**		436042	**S**
436004	**S**	LE	436017	**S**	LE	436030	**S**		436043	**S**
436005	**S**	LE	436018	**S**	LE	436031	**S**		436044	**S**
436006	**S**	LE	436019	**S**		436032	**S**		436045	**S**
436007	**S**	LE	436020	**S**		436033	**S**		436046	**S**
436008	**S**	LE	436021	**S**		436034	**S**		436047	**S**
436009	**S**	LE	436022	**S**		436035	**S**		436048	**S**
436010	**S**	LE	436023	**S**		436036	**S**		436049	**S**
436011	**S**	LE	436024	**S**		436037	**S**		436050	**S**
436012	**S**	LE	436025	**S**		436038	**S**		436051	**S**
436013	**S**	LE	436026	**S**		436039	**S**		436052	**S**

| 436053 **S** | 436055 **S** | 436057 **S** | 436059 **S** |
| 436054 **S** | 436056 **S** | 436058 **S** | 436060 **S** |

Names:

436003 MAUBERGE-RATINGEN
436005 HIRSON/CHARLEROI
436006 CHAMPIGNUILLE VILLE

CLASS BB 80000   Bo-Bo

These are Class BB 8100 locos converted for empty coaching stock movements from Masséna to Paris Austerlitz. Modifications are restricted to the reduction in maximum speed, removal of multiple operation cables and equipment with radio. In the case of locos converted from two locos, the new loco is a combination of the body of one and the bogies of the other. Conversions stopped after 12 locos of 27 originally programmed to save money. Instead, Class BB 8500 are being downgraded for this work. Details as Class BB 8100 except:

Modified: 1995–98 by SNCF Béziers works.
Max. Speed: 100 km/h.

180001	(8189)	**C**	PO	180005	(8139)	**C**	PO	180009	(8162)	**C**	PO
180002	(8161)	**C**	PO	180006	(8166)	**C**	PO	180010	(8188)	**C**	PO
180003	(8126)	**C**	PO	180007	(8121)	**C**	PO	180011	(8185)	**C**	PO
180004	(8175)	**C**	PO	180008	(8220)	**C**	PO	180012	(8193)	**C**	PO

1.2. DIESEL LOCOMOTIVES

All diesel locomotives are livery **D** (blue and grey with white lining) unless otherwise shown.

CLASS BB 62400   Bo-Bo

In 1990 SNCF bought 44 of these ex NS diesels for work on the construction of the TGV Nord Europe line. They were later used on the TGV Jonction Paris avoiding line but almost all were stored at Longueau depot for 5 years then reactivated for the TGV Méditeranée in 1999. The last four digits of the number are the former NS number. The four locos at Longueau are used on test trains around Paris.

Built: 1954–57.   **Builder:** Alsthom.
Engine: SACM MGO V12A SHR (625 kW).
Transmission: Electric. Four Alsthom TA637 traction motors.
Heating: None.   **Weight:** 60 tonnes.
Max. T.E.: 161 kN.   **Length:** 12.52 m.
Wheel Dia.: 1000 mm.   **Max. Speed:** 80 km/h.
Class Specific Livery: S NS. Grey with yellow cabs and front panels.
Non-Standard Livery: N 662450/501 are NS maroon and 663413 is NS blue.

662403	S	AV	662430	S	AV	662456	S	AV	662501	N	AV
662405	S	AV	662432	S	AV	662458	S	AV	662502	S	AV
662406	S	AV	662439	S	AV	662459	S	AV	662504	S	AV
662407	S	AV	662440	S	LO	662462	S	AV	662506	S	AV
662409	S	AV	662443	S	AV	662465	S	AV	662508	S	AV
662412	S	AV	662444	S	AV	662466	S	AV	662510	S	AV
662413	N	AV	662449	S	AV	662467	S	AV	662513	S	AV
662414	S	AV	662450	N	AV	662470	S	AV	662518	S	AV
662418	S	LO	662452	S	AV	662477	S	AV	662526	S	LO
662424	S	AV	662454	S	AV	662491	S	AV	662528	S	LO
662429	S	AV									

CLASS BB 63000   Bo-Bo

Classes BB 63000, 63400 and 63500 are all virtually identical and form a large family of over 800 locomotives. These low powered locomotives are found on station pilot duties, freight trips and general shunting duties and appear all over France. Following loss of freight traffic and replacement by Class Y 8000 shunters, this class is now being withdrawn quickly. Several have been sold into industrial use. A number have been converted to Class BB 64800.

Built: 1953–64.   **Builder:** Brissonneau and Lotz.
Engine: Sulzer 6LDA22B (440 kW) (63003–68), Sulzer 6LDA22C (440 kW) (63074–108), Sulzer 6LDA22C (535 kW) (63111–127), Sulzer 6LDA22D (535 kW) (63131–193), Sulzer 6LDA22E (550 kW) (63196–250).
Transmission: Electric. Four B&L 453-29 traction motors.
Heating: None.   **Weight:** 64–69 tonnes.
Max. T.E.: 167 kN.   **Length:** 14.68 m.
Wheel Dia.: 1050 mm.   **Max. Speed:** 90 km/h.

63003	V	TP	663060	J	PO	63098	V	NV	63135	V	NV
63004	J	TP	663061	V	PO	63099	J	DP	63136	J	PV
63005	V	TP	63062	V	NV	63100	J	TP	63138	V	MB
63006	V	CB	63067	V	MB	63107	V	TP	63140	J	LE
663007	V	PO	63068	J	DP	663108	V	PO	63142	V	LE
63010	V	CB	63074	V	CB	63111	V	CB	663144	V	PO
63015	J	VG	63078	V	CB	63113	V	PV	63145	J	LE
63016	J	NV	663082	J	PO	63116	V	CB	663147	V	PO
63017	J	MB	63085	J	DP	63122	J	TP	63151	V	TP
63018	J	MB	663088	V	PO	63127	J	CB	63152	V	TP
663037	V	PO	63094	V	TP	63131	V	PV	63156	V	TP
63048	J	MB	63095	J	CB	63133	V	MB	63157	V	TP
63056	J	TP	63096	V	NV	63134	V	PV	63158	V	TP

63160	J	PV	63182	J	LE	63205	J	DP	63232	J	DP
63161	J	PV	63184	V	MB	63207	V	TP	63233	J	DP
63162	V	PV	63185	V	MB	63209	J	LE	63237	J	DP
63165	J	PV	63187	V	DP	163211	V	PO	63239	V	LE
63166	J	PV	63188	J	TP	63216	V	PV	63240	V	PV
63167	V	DP	63189	J	PV	63217	V	DP	163241	V	PO
63168	J	LE	663192	V	PO	63222	V	MB	63243	V	TP
63170	V	PV	63193	J	DP	163225	V	PO	63244	V	DP
63177	J	PV	63196	V	PV	63226	J	DP	163248	V	PO
63179	V	MB	63197	J	LE	63227	J	DP	63249	J	TP
63180	V	PV	63198	J	NV	63228	J	DP	63250	J	TP
63181	J	PV	63200	J	DP						

CLASSES BB 63400 & BB 63500 Bo-Bo

These two classes are identical but Class BB 63400 are numbered separately as they were financed by the Eurofima organisation. The class is a more powerful version of Class BB 63000 but with many detail variations within the class, the most important being the batches which can work in multiple. A number of the class were converted into Class BB 64700.

Built: 1956–71. **Builder:** Brissonneau and Lotz.
Engine: SACM MGO V12SH (605 kW).
Transmission: Electric. Four B&L 453-29 traction motors.
Heating: None. **Weight:** 64–68 tonnes.
Max. T.E.: 167 kN. **Length:** 14.68 m.
Wheel Dia.: 1050 mm. **Max. Speed:** 90 km/h.

m Multiple working fitted.
e e.t.h. fitted.
c Equipped with cab signalling for maintenance work on TGV Atlantique line.

Class BB 63400.

63401	V	NB	63407	V	NB	63413	J	LE	63419	V	VG
63402	V	VG	63408	V	BD	63414	V	VG	63420	J	NB
63403	V	NB	63409	V	LN	63415	V	VG	63421	J	NB
63404	V	SO	63410	V	NB	63416	V	VG	63422	V	VG
63405	V	NB	63411	V	AC	63417	V	NB	63423	V	PV
63406	V	NB	63412	J	NB	63418	V	VG			

Class BB 63500.

63501	V	MB	63525	J	SO	63549	V	LV	63573	V	LE
63502	V	LE	63526	V	SO	63550	V	TL	63574	J	LN
63503	V	AC	63527	V	AC	63551	J	BD	63575	V	MZ
63504	V	BD	63528	V	SB	63552	V	PV	63576	V	LN
63505	J	SO	63529	J	SO	63553	J	AC	63577	V	TL
63506	J	NB	63530	J	SO	63554	J	VG	63578	V	BD
63507	V	VG	63531	J	MZ	63555	J	RS	63579	V	AV
63508	J	AC	63532	J	AC	63556	J	SO	63580	V	TL
63509	J	RS	63533	V	LE	63557	V	TL	63581	V	VG
63510	V	PO	63534	V	VG	63558	V	SO	63582	V	TL
63511	J	SO	63535	V	RS	63559	V	TL	63583	V	TL
63512	J	SO	63536	V	PV	63560	V	LE	63584	V	AV
63513	J	SO	63537	J	SO	63561	J	SO	63585	V	VG
63514	J	VG	63538	V	TL	63562	V	LV	63586	J	BD
63515	V	VG	63539	V	SO	63563	J	SO	63587	V	SB
63516	V	SO	63540	V	TL	63564	V	AC	63588	J	PV
63517	J	SB	63541	J	AC	63565	V	AV	63589	V	LN
63518	V	AC	63542	V	AV	63566	J	LE	63590	V	AC
63519	J	SO	63543	V	VG	63567	J	AC	63591	J	VG
63520	V	AC	63544	V	AV	63568	J	AC	63592	V	SB
63521	J	SO	63545	V	LV	63569	J	AV	63593	V	PV
63522	J	LE	63546	V	LE	63570	V	LE	63594	V	PV
63523	J	LV	63547	J	BD	63571	V	SO	63595	V	TL
63524	V	SO	63548	V	LV	63572	V	PO	63596	V	SB

#				#				#				#			
63597	J		LE	63665	V		MZ	63730	J	m	SB	63798	J		AC
63598	J		SO	63666	J		MZ	63731	J	m	MZ	63799	J		AC
63599	J		LE	63667	J		VG	63732	V	m	MZ	63800			AC
63600	V		BD	63668	V		LN	63733	V	m	LN	63801	J		PV
63601	J		BD	63669	V		VG	63734	J	m	LN	63802	V		AC
63602	J		AC	63670	V		MZ	63735	J	m	MZ	63803	V		AC
63603	J		SO	63671	V		AV	63736	J	m	MZ	63804	J		AC
63604	V		NB	63672	J		BD	63737	V	m	LN	63805	V		VG
63605	J		BD	63673	V		LN	63738	J	m	LN	63806	J		PV
63606	V		BD	63674	V		SO	63739	J	m	LN	63807	J		PV
63607	J		SB	63675	V		LV	63740	J	m	LN	63808	V		SO
63608	V		MB	63676	V		AV	63741	V	m	MZ	63809	J		AC
63609	J		BD	63677	J		MZ	63742	J	m	MZ	63810	J		AC
63610	J		LV	63678	V		SO	63743	J	m	PV	63811	V	m	MZ
63611	J		RS	63679	V		PO	63744	J	m	LN	63812	J	m	MZ
63612	J		SO	63680	V		MZ	63745	J	m	LN	63813	J	m	AV
63613	V		SO	63681	V		MZ	63746	V	m	MZ	63814	V	m	AV
63614	J		SO	63682	V		SO	63747	J	m	PV	63815	V	m	PV
63615	V		SO	63683	V		BD	63748	J	m	MZ	63816	V	m	MZ
63616	V		SO	63684	J		BD	63749	V	m	MZ	63817	V	m	AV
63617	V		SB	63685	J		LE	63750	J	m	MZ	63818	V	m	LV
63618	V		MZ	63686	V		PV	63751	V		VG	63819	J	m	MZ
63619	V		SB	63687	J		AC	63752	J		SB	63820	V	m	MZ
63620	V		LV	63688	J		LV	63754	J		AV	63821	V	m	LV
63621	V		SO	63689	J		LV	63755	V		LV	63822	J	m	SO
63623	J		LN	63690	V		SB	63756	V		VG	63823	J	m	MZ
63624	V		AV	63691	V		SB	63757	V		RS	63824	J	m	MZ
63625	V		LE	63692	J		LV	63758	V		LV	63825	J	m	AV
63626	V		LE	63693	V		LV	63759	V		LV	63826	V	m	PV
63627	V		LV	63694	V		LV	63760	V		PO	63827	J	m	MZ
63628	J		LE	63695	V		MZ	63761	V		LN	63828	V	m	MZ
63629	V		LV	63696	V		MZ	63762	J		LN	63829	V	m	SB
63630	V		VG	63697	J		LV	63763	J		LE	63830	J	m	AV
63631	J		RS	63698	V		BD	63764	J		LE	63831	V	m	AV
63632	V		PV	63699	V		AV	63765	J		PV	63832	V	m	LE
63633	J		BD	63700	V		MZ	63766	J		LN	63833	J	m	MZ
63634	V		LV	63701	V		SB	63767	V		BD	63834	V	m	PV
63635	J		AV	63702	J		AV	63768	V		NB	63835	V	m	MZ
63636	V		PV	63703	V		LN	63770	J		NB	63836	J	m	LG
63638	V		LN	63704	V		LN	63771	V		VG	63837	V	m	AV
63639	V		SB	63705	J		LV	63772	J		LN	63838	V	m	AV
63640	V		LV	63706	V		LE	63773	J		LN	63839	J	m	LE
63641	V		LV	63707	V		VG	63774	V		PV	63840	V	m	MZ
63642	V		LE	63708	V		LV	63775	V		BD	63841	V	m	LE
63643	V		LN	63709	J		PV	63776	J		LN	63842	J	m	LG
63645	V		SO	63710	J		AV	63777	V		LN	63843	V	m	MZ
63646	V		LV	63711	V		PV	63778	V		LE	63844	V	m	MZ
63647	J		BD	63712	J		VG	63779	J		VG	63845	V	m	MZ
63648	V		NB	63713	V		LV	63780	V		LV	63846	V	m	AV
63649	J		VG	63714	V		LE	63781	J		MZ	63847	V	m	MZ
63650	J		SO	63716	V		MB	63782	V		BD	63848	J	m	PV
63651	V		MZ	63717	V		LE	63783	J		PV	63849	V	m	MZ
63652	V		LN	63718	V		SB	63784	V		LV	63850	V	m	MZ
63653	V		SO	63719	V		PV	63785	V		LV	63851	V	m	MZ
63654	V		BD	63720	V		AV	63786	V		LE	63852	V	m	MZ
63655	V		MZ	63721	V	m	LE	63787	V		BD	63853	V	m	LE
63656	V		LV	63722	V	m	SB	63788	V		PV	63854	V	m	LV
63657	J		AV	63723	V	m	SB	63789	V		LV	63855	V	m	LG
63658	J		BD	63724	V	m	LN	63790	V		LV	63856	J	m	LN
63659	V		AV	63725	V	m	SB	63791	J		LE	63857	J	m	SO
63660	J		NB	63726	V	m	MZ	63792	J		AC	63858	V	m	MZ
63661	V		MZ	63727	V	m	SB	63794	J		AC	63859	V	m	LV
63663	V		PO	63728	J	m	SB	63796	J		LN	63860	V	m	SB
63664	V		LE	63729	J	m	LN	63797			PV	63861	V	m	MZ

No.				No.				No.				No.			
63862	V	m	SO	63923	J		LE	63982	V	m	BD	64031	V		SO
63863	V	m	MZ	63924	J		LE	63983	V	m	LG	64032	V		LG
63864	V	m	AV	63925	V		MZ	63984	J	m	LN	64033	J		MZ
63865	J	m	LV	63926	J		VG	63985	J	m	LG	64034	V		SO
63866	V	m	SO	63927	J		VG	63986	J	m	BD	64035	V		AV
63867	V	m	MZ	63928	J		LV	63987	J	m	BD	64036	V		MZ
63868	V	m	MZ	63929	J		LN	63988	J	m	LN	64037	V		AC
63869	J	m	LG	63930	J		PV	63989	J	m	LG	64038	J		AV
63870	V	m	SB	63931	V		MZ	63990	J	m	LG	64039	V		MZ
63871	V	m	MZ	63932	V		LV	63991	J	m	LN	64040	V		LN
63872	J	m	MZ	63933	V		NB	63992	V	m	LV	64041	V		SO
63873	V	m	SB	63934	V		LV	63993	J	m	BD	64042	V		SO
63874	V	m	SB	63935	J		LN	63994	J	m	LG	64043	V		BD
63875	J	m	SB	63936	J		LN	63995	J	m	LN	64044	J		TL
63876	V	m	SB	63938	V		PV	63996	V	m	SO	64045	V		MZ
63877	J	m	SB	63939	V		RS	63997	V	m	PV	64046	V		PV
63878	J	m	SB	63940	J		LV	63998	V	m	PV	64047	V		RS
63879	V	m	SB	63941	J		NB	63999	J	m	SB	64048	V		RS
63880	J	m	SO	63942	V		MZ	64000	J	m	PV	64049	V		MB
63881	V	m	SB	63944	J		BD	64001	V	m	BD	64050	J		AV
63882	V	m	MZ	63947	J		BD	64002	V	m	BD	64051	J		MZ
63883	J	m	SB	63948	V		BD	64003	J	m	SO	64052	V		RS
63884	V	m	SB	63950	V		PV	64004	J	m	LG	64054	V		BD
63885	V	m	LN	63951	V		LV	64005	J	m	BD	64055	V		PV
63890	V		LV	63952	V		MZ	64006	J	m	BD	64056	V		AC
63891	V		PV	63953	J		PV	64007	J	m	MZ	64057	J		VG
63893	V		PV	63954	V		PV	64008	J	m	MZ	64058	J		LE
63894	V		PV	63955	V		LG	64009	V	m	SO	64059	J		SO
63895	V		MB	63956	V		LN	64010	J	m	SO	64060	J		MZ
63896	V	e	AV	63957	V		LG	64011	V	m	LG	64061	J		SB
63897	V		NB	63958	J		RS	64012	J	m	LG	64062	J		SB
63898	J		SB	63960	V		MB	64013	J	m	SO	64063	J		PV
63899	V		LE	63961	V		NB	64014	J	m	SO	64064	J		MZ
63900	V		AV	63962	V		VG	64015	J	m	SO	64065	V		LN
63901	V	e	AV	63964	J		TL	64016	V	m	BD	64066	J		LN
63902	V	e	PV	63965	J	c	AC	64017	V	m	BD	64067	J		LE
63903	V		SO	63966	V		MZ	64018	V	m	BD	64068	J		LE
63905	V		MB	63967	J		NB	64019	V	m	SO	64069	J		LN
63906	V	e	PV	63968	J		RS	64020	J	m	SO	64070	J		AV
63907	V		RS	63969	V		MB	64021	V		LE	64071	J		AV
63911	V		SB	63970	J		MZ	64022	V		SO	64072	V		AV
63912	J		SB	63971	V		LV	64023	V		AV	64073	J		AC
63913	V		MZ	63972	V		AV	64024	V		LV	64074	J		SB
63914	V		PV	63973	V		MZ	64025	V		SO	64075	J		AV
63915	V		SO	63975	V		LV	64026	V		MB	64076	V		PV
63917	V		SB	63977	J		MZ	64027	V		LG	64077	V		PV
63919	V		MZ	63978	J		TL	64028	V		LE	64079	V		PV
63921	V		SO	63979	J	c	AC	64029	J		AV	64080	V		PV
63922	V		LV	63981	J	m	BD	64030	V		PV				

CLASS BB 64700/TBB 64800   Bo-Bo+Bo-Bo

With freight train weights continuing to increase the SNCF required shunters of greater tractive effort. SNCF decided to go back to a system previously tried with Class C 61000, where a number of motored trucks (Class TC 61100) were coupled to them. Class BB 63500 was decided on as the master unit and Nevers Works was given the job of rebuilding these locos which are finished off similar to Class BB 66700. Sotteville Quatre Mares Works was given the job of converting Class BB 63000s into the new mates (motors assisting tractive effort). Here the work has been more drastic. The cab has been removed as it is unnecessary but the main frame has been shortened and the two motor bogies are much closer. The overall length of the Class BB 64700 remains the same as its predessor but the Class TBB 64800 measures only 11.39 m. As there are no fuel tanks and no diesel engine in the mate a large deadweight has been added to give good adhesion. Locos are used in yards at Miramas (AV), Sibelin (LV), Woippy (MZ), Hausbergen (SB), Sotteville (SO), Dunkerque and Somain (LE).

Details as 2 x Class BB 63500 except:

Max. T.E.: 300 kN. **Weight:** 63 + 63 tonnes.
Max. Speed: 80 km/h. **Length:** 14.68 m. + 11.39 m.

Class BB 64700 Locomotives.

464701	(63920)	J	AV	464709	(63946)	J	MZ	464717	(63937)	J	LE
464702	(63976)	J	LV	464710	(63910)	J	SB	464718	(63908)	J	AV
464703	(63889)	J	LV	464711	(63974)	J	SB	464719	(63892)	J	LE
464704	(63959)	J	AV	464712	(63886)	J	SB	464720	(63949)	J	LE
464705	(63909)	J	AV	464713	(63945)	J	SO	464721	(63888)	J	MZ
464706	(63644)	J	MZ	464714	(63904)	J	SO	464722	(63916)	J	SO
464707	(63980)	J	MZ	464715	(63918)	J	SO	464723	(63943)	J	LE
464708	(63887)	J	MZ	464716	(63963)	J	LE				

Class TBB 64800 Mates.

464801	(63024)	J	AV	464808	(63070)	J	MZ	464814	(63030)	J	SO
464802	(63057)	J	LV	464809	(63051)	J	MZ	464815	(63063)	J	SO
464803	(63043)	J	LV	464810	(63089)	J	SB	464816	(63025)	J	LE
464804	(63080)	J	AV	464811	(63022)	J	SB	464817	(63047)	J	LE
464805	(63001)	J	AV	464812	(63075)	J	SB	464818	(63034)	J	AV
464806	(63014)	J	MZ	464813	(63086)	J	SO	464819	(63093)	J	LE
464807	(63059)	J	MZ								

CLASS CC 65500 Co-Co

The first heavy duty diesel introduced for freight work around the Grande Ceinture route in Paris. They were made redundant by electrification and the introduction of dual-voltage electric locomotives on transfer freights. Saved from the scrapyard by the need to have powerful locomotives for use on construction trains on LGV Sud Est, they had reprieves for work on the LGV Atlantique and the LGV Rhône-Alpes around Lyon. They were stored for two years at Vénissieux before being transferred to Avignon from 1997 for work on the LGV Méditerranée. Who knows when they will be withdrawn? Known as "Dakotas" after the aircraft, perhaps because the latter were also indestructible. These locos are officially renumberered with a '6' prefix, but not in practice, since they have numberplates.

Built: 1955–59. **Builders:** CAFL/CEM.
Engine: Sulzer 12LDA28 (1470 kW).
Transmission: Electric. Six CEM GDTM 532 traction motors.
Heating: None. **Weight:** 123 tonnes.
Max. T.E.: 359 kN. **Length:** 19.42 m.
Wheel Dia.: 1200 mm. **Max. Speed:** 80 km/h.

65501	V	AV	65515	V	AV	65521	V	AV	65530	V	AV
65502	V	AV	65516	V	AV	65524	V	AV	65531	V	AV
65503	V	AV	65517	V	AV	65527	V	AV	65533	V	AV
65506	V	AV	65519	V	AV	65529	V	AV	65534	V	AV
65508	V	AV	65520	V	AV					

CLASS BB 66000 Bo-Bo

A mixed traffic locomotive once found on passenger trains but with the introduction of electric heating they are not now found on this type of work. At one time they worked in multiple either side of a boiler van. Class BB 66400 have taken over local passenger train work while Classes BB 67300 and BB 67400 work the heavier trains. Some were rebuilt as Class BB 66600 (now all withdrawn) and others as Class BB 66700. Apart from the majority of the class, which have a low level of activity on a variety of local freights, a number of the earliest locos are usually in use on construction trains. They are now mainly at Avignon for work on the LGV Méditerranée.

Built: 1959–68. **Builders:** CAFL/CEM/Alsthom/Fives-Lille.
Engine: SACM MGO V16BSHR (1030 kW).
Transmission: Electric. Four Alsthom TA648A1 traction motors.
Heating: None. **Weight:** 66/67 tonnes.

Max. T.E.: 167 kN.
Wheel Dia.: 1100 mm.
Length: 14.90 m.
Max. Speed: 120 km/h.

Multiple working fitted. Some have snowploughs.

666001	AV	466071	TL	466153	SO	466221	LG
666002	AV	466072	TL	466154	NV	466222	AV
666003	TP	666073	TP	466155	NV	466223	LN
666004	AV	466075	TL	466156	TL	466224	SO
666006	AV	666077	TP	466157	TL	466225	SO
666007	AV	666078	TP	466159	TL	466226	SO
666008	AV	666079	TP	466160	LN	466227	LN
666013	TP	466082	TL	466161	TP	466228	NV
666014	AV	466083	TL	466162	TP	466229	SO
666016	TP	466084	TL	466163	TP	466230	TP
666018	AV	466085	TL	466164	TP	466231	TP
666019	TP	466086	TL	466165	TP	466232	TP
666020	AV	466088	LG	466167	TP	466233	TP
666021	AV	466089	TP	466168	TP	466234	TP
666022	AV	466090	TP	466169	TP	466235	TP
666023	AV	466091	LN	466170	TP	466236	TP
666024	AV	466092	LG	466171	TP	466237	TP
666025	AV	466093	LG	466175	LN	466238	TP
666026	TP	466094	LN	466179	SO	466239	TP
666027	AV	466095	LN	466180	SO	466240	TP
666028	AV	466096	LN	466181	SO	466241	TP
666029	AV	466097	LG	466182	SO	466242	NV
666031	AV	466099	LN	466183	SO	466243	NV
666032	AV	466100	LN	466184	NV	466244	NV
666033	AV	466103	LG	466185	NV	466245	NV
666034	AV	466104	LG	466186	SO	466246	NV
466035	TL	466105	LG	466187	TP	466248	NV
466036	TL	466107	LN	466188	TL	466249	LN
666037	AV	466109	TL	466189	AV	466250	NV
666038	AV	466110	LN	466190	LG	466251	LN
666041	AV	466111	TP	666191	AV	466252	SO
666042	LN	466112	TP	466192	LN	466253	TP
666043	AV	466113	LN	466193	TP	466254	LG
666044	TP	466114	LN	466194	LG	466255	TP
666045	AV	466115	TL	666195	AV	466256	SO
466046	TL	466116	LN	466196	LN	466257	LG
466047	TL	466117	TP	666197	AV	466258	SO
466048	TL	466118	LN	666198	AV	466259	NV
666049	TP	466119	LG	466199	AV	466260	LG
466050	TL	466120	NV	466200	LN	466261	LG
466051	TL	466121	LG	466201	LN	466262	TP
466052	TL	466122	LG	466202	LG	466263	SO
666053	TP	466123	AV	466203	LN	466264	SO
666054	AV	466124	TP	466204	NV	466265	TP
666055	AV	466125	TP	466205	LG	466266	TP
466056	TL	466126	LN	466206	AV	466267	LN
666057	TP	466127	TP	466207	TP	466268	TP
666058	AV	466128	TP	466208	SO	466269	LG
666059	NV	466129	LG	466209	TP	466270	LN
666060	TP	466130	LG	466210	AV	466271	LN
466061	TP	466131	TL	666211	AV	466272	TL
466062	TL	466133	TL	466212	LN	466273	TP
666063	AV	466135	NV	466213	SO	466274	LN
466064	TL	466140	TP	466214	SO	466275	LN
666065	AV	466141	TL	666215	AV	466276	LN
666066	AV	466142	LN	466216	LN	466277	LN
666067	AV	466145	LE	666217	AV	466278	SO
666068	TP	466147	NV	466218	SO	466279	LG
666069	NV	466150	TP	466219	NV	466280	LN
466070	TL	466151	TP	466220	LN	466281	LG

466282	VE	466292	LN	466301	SO	466310	TP
466283	LG	466293	NV	466302	LG	466311	TL
466284	LN	466294	SO	466303	AV	466312	SO
466285	SO	466295	TP	466304	LN	466313	LG
466286	LG	466296	LN	466305	LN	466314	LG
466287	TP	466297	AV	466306	LG	466315	LG
466288	LN	466298	AV	466307	LG	466316	AV
466289	LG	466299	AV	466308	LN	466317	TL
466290	AV	466300	LN	466309	LN	466318	SO
466291	AV						

CLASS BB 66400   Bo-Bo

This class is a development of Class BB 66000 and incorporates three-phase transmission. All are fitted with electric train heating and almost all are push-pull fitted. This feature is used for passenger trains around Lille, Creil, Clermont-Ferrand and Nancy. Apart from this, most locos are used on freight. The class is also used in multiple on passenger trains on the Rouen–Caen–Rennes route (Friday–Sunday) and on Laroche-Migennes to Auxerre.

Built: 1968–71.   **Builders:** CAFL/CEM/Alsthom/Fives-Lille.
Engine: SACM MGO V16BSHR (1030 kW).
Transmission: Electric. Four Alsthom TA648H2 three phase traction motors.
Heating: Electric.   **Weight:** 64 tonnes.
Max. T.E.: 167 kN.   **Length:** 14.97 m.
Wheel Dia.: 1100 mm.   **Max. Speed:** 120 km/h.

Multiple working fitted.

p Push-pull fitted.

466401	p	LN	566428	p	NV	566455	p	LN	466481	p	CY
466402	p	LN	566429	p	LN	566456	p	LN	466482	p	NV
466403	p	LN	466430	p	NV	466457	p	CY	566483	p	LN
466404	p	LN	466431	p	CY	466458	p	NV	566484	p	LN
466405	p	LN	466432	p	NV	566459	p	LN	566485	p	LN
466406	p	LN	466433	p	CY	566460	p	LN	466486	p	CY
466407	p	LN	466434	p	CY	566461	p	LN	466487	p	CY
466408	p	LN	466435	p	NV	566462	p	LN	466488	p	CY
466409	p	LN	466436	p	CY	466463		NV	566489	p	LN
466410	p	LN	466437	p	CY	466464	p	NV	566490	p	LN
466411	p	LN	466438	p	CY	566465		LN	466491	p	CY
466412	p	CY	466439	p	NV	466466		NV	466492	p	CY
466413	p	CY	466440	p	CY	466467	p	NV	466493	p	CY
466414	p	CY	466441	p	CY	466468		NV	466494	p	CY
466415	p	CY	466442	p	CY	466469	p	NV	466495	p	CY
466416	p	CY	466443	p	CY	466470		NV	566496	p	LN
566417	p	LN	466444	p	CY	466471		NV	466497	p	NV
466418	p	NV	566445	p	LN	466472	p	NV	466498	p	NV
566419	p	LN	466446	p	CY	466473		CY	466499	p	CY
466420	p	CY	466447	p	CY	466474	p	CY	466500	p	NV
466421	p	CY	466448	p	CY	466475		NV	466501	p	NV
466422	p	CY	466449	p	CY	566476	p	LN	466502	p	NV
466423	p	CY	566450	p	LN	466477	p	CY	466503	p	CY
466424	p	CY	566451	p	LN	466478	p	CY	566504	p	LN
466425	p	CY	566452	p	LN	466479	p	CY	566505	p	LN
466426	p	CY	566453	p	LN	566480	p	LN	466506	p	CY
466427	p	CY	566454	p	LN						

CLASS BB 66700   Bo-Bo

These are converted Class BB 66000. The ever increasing weight of wagons has led to the need for more powerful shunting locomotives. These locomotives have been regeared at Nevers works and the weight increased slightly. The locos hump shunt and haul freight at Dijon Gevrey (DP), Dunkerque (LE), Hourcade (BD) Mulhouse Nord (SB), St. Pierre-des-Corps (TP) and Sibelin (LV) yards.

Built: 1985–91.   **Builders:** CAFL/CEM/Alsthom/Fives-Lille.
Engine: SACM MGO V16BSHR (1030 kW).
Transmission: Electric. Four Alsthom TA648A1 traction motors.
Heating: None.   **Weight:** 71 tonnes.
Max. T.E.: 220 kN.   **Length:** 14.89 m.
Wheel Dia.: 1100 mm.   **Max. Speed:** 90 km/h.

466701	(66146)	J	LV	466709	(66148)	J	DP	466717	(66149)	J	TP
466702	(66080)	J	LV	466710	(66134)	J	LE	466718	(66173)	J	LE
466703	(66166)	J	LV	466711	(66158)	J	DP	466719	(66076)	J	BD
466704	(66174)	J	TP	466712	(66144)	J	LE	466720	(66074)	J	BD
466705	(66152)	J	LE	466713	(66139)	J	TP	466721	(66136)	J	BD
466706	(66172)	J	SB	466714	(66143)	J	LE	466722	(66138)	J	BD
466707	(66176)	J	SB	466715	(66081)	J	LE	466723	(66137)	J	DP
466708	(66178)	J	SB	466716	(66177)	J	LE	466724	(66087)	J	LE

CLASS BB 67000   B-B

This is the first of the SNCF big diesels that played a part in the elimination of steam workings. These and subsequent series were one of the first to have the exterior styling by Paul Arzens who has since been responsible for most SNCF locomotive body designs. Originally a mixed traffic locomotive with a two gear bogie, they are now regarded as freight only and the bogie geared accordingly. Never fitted with boiler equipment, they used to operate with boiler vans. Many have been rebuilt into Classes BB 67200 or BB 67300 and the missing numbers will be found under those series except 67036 which became e.t.h. prototype 67291 then 67390. Locos mainly work from Fos-sur-Mer and Miramas yard from where pairs of locos top-and-tail ore trains to Gardanne.

Built: 1963–68.   **Builders:** Brissonneau and Lotz/MTE.
Engine: SEMT 16PA4 (1470 kW).
Transmission: Electric. Two SW 9209 monomotors.
Heating: None.   **Weight:** 80 tonnes.
Max. T.E.: 304 kN.   **Length:** 17.09 m.
Wheel Dia.: 1150 mm.   **Max. Speed:** 90 km/h.

Multiple working fitted within class and with Classes BB 67200, A1A-A1A 68000 and A1A-A1A 68500.

467002	AV	467017	AV	467033	AV	467063	AV
467003	AV	467019	AV	467035	AV	467064	AV
467005	AV	467020	AV	467038	AV	467066	AV
467009	AV	467022	AV	467044	AV	467067	AV
467010	AV	467024	AV	467049	AV	467068	AV
467012	AV	467025	AV	467053	AV	467072	AV
467013	AV	467026	AV	467055	AV	467083	AV
467014	AV	467027	AV	467060	AV	467084	AV
467015	AV	467031	AV	467062	AV	467097	AV

CLASS BB 67200   B-B

With the introduction of the LGV Sud Est route it was realised that some locomotives would be required that could operate over the line on ballast trains and in emergencies. The line does not have conventional signalling and thus 30 Class BB 67000 were modified and fitted with cab signalling and train-signal box radio. With the construction of the LGV Atlantique, a further 16 were converted. Like Class BB 67000 their bogies are locked onto the freight gear ratio. The class now have no regular freight workings and are based at Paris Charolais, Laroche-Migennes, Montchanin, Vénissieux and Portes-les-Valence on the LGV Sud Est (locos from NV), Paris Vaugirard, Chartres and St. Pierre-des-Corps (TP) on the LGV Atlantique and La Plaine, Lille Fives and Calais Fréthun on the LGV Nord Europe (LN). From 1996, 16 NV locos were being used for track renewal on the LGV Sud Est.

Details as BB 67000. Converted 1980–94.

Snowploughs fitted. Fitted with TVM300 (TVM430*) cab signalling.

167201	(67006)	NV	167202	(67011)	NV	167203	(67040)	NV

167204	(67034)		NV	667225	(67029)	NV	667246	(67050)		NV
167205	(67037)		NV	667226	(67028)	NV	167247	(67074)		LN
167206	(67030)		NV	667227	(67007)	NV	167248	(67071)		LN
167207	(67021)	*	NV	667228	(67039)	NV	167249	(67069)		LN
167208	(67008)	*	NV	667229	(67004)	NV	667250	(67080)		NV
167209	(67118)	*	NV	667230	(67018)	NV	667251	(67086)		NV
167210	(67120)	*	LN	167231	(67048)	TP	167252	(67076)		LN
667211	(67108)	*	NV	167232	(67043)	TP	167253	(67079)		LN
667212	(67122)	*	NV	667233	(67046)	NV	167254	(67088)		LN
167213	(67115)	*	LN	167234	(67051)	TP	167255	(67077)		LN
667214	(67123)	*	NV	167235	(67041)	TP	167256	(67085)		LN
667215	(67102)	*	NV	167236	(67042)	TP	667257	(67001)		NV
667216	(67121)	*	NV	667237	(67054)	NV	667258	(67016)		NV
667217	(67117)	*	NV	167238	(67057)	TP	667259	(67032)		NV
667218	(67112)		NV	167239	(67052)	TP	667260	(67065)		NV
667219	(67091)		NV	167240	(67056)	TP	667261	(67073)		NV
667220	(67114)		NV	167241	(67059)	TP	667262	(67023)		NV
667221	(67081)		NV	167242	(67045)	TP	667263	(67090)		NV
667222	(67078)		NV	167243	(67047)	TP	667264	(67087)		NV
667223	(67082)		NV	167244	(67061)	TP	667265	(67089)		NV
667224	(67103)		NV	667245	(67058)	TP	667266	(67070)		NV

CLASS BB 67300 — B-B

As mentioned under Class BB 67000, 67036 was modified to provide e.t.h. As 67291 and became the prototype for this class. The production series featured other improvements such as three-phase transmission. Later, rather than build more new locomotives, some of Class BB 67000 were converted and the old numbers of these are shown below. A mixed traffic locomotive with some fitted out for working push-pull trains. 67325/40/66 were withdrawn in late 1990 after accidents. CB locos work mainly around the Alps, especially from Chambéry to Valence, RS locos mainly work Rennes-St. Malo push-pull services whilst TP locos double-head Paris Montparnasse to Granville amongst other duties.

Built: 1967–69. **Builders:** Brissonneau and Lotz/MTE.
Engine: SEMT 16PA4 (1764 kW).
Transmission: Electric. Two SW 9209 monomotors.
Heating: Electric. **Weight:** 80 tonnes.
Max. T.E.: 202 kN. **Length:** 17.09 m.
Wheel Dia.: 1150 mm. **Max. Speed:** 140 km/h.

Multiple working fitted within class and with Class BB 67400. Odd examples have snowploughs.

p push-pull fitted.

467301		CB	567318	p	RS	467336		CB	567354	p	CB
467302		CB	467319		RS	467337		RS	467355		CB
567303	p	RS	467320		RS	467338	**P**	CB	567356	p	RS
567304	p	RS	467321		TP	467339		TP	467357		CB
567305	p	CB	467322		RS	567341	p	CB	467358		CB
567306	p	CB	467323		TP	467342		CB	467359		CB
467307		TP	467324		TP	467343		CB	467360		CB
467308		TP	567326	p	RS	567344	p	CB	467361		CB
467309		TP	467327		CB	567345	p	TP	467362		TP
467310		TP	467328		TP	467346		CB	467363		CB
467311		RS	467329		CB	467347		CB	467364		CB
467312		TP	467330		TP	567348	p	RS	467365		CB
467313		TP	467331		TP	567349	p	RS	467367		CB
467314		TP	467332		TP	467350		TP	467368		TP
467315		TP	467333		TP	567351	p	RS	467369		CB
467316		TP	467334		TP	567352	p	RS	467370		CB
467317		TP	467335		CB	467353		CB			

Locos converted from Class BB 67000.

567371	(67092)	p	RS	567373	(67110)	**P**	p	RS	567375	(67116)	**P**	p	RS
567372	(67107)	p	RS	567374	(67109)		p	RS	567376	(67095)		p	RS

567377	(67104)	p RS	567382	(67101)	p CB	567387	(67124)	p CB
567378	(67098)	p RS	567383	(67119)	p CB	567388	(67096)	p CB
567379	(67113)	p RS	567384	(67099)	p RS	567389	(67093)	p RS
567380	(67100)	p TP	567385	(67105)	p CB	567390	(67291)	p TP
567381	(67111)	p CB	567386	(67094)	p TP			

Name: 67344 LA BERNERIE EN RETZ

CLASS BB 67400   B-B

This class used to be the first sight at Calais Maritime for visitors from Britain in the days before Eurostar but now Class CC 72000 has taken over in this area. The class represents another development of the Class BB 67000 series. Three-phase transmission and e.t.h. fitted they can be found virtually all over the system on freight and passenger duties. One gear ratio. The bogies are the same as on Classes BB 7200/15000/22200/26000 but with a shorter wheelbase. Since the last edition, allocations have been regrouped, CY locos going to SB, RS to BD and Caen to LN. Locos are used on push-pull duties around Lille (LN), Toulouse (LG), Marseille (MB), Clermont-Ferrand (NV) Paris Est and Strasbourg (SB).

Built: 1969–75.
Builders: Brissonneau and Lotz/MTE.
Engine: SEMT 16PA4 (1765 kW).
Transmission: Electric. Two Jeumont-Schneider CTS66.43.4 three-phase monomotors.
Heating: Electric.
Weight: 83 tonnes.
Max. T.E.: 285 kN.
Length: 17.09 m.
Wheel Dia.: 1260 mm.
Max. Speed: 140 km/h.

Multiple working fitted within class and with Class BB 67300. Some have snowploughs.

p push-pull fitted.

No.	p	Dep	No.	p	Dep	No.	p	Dep	No.	p	Dep
567401	p	NV	567438	p	MB	567475		BD	567512	p	SB
567402		BD	467439	p	LN	567476		BD	567513	p	SB
567403		BD	467440		NV	567477		BD	567514	p	SB
567404		BD	567441		BD	467478	p	NV	567515	p	SB
567405	p	MB	567442		BD	467479	p	NV	567516	p	SB
467406		NV	567443		BD	567480		BD	567517	p	SB
467407		NV	467444		NV	467481	p	NV	567518	p	SB
567408		BD	567445		BD	567482	p	MB	567519	p	SB
567409	p	SB	567446		BD	467483	p	LN	567520	p	SB
467410		NV	567447		BD	567484	p	MB	567521	p	SB
567411	p	SB	467448	p	NV	467485	p	LN	567522	p	SB
567412		BD	467449	p	NV	467486	p	LN	567523	p	SB
567413	p	SB	467450	p	NV	567488	p	MB	567524	p	SB
467414	p	LN	467451		LN	567489	p	MB	467525	p	NV
567415		SB	467453	p	NV	467490	p	NV	567526	p	SB
567416	p	LG	467454		LN	467491	p	NV	467527		NV
567417		BD	467455	p	NV	467492		LN	567528	p	LN
567418		BD	467456	p	SB	567493	p	MB	467529		LN
567419	p	SB	467457	p	MB	567494	p	NB	567530	p	SB
567420		BD	467458	p	NV	567495	p	MB	467531	p	NV
567421		BD	467459	p	LN	567496	p	MB	467532		NV
567422	p	SB	467460	p	NV	567497	p	MB	567533	p	SB
567423	p	SB	467461		LN	567498	p	SB	467534		NV
567424		BD	467462	p	NV	567499	p	SB	467535	p	NV
567425	p	LN	467463	p	NV	567500		BD	467536		NV
467426		NV	567464	p	SB	467501		NV	467537	p	LN
567427		BD	467465		LN	467502		NV	567538		BD
567429		BD	467466		LN	467503		NV	467539		NV
567430	p	LN	467467		LN	467504		NV	467540	p	LN
567431		BD	567468		BD	467505	p	NV	567541	p	MB
467432		NV	467469	p	NV	467506	p	NV	567542	p	MB
567433	p	SB	567470		BD	467507	p	NV	567543	p	LN
567434	p	SB	567471		BD	467508		NV	467544		NV
567435		BD	467472		NV	467509		NV	567545	p	NV
567436		BD	567473		BD	567510	p	SB	567546	p	NV
567437		BD	467474		LN	567511	p	SB	567547	p	NV

567548	p	NV	567569	p	SB	567590	p	LN	567611	p	LG
567549	p	MB	567570	p	SB	567591	p	LN	567612	p	BD
467550		NV	567571	p	SB	567592	p	LN	567613		LG
467551		NV	567572	p	SB	567593	p	LN	567614	p	LG
467552		NV	567573	p	MB	567594	p	LN	567615	p	LG
467553	p	NV	567574	p	NV	567595	p	LN	567616	p	LG
567554		MB	567575	p	NV	567596	p	LN	567617	p	LN
567555		NV	567576	p	NV	567597	p	LN	567618	p	LN
567556		NV	567577	p	NV	567598	p	LN	567619	p	LN
567557		NV	567578	p	MB	567599	p	LN	567620	p	LN
567558	p	MB	567579	p	LN	567600	p	SB	567621	p	LG
567559	p	LN	567580	p	MB	567601	p	LN	567622	p	LG
567560	p	MB	567581	p	NV	567602	p	LN	567623	p	BD
567561	p	MB	567582	p	SB	567603	p	SB	567624		LG
567562	p	NV	567583	p	SB	567604	p	LN	567625		LG
467563		LN	567584	p	SB	567605	p	LN	567626		LN
567564		NV	567585	p	LN	567606	p	LN	567627	p	LG
567565	p	MB	567586	p	SB	567607	p	LN	567628		LG
567566	p	NV	567587	p	SB	567608	p	LN	567629		BD
567567	p	NV	567588	p	SB	567609	p	LN	567631		BD
567568	p	MB	567589	p	LN	567610	p	LN	567632		LG

Names:

567530	ROMILLY-SUR-SEINE	567581	NEVERS
567575	DRAGUIGNAN	567620	ABBEVILLE
567580	MONTPELLIER		

CLASSES A1A-A1A 68000 & A1A-A1A 68500 — A1A-A1A

These two classes are identical except for the different engines. Because of this there have been several conversions from one to another. Five Class A1A-A1A 68500 were re-engined with Sulzer engines acquired from and originally tested on British Railways Class 48 (D1702–D1706). In 1995/6, several Class A1A-A1A 68000 were converted to Class A1A-A1A 68500 due to a high number of cracks in the Sulzer power units. 68510 was rebuilt as 68085 then again as 68534! AGO engines were recovered from Class A1A-A1A 68500 bodies and installed in Class A1A-A1A 68000 bodies which had received mid-life overhauls. Both classes are usually used in pairs on freight, mainly around the Paris–Belfort line and around Paris (CY locos) and around Thouars and on the Tours–Le Mans–Rouen line (SO). Locos are often outbased for ballast trains on construction work and are being used on the LGV Méditeranée project.

Built: 1963–68. **Builders:** CAFL/CEM/Fives-Lille.
Engine: Sulzer 12LVA24 (1950 kW) (Class A1A-A1A 68000), SACM AGO 12DSHR (1985 kW) (Class A1A-A1A 68500).
Transmission: Electric. Four CEM GDTM 544 traction motors.
Heating: None. **Weight:** 102–104 tonnes.
Max. T.E.: 298 kN. **Length:** 17.92 m.
Wheel Dia.: 1250 mm. **Max. Speed:** 130 km/h.

Multiple working fitted within both classes. Some fitted with snowploughs.

Class A1A-A1A 68000.

468001	CY	468018	CY	468037	CY	468051	SO
468002	CY	468020	CY	468038	CY	468052	SO
468003	CY	468021	CY	468039	CY	468053	SO
468004	CY	468023	CY	468040	CY	468054	SO
468005	CY	468025	CY	468041	CY	468055	SO
468006	SO	468026	CY	468042	CY	468056	SO
468007	CY	468027	TP	468043	SO	468057	SO
468008	CY	468029	SO	468044	SO	468058	SO
468010	CY	468031	CY	468045	CY	468059	SO
468011	CY	468032	CY	468046	CY	468060	SO
468012	CY	468033	SO	468047	CY	468061	CY
468013	CY	468034	CY	468048	SO	468064	SO
468014	SO	468035	CY	468049	SO	468065	SO
468015	CY	468036	CY	468050	SO	468066	SO

468067	SO	468072	SO	468076	SO	468081	SO
468068	SO	468073	SO	468078	SO	468082	SO
468070	SO	468074	SO	468079	SO	468083	SO
468071	SO	468075	SO	468080	SO	468084	CY

Old Numbers:

468005 (68501) | 468082 (68529) | 468083 (68525) | 468084 (68508) |

Class A1A-A1A 68500.

668503	CY	668515	CY	668523	CY	668530	CY
668504	CY	668518	CY	668524	CY	668531	CY
668505	CY	668519	CY	668526	CY	668532	CY
668506	CY	668520	CY	668527	CY	668532	CY
668507	CY	668521	CY	668528	CY	668534	CY
668509	CY	668522	CY	668529	CY	668535	CY
668512	CY						

Old Numbers:

468529 (68030) | 468531 (68009) | 468533 (68017) | 468534 (68085) | 468535 (68019)
468530 (68022) | 468532 (68024) |

CLASS CC 72000   C-C

This is SNCF's really big diesel and features monomotor bogies with gear selection. The low gear is intended for freight work but is also used when hauling passenger trains over difficult routes such as Lyon–Roanne–St.Germain des Fosses. After surmounting the gradients out of Lyon the express gear ratio is selected whilst station duties are undertaken at Roanne. There have been several changes to use in recent years. Electrification has driven the class away from the west of France. They continue to be in charge of almost all expresses and much of the freight on the Paris–Belfort line (CY locos), on freight between Tours and Dijon and on Tours–Lyon and Bordeaux–Lyon passenger trains. In 1995, the class started to be used on the Chambéry–Valence line. Since 1996, CY locos have been diagrammed on Amiens–Calais passenger services. 72061/2/4 are to receive special couplings in 1999 to allow haulage of TGV-A sets between Nantes and Les Sables d'Olonne and will be renumbered 72101-3.

Built: 1967–74.   **Builders:** Alsthom.
Engine: SACM AGO V16ESHR (2650 kW). [† Pielstick V16PA4-VGA (2350 kW)].
Transmission: Electric. Two Alsthom TAO 656B1 monomotors.
Heating: Electric.   **Weight:** 114/118 tonnes.
Max. T.E.: 362/189 kN.   **Length:** 20.19 m.
Wheel Dia.: 1140 mm.   **Max. Speed:** 85/160 (85/140*)km/h.

Electro-pneumatic braking. Driver-guard communication (not *).

472001		*	CY	ANNONAY	472022		CY	VILLEMOMBLE
472002		*	CY		172023		NV	
472003		*	CY		472024		CY	PONT-AUDEMER
472004		*	CY		172025		NV	TARARE
472005		*	CY		472026		CY	LUXEUIL-LES-BAINS
472006	P	*	CY		472027		CY	
472007		*	CY		472028		CY	
472008		*	CY		472029		CY	
472009		*	CY		472030	P	CY	CHALINDREY
472010		*	CY	BOURG ARGENTAL	472031		CY	FOUGEROLLES
472011		*	CY		472032		CY	
472012		*	CY		472033		CY	
472013		*	CY		472034		CY	
472014		*	CY		472035		CY	
472015		*	CY	PARAY-LE-MONIAL	172036		CY	THANN
472016		*	CY		172037		CY	
172017		*	NV		172038		CY	NANGIS
472018		*	CY		172039		CY	
472019		*	CY		172040	P	CY	
472020		*	CY		172041		CY	CHAUMONT
172021			NV		172042		NV	

172043		CY	LANGRES	472069	NV	
172044	†	CY		472070	NV	
172045		CY		472071	NV	MARSEILLE
172047		CY		172072	CY	SAINT-MALO
172048		CY	HAUTE SAÔNE	472073	NV	
172049		CY		172074	CY	TOULON
172050		NV	LAPALISSE-EN-BOURBONNAIS	172075	† CY	
172051		CY		172076	CY	
172052		NV	LA BAULE	172077	CY	NOISY-LE-SEC
172053		CY	MONTAUBAN DE BRETAGNE	172078	CY	
172054		NV		172079	CY	
172055		NV		172080	CY	MULHOUSE
172056		CY	LA BOURBOULE	472081	NV	
172057		NV		172082	CY	PROVINS
172058		NV		472083	NV	
172059		NV		472084	NV	
172060		CY	GRAY	472085	NV	
172061		NV	AMPLEPUIS	172086	CY	
172062		NV		472087	NV	
172063		CY	LA ROCHE-SUR-YON	472088	NV	
172064		NV		472089	NV	
472065		NV		172090	CY	BELFORT
172066		CY		472091	NV	LURE
472067		NV		472092	NV	
172068		CY				

EWS CLASS 37   Co-Co

At the time of writing, SNCF was hiring a number of English, Welsh and Scottish Railway Class 37 locos for construction work on the LGV Méditeranée. Locos selected so far are detailed below, but are subject to change. It is not known exactly how long the locos will remain in France. Details of this class can be found in 'British Railways Pocket Book No.1: Locomotives' and 'British Railways Locomotives and Coaching Stock' (both published annually).

37010	37097	37201	37261	37686
37037	37100	37212	37293	37693
37046	37133	37218	37294	37696
37059	37140	37221	37376	37708
37069	37162	37225	37515	37715
37071	37170	37238	37672	37890
37073	37185	37242	37683	37891
37074	37196	37250	37685	

▲ CC 1112 at Villeneuve St Georges on 9th August 1995. **Pete Moody**

▼ BB 7292 passes Vias Airport with the eastbound Catalan Talgo service on 1st July 1996.
Peter Fox

A southbound freight, hauled by CC 7002, passes Cruas in the Rhône Valley on 15th May 1996.

Les Nixon

▲ BB 8191 heads west through Marseillan-Plage on 1st June 1995 with a rake of car carrying wagons.
Chris Wilson

▼ BB 8606 and BB 8644 stand at La-Tour-de-Carol with the 19.36 to Paris Austerlitz on 3rd July 1997.
Peter Fox

▲ BB 9217 passes Carcassonne with an express heading west towards Toulouse on 29th September 1994. **Les Nixon**

▼ BB 9641 and BB 9642 carry a special livery and operate Tours to St Pierre-des-Corps shuttle services connecting with TGVs. 9641 is seen here at Tours during August 1991. **David Haydock**

▲ BB 9703 in special livery at Villeneuve St Georges on 11st March 1999 with the 13.45 Paris Gare de Lyon–Laroche-Migennes. **David Haydock**

▼ "Corail Plus" liveried BB 15016 stands at Metz with a Frankfurt (Main)–Paris Est service in November 1997. **David Haydock**

CC 12143 passes Hettange with a mixed freight on 31st May 1996.

Phil Marshall

▲ BB 16027, in "Corail Plus" livery, stands at Douai with the evening Lille Flandres–Rouen service on 12th May 1998.   **David Haydock**

▼ BB 16768 and BB 16677 haul a 2400 tonne Dunkerque–Gandrange iron ore train through Douai on 12th May 1998. Note the differing bodyside grilles.   **David Haydock**

▲ BB 17066 in "Ile de France" livery at Noisy-le-Sec at the head of a train of double-decker stock forming the 09.26 Paris Est–Meaux.   **David Haydock**

▼ BB 22341 at Menton hauling the overnight "Flandres-Riviera", the 20.02 Calais-Ville–Ventimiglia on the morning of 21st June 1999.   **Peter Fox**

▲ BB 25236 heads the 14.40 St Gervais–Lyon Part Dieu past the goods yard at Annecy on 31st July 1992. This is the last green liveried loco of its class, and is to be retained in this livery. **Michael J. Collins**

▼ BB 25622 and 25501 head a southbound mixed freight through Villeneuve St Georges on 11th March 1999. **David Haydock**

▲ 'Sybic' No. BB 26145 at Woippy with a mixed freight on 30th May 1996.   **Phil Marshall**

▼ 'Astride' BB 36001 coupled to a test train at Dijon on 7th September 1996.   **Sandy Foott**

▲ One of twelve Class BB 8100 converted for shunting duties, BB 80001 stands at Paris Austerlitz with the empty stock of an overnight train on 11th June 1996. **David Haydock**

▼ Ex-NS Class BB 62400 locomotives returned to traffic in 1999 after five years in store. Several of the class, headed by 62453, are seen here at Longueil Sainte Marie in September 1991. **David Haydock**

▲ BB 63179 stands beside BB 64717 outside Lens depot in June 1992. 64717 had just been converted for heavy shunting in Somain and Grande Synthe yards. **David Haydock**

▼ Class CC 65500 were taken out of store in 1999 for use on LGV Méditerranée construction trains. Here, CC 66529 stands at La Plaine depot (Paris) in November 1989. **David Haydock**

▲ BB 66409 leaves Tournai on 11th March 1994 with the 09.47 service to Lille Flandres. **Chris Wilson**

▼ BB 67362 and BB 67368 at Romans-sur-Isère on 9th April 1994. **Paul D. Shannon**

▲ One of twenty four Class BB 66000 converted to Class BB 66700 for heavy shunting work, BB 66713 stands at Lens depot on 18th May 1992. **David Haydock**

▼ BB 67609 leading a pair of RIO push-pull sets forms the 12.25 Lille Flandres–Boulogne-Ville TER service near Renescure on the Calais to Hazebrouck line on 7th October 1995. **Chris Wilson**

▲ A1A 68523 and A1A 68506 with a ballast train on the Nord Europe high-speed line at Monchy-le-Preux on19th February 1992. **David Haydock**

▼ CC 72041 at Oissel, near Sotteville, on 12th March 1993, shortly after receiving an overhaul at Quatre Mares works. **Chris Wilson**

▲ Only a few Class T 2000 RTG 'Turbotrains' are now left in stock. During their heyday, an unidentified set arrives at Lisieux on a Cherbourg–Paris service. **David Haydock**

▼ X 2146 at Lannion on 5th July 1993. **Chris Wilson**

1.3. TURBOTRAINS

CLASS T 1000 ETG

In 1967 SNCF converted DMU X 4375 and trailer 8579 into an experimental gas turbine unit. X 4375 had new cab provided but the diesel motor and transmission retained. The trailer car also had a new cab fitted but this received a gas turbine power unit and was renumbered to X 2061. After detailed testing it was decided to order a production series of 4 car sets. These became the ETGs ("Élément à turbine à gaz") where the T 1000 are the gas turbine cars and T 1500 the diesel cars. For many years the class was allocated to Vénissieux but they have moved to Lyon Vaise. The remaining cars are now stored but will be available for use if required until March 2000.

Built: 1969–72. **Builders:** ANF/SFAC.
Engines: Turmo IIIH1 (830 kW) + Saurer SDHR (330 kW).
Transmissions: Hydraulic. Voith L411u + mechanical.
Formation: TB + TRA + TRB + TBD.
Accomodation: –/44 + 56/– + –/54 + –/48.
Weight: 42 + 28 + 33 + 44 tonnes.
Length: 22.84 + 20.75 + 20.75 + 22.84 m.
Max. Speed: 160 km/h.

T 1002	21002	51002	T 1502	D	LV (S)
T 1006	21006	51006	T 1506	D	LV (S)
T 1009	21009	51009	T 1509	D	LV (S)

CLASS T 2000 RTG

These units are 5 car sets with a gas turbine power car at each end. These are known as RTG sets ("Rame à turbine à gaz"). The odd numbered power cars have a slightly more powerful turbine and once on the move the lower powered one is usually shut down. Units are all now fitted for multiple working where previously two drivers were necessary. Following electrification, the class has been withdrawn from the Paris–Cherbourg and Strasbourg–Lyon routes. Power cars T 2077 and T 2081 have been taken to form the Bombardier "axis" tilting test train. 72057 has been reserved for Mulhouse museum. Remaining duties include Lyon–Bordeaux. The trains are being replaced by Class X 72500 DMUs.

Note: Catering vehicles are buffet cars except 52018 which has a kitchen.

Built: 1972–76. **Builders:** ANF/MTE.
Engines: Turmo XII (1200 kW) (odd), Turmo IIIF1 (820 kW) (even).
Transmission: Hydraulic. Voith L411r.
Formation: TBD + TRAB (TRB*) + TRA + TRBr + TBD.
Accommodation: –/48 1T + 29/40 2T + 60/– + –/44 & 24 chairs 1T (–/64 2T*) + –/48 1T.
Weight: 54 + 38 + 42 + 37 + 54 tonnes.
Length: 26.23 + 25.51 + 25.51 + 25.51 + 26.23 m.
Max. Speed: 160 km/h.

Most are fitted with train-signal box radio and cowcatchers.

T 2013	32007	22007	52007	T 2014	0		VE	RIORGES
T 2021	32011	22011	52011	T 2022	0		VE	BESANÇON
T 2031	32016	22016	52016	T 2032	0		VE	MONTLUÇON
T 2033	32017	22077	52017	T 2034	0		VE	NANTES
T 2036	32018	22018	52018	T 2035	0	*	VE	PÉRIGUEUX
T 2049	32001	22001	52001	T 2002	0		VE	AIX-LES-BAINS
T 2053	32013	22013	52013	T 2026	0		VE	EYGURANDE-MERLINES

1.4. DIESEL RAILCARS & MULTIPLE UNITS

In France there are many services operated by single unit diesel railcars which tow trailers. At the end of the journey it is necessary to run round the trailer. However, as the trailers are through wired for multiple working, trains often run with a railcar at each end with a trailer or trailers sandwiched between them. Those railcars with a '9' prefix were built specially for regional councils. Increasing numbers of the others are being repainted in regional colours.

All diesel railcars and multiple units are livery **X** unless otherwise shown.

CLASS X 2100 — SINGLE RAILCAR

This class helped to replace the ageing Classes X 2400 and X 3800. Toulouse units are mainly used on Toulouse–Auch, Rennes units all over Brittany and Limoges units in common with Class X 2200.

Built: 1980–83.
Engine: Saurer S1DHR (440 kW).
Type: XABD.
Weight: 44 tonnes.
Wheel Arrangement: B-2.
Builders: ANF/Schneider.
Transmission: Hydraulic. Voith T420r.
Accommodation: 8/48 1T.
Length: 22.40 m.
Max. Speed: 140 km/h.

Hydrodynamic braking. Multiple working with Classes X 2200, X 2800, XR 6000 and XR 6200 up to a maximum of 3 railcars and 3 trailers.

Note: 92104 was renumbered from 2133.

X 2101	M	TL	X 2115	G	RS	X 2128	M	TL	X 2142	G	RS
X 2102	M	TL	X 2116	G	RS	X 2129	M	LG	X 2143	G	RS
X 2103	M	TL	X 2117	G	RS	X 2130	M	TL	X 2144	G	RS
X 2104	M	TL	X 2118	G	RS	X 2131	M	LG	X 2145	G	RS
X 2105	M	TL	X 2119	M	LG	X 2132	M	TL	X 2146	G	RS
X 2106	M	TL	X 2120	M	TL	X 2134	G	RS	X 2147	G	RS
X 2107	M	TL	X 2121	M	TL	X 2135	G	RS	X 2148	G	RS
X 2108	G	RS	X 2122	M	LG	X 2136	G	RS	X 2149	M	LG
X 2109	G	RS	X 2123	G	RS	X 2137	G	RS	X 2150	G	TL
X 2110	G	RS	X 2124	G	RS	X 2138	G	RS	X 92101	M	NB
X 2111	G	RS	X 2125	M	TL	X 2139	G	RS	X 92102	M	NB
X 2112	G	RS	X 2126	M	LG	X 2140	G	RS	X 92103	M	NB
X 2113	G	RS	X 2127	M	LG	X 2141	G	RS	X 92104	M	TL
X 2114	G	RS									

Names:

X 2132	DUNIÈRES.
X 92101	LES PAYS DE LA LOIRE
X 92102	LES PAYS DE LA LOIRE
X 92103	LES PAYS DE LA LOIRE
X 92104	CONSEIL RÉGIONAL MIDI-PYRÉNEES

CLASS X 2200 — SINGLE RAILCAR

An improved version of Class X 2100 with a modified interior. Limoges units cover a very wide area from the Massif Central to La Rochelle and Mont-de-Marsan. Tours units are mainly used on the line to Vierzon. In 1996, 7 units were transferred to MB to give better comfort and acceleration on the mountainous Nice–Cuneo line.

Built: 1985–88.
Engine: Saurer S1DHR (440 kW).
Type: XABD.
Weight: 43 tonnes.
Wheel Arrangement: B-2.
Non-standard Livery: N Stainless steel body with blue upper bodyside.
Builders: ANF/Schneider.
Transmission: Hydraulic. Voith T320r.
Accommodation: 8/46 1T.
Length: 22.40 m.
Max. Speed: 140 km/h.

Hydrodynamic braking. Multiple working with Classes X 2100, X 2800, XR 6000 and XR 6200.

X 2201	R	LG	X 2204	R	MB	X 2207	B	TP	X 2210	B	TP
X 2202	B	LV	X 2205	B	TP	X 2208	B	TP	X 2211	B	TP
X 2203	R	MB	X 2206	B	TP	X 2209	B	TP	X 2212	B	TP

X 2213	R	MB	X 2226	R	LG	X 2238	R	LG	X 2250	N	TP
X 2215	R	MB	X 2227	R	LG	X 2239	R	LG	X 2251	R	LG
X 2216	R	MB	X 2228	R	LG	X 2240	R	LG ·	X 2252	R	LG
X 2217	R	MB	X 2229	R	LG	X 2241	R	LG	X 2253	R	LG
X 2218	R	LG	X 2230	R	LG	X 2242	R	LG	X 2254	R	LG
X 2219	R	LG	X 2231	R	LG	X 2243	R	LG	X 2255	R	LG
X 2220	R	LG	X 2232	R	LG	X 2244	R	LG	X 2256	R	LG
X 2221	R	LG	X 2233	R	LG	X 2245	R	LG	X 2257	R	MB
X 2222	R	LG	X 2234	R	LG	X 2246	R	LG	X 92201	G	SO
X 2223	R	LG	X 2235	R	LG	X 2247	R	LG	X 92202	M	TL
X 2224	R	LG	X 2236	R	LG	X 2248	R	LG	X 92203	Y	TL
X 2225	R	LG	X 2237	R	LG	X 2249	R	LG			

Names:

X 2201	LIMOUSIN
X 2205	CLOYES-SUR-LE-LOIR
X 92201	NORMANDIE
X 92202	CONSEIL RÉGIONAL MIDI-PYRÉNÉES
X 92203	LANGUEDOC ROUSSILLON

CLASS X 2400   DEPARTMENTAL RAILCAR

This class of powerful railcars have now all been withdrawn except X 2464 which is in departmental service as a signal department test car and is equipped with video cameras.

Built: 1953.
Engines: Two Renault 517G (255 kW).
Type: XABDP.
Weight: 43 tonnes.
Wheel Arrangement: B-B.
Non-standard Livery: N Corail livery of two-tone grey lined in orange.

Builder: Decauville.
Transmission: Mechanical.
Accommodation: 12/56 1T.
Length: 27.73 m.
Max. Speed: 120 km/h.

X 2464   **N**   NV

CLASS X 2700   RGP TWO-CAR DEPARTMENTAL UNIT

This departmental unit was formed in 1987 from two power cars of former RGP sets (see below). The set was converted from power cars 2707 and 2714 at Bordeaux Works and is used as an ultrasonic rail tester. Numbered as X 2700, it is also known as V4. In each power car the outer engine has been replaced by test equipment leaving the inner engine in each car.

Built: 1954–55.
Engines: One Renault 517G (250 kW) per car.
Weight:
Wheel Arrangement: 2-B + B-2.
Non-standard Livery: N Corail livery of two-tone grey lined in orange.

Builder: Decauville.
Transmission: Mechanical.
Length: 26.63 + 26.63 m.
Max. Speed: 120 km/h.

X 2700   X 2700 **N**   NV

CLASS X 2720   RGP TWO-CAR UNITS

This class was formerly two separate classes. The units are also known as "Rames à Grand Parcours" (RGP). Unlike Class X 2700, they have one large engine instead of two smaller ones. The X 2770 series were former TEE units and were renumbered in the series X 2739–49 when refurbished in 1984–92. The refurbishment consists of fitting new cabs similar to those on the Class X 2200 railcars, new seats and automatic doors. Driving trailers X 7721–32 were renumbered X 7757–68 prior to refurbishing and were renumbered in the same series when refurbished. However they did not necessarily regain their original number. All units are now allocated to LV and operate mainly on the Nîmes–Clermont Ferrand, Lyon–St. Claude and Valence–Chambéry lines.

Built: 1955–56.
Engine: SACM MGO V12SH (605 kW).
Formation: XBD + XRABx.
Weight: 53 + 32 tonnes.
Wheel Arrangement: B-2 + 2-B.

Builders: De Dietrich/SACM.
Transmission: Hydraulic. Mekydro K104u.
Accommodation: –/60 + 24/54 (*24/52).
Length: 26.63 + 26.05 (25.53 unrefurbished) m.
Max. Speed: 140 km/h.

X 2721	7721	**Y**		LV	X 2722	7722	**Y**	*	LV	X 2723	7723 **Y** * LV

X 2724	7724	Y		LV		X 2734	7734	Y		LV		X 2742	7742	Y		LV
X 2725	7725	Y		LV		X 2735	7735	Y	*	LV		X 2743	7743	Y		LV
X 2726	7726	Y		LV		X 2736	7736	B	*	LV		X 2744	7744	Y		LV
X 2727	7727	Y		LV		X 2737	7737	Y		LV		X 2745	7745	B		LV
X 2728	7728	B	*	LV		X 2738	7738	R		LV		X 2746	7746	Y		LV
X 2730	7730	Y	*	LV		X 2739	7739	Y		LV		X 2747	7747	Y		LV
X 2731	7731	Y	*	LV		X 2740	7740	Y		LV		X 2748	7748	Y		LV
X 2732	7732	Y		LV		X 2741	7741	Y		LV		X 2749	7749	Y		LV
X 2733	7733	B	*	LV												

Name: X 2745 CREST

CLASS X 2800   SINGLE RAILCAR

These sets have all been refurbished and are known as "Massif Central sets", although they also work in the Jura. In 1995, 15 units were modified for 140 km/h operation to replace Class T 1000 around Nevers and Clermont-Ferrand.

Built: 1957–62.
Engine: MGO V12SH (605 kW).
Type: XABD.
Weight: 53 tonnes.
Wheel Arrangement: B-2.

Builders: Decauville/Renault.
Transmission: Hydraulic. Mekydro K104u.
Accommodation: 12/50 1T (†24/34 1T).
Length: 27.73 m.
Max. Speed: 120 km/h (*140 km/h).

Multiple working with Classes X 2100, X 2200, XR 6000 and XR 6200.

X 2801	M	LG	X 2833	M †	TL	X 2863	M *	LV	X 2894	M	LG
X 2802	M *	LV	X 2834	M	LV	X 2866	M	LV	X 2895	M	LV
X 2804	M	LG	X 2835	M	LV	X 2867	M	LG	X 2896	M	LV
X 2805	M	LG	X 2836	M	TL	X 2868	M	LV	X 2897	M	LG
X 2806	M *	LV	X 2837	M	LV	X 2869	M *	LV	X 2898	M	LV
X 2807	M	LV	X 2838	M	LV	X 2870	M	LV	X 2900	M *	LV
X 2808	M	LG	X 2840	M	LG	X 2871	M	LG	X 2901	M	LG
X 2809	M	LG	X 2842	M	LG	X 2872	M	LG	X 2902	M	LG
X 2810	M	LV	X 2843	M	LV	X 2873	M	LV	X 2903	M †	TL
X 2811	M	LV	X 2844	M	LV	X 2874	M	LV	X 2904	M	LG
X 2812	M	LG	X 2845	M	LV	X 2875	M	LG	X 2905	M	LG
X 2813	M	LG	X 2846	M	LV	X 2876	M	LG	X 2906	M	LG
X 2814	M	LG	X 2847	M	LG	X 2877	M	LV	X 2907	M	LG
X 2816	M *	LV	X 2848	M	LV	X 2878	M *	LV	X 2908	M	LG
X 2817	M	TL	X 2849	M	LG	X 2879	M *	LV	X 2909	M †	TL
X 2819	M *	LV	X 2850	M	LV	X 2880	M	LG	X 2910	M *†	LV
X 2820	M †	LG	X 2851	M	LG	X 2883	M	LG	X 2911	M †	LV
X 2822	M	TL	X 2852	M	LV	X 2885	M	LG	X 2912	M	LV
X 2823	M *	LV	X 2853	M *†	LV	X 2886	M	LG	X 2913	M	LG
X 2824	M	LV	X 2855	M	LV	X 2887	M	LG	X 2914	M *	LV
X 2825	M *	LV	X 2856	M	LG	X 2888	M	LG	X 2915	M	LG
X 2827	M *	LV	X 2857	M	LG	X 2889	M	LG	X 2916	M	LV
X 2828	M	LV	X 2858	M	LV	X 2890	M	LG	X 2917	M	LG
X 2829	M	LV	X 2859	M	LV	X 2892	M	LG	X 2918	M	LG
X 2830	M	LG	X 2860	M	LV	X 2893	M	TL	X 2919	M	LG
X 2832	M	LG	X 2862	M	LV						

CLASS X 3800   SINGLE RAILCAR

These classic diesel railcars are known as "Picassos" because of the strange location of the driving cab (on the roof!) and the fact that the driver has to sit side on instead of facing the direction of travel! They were built with one cab as a means of providing a cheap unit that would help to keep branch lines open, the roof cab meaning that the driver did not have to change ends during reversals en route. The remaining units are in departmental use and have modified front windows for better observation. Many have also been preserved.

Built: 1951–62.
Engine: Renault 517G (250 kW).

Builders: ANF/De Dietrich/Renault/Saurer.
Transmission: Mechanical.

Type: XBD or XABD. **Accommodation**: –/62 1T or 12/32 1T.
Weight: 53 tonnes. **Length**: 27.73 m.
Wheel Arrangement: B-2. **Max. Speed**: 120 km/h.
Non-standard Livery: **N** X 3896 is in pale green lined in white, X 3997 is in Corail livery of two-tone grey lined in orange.

X 3896 **N** PV | X 3997 **N** PV |

CLASSES X 4300 & X 4500 TWO-CAR UNITS

These two-car DMUs represent the 1960s generation of DMUs. Introduced in 1963, similar units continued to be built until 1981s. Their introduction led to mass withdrawals of old units many of which dated from pre-war days. The only difference between the two classes is the engine. The trailer cars have different proportions of first and second class and power cars of either class operate with either an XR 8300 or an XR 8500 driving trailer to match seating demand. Formations now tend to be permanent. Both classes are being modernised. The ends have been altered and are now similar to the recently-delivered RRR push-pull sets with large and one small window. The class operate all over France on diesel lines. In 1996, the class started to receive "mini" overhauls in which bench seats were replaced by those from "Pays de la Loire" Class X 4630. Further mini-overhauls are to be applied to Picardie units in 1999–2000. The modified units are painted in regional colours without changes to cabs. With the introduction of Class X 72500 and X 73500 plus continued electrification withdrawal of non-refurbished units is accelerating.

Built: 1963–70. **Builder**: ANF.
Engines: Poyaud C6150SRT (330 kW) (X 4300), Saurer SDHR (330 kW) (X 4500).
Transmission: Mechanical. De Dietrich. **Formation**: XBD + XRABx.
Accommodation: –/60 1T + 12/69 1T (XR 8300), 24/49 1T (XR 8500), (r –/52 1T + 20/52 1T).
Weight: 35 (X 4300), 36 (X 4500) + 23 tonnes. **Length**: 21.24 + 21.24 m (r 21.74 + 21.74 m).
Wheel Arrangement: B-2 + 2-2. **Max. Speed**: 120 km/h.

Note: X 4365 became a turbotrain prototype. X 4624/5/6 were rebuilt from X 4351/71/85 respectively.

r Refurbished units. .

No	No	B	r	Code	No	No	B	r	Code	No	No	B	r	Code
X 4301	8301			TP	X 4340	8325			TP	X 4377	8359	B	r	MZ
X 4302	8302			MZ	X 4341	8326			MZ	X 4378	8578	B	r	MZ
X 4303	8557			NV	X 4342	8340			MZ	X 4379	8588			MZ
X 4304	8559			MZ	X 4343	8337			MZ	X 4380	8580			MZ
X 4307	8507			NV	X 4344	8342			MZ	X 4381	8582	B	r	MZ
X 4308	8303			TP	X 4346	8555	B	r	NV	X 4383	8602			MZ
X 4309	8330			TP	X 4348	8328			MZ	X 4384	8603	B	r	MZ
X 4310	8331			NV	X 4349	8598	B	r	MZ	X 4386	8539			NV
X 4312	8306			TP	X 4350	8329			MZ	X 4387	8606			MZ
X 4313	8309			TP	X 4352	8339			MZ	X 4388	8607	B	r	NV
X 4314	8310			TP	X 4353	8343			MZ	X 4389	8608	B	r	MZ
X 4316	8312			TP	X 4355	8345			MZ	X 4391	8610	B	r	TP
X 4317	8517			MZ	X 4356	8344			TP	X 4392	8611	B	r	MZ
X 4320	8520			MZ	X 4357	8347			MZ	X 4393	8612	B	r	TP
X 4322	8313			MZ	X 4358	8581	B	r	MZ	X 4394	8501			MZ
X 4323	8314			MZ	X 4359	8568			MZ	X 4395	8549			MZ
X 4324	8533			MZ	X 4360	8527	B	r	TP	X 4396	8363			NV
X 4325	8315			MZ	X 4361	8570			NV	X 4397	8560			MZ
X 4326	8316			MZ	X 4363	8577			MZ	X 4398	8605			MZ
X 4327	8317			MZ	X 4364	8354	B	r	MZ	X 4400	8542	B	r	TP
X 4328	8318			MZ	X 4366	8356	B	r	MZ	X 4401	8367			MZ
X 4329	8540			NV	X 4368	8357	B	r	MZ	X 4402	8502	B	r	TP
X 4330	8543			MZ	X 4369	8361	B	r	MZ	X 4403	8369	B	r	TP
X 4331	8319			MZ	X 4370	8355	B	r	TP	X 4404	8366			NV
X 4333	8544			NV	X 4372	8348	B	r	TP	X 4406	8506	B	r	MZ
X 4334	8545			NV	X 4373	8518	B	r	MZ	X 4407	8626	B	r	TP
X 4335	8321			MZ	X 4374	8589			MZ	X 4408	8573	B	r	MZ
X 4336	8322			MZ	X 4375	8351			NV	X 4409	8628			MZ
X 4337	8554			NV	X 4376	8352	B	r	MZ	X 4410	8569			MZ

No	Trailer		Livery	No	Trailer		Livery	No	Trailer		Livery
X 4411	8532	B r	MZ	X 4517	8389		LN	X 4571	8590		LN
X 4412	8631	B r	MZ	X 4518	8629		LN	X 4572	8378		LN
X 4413	8591		NV	X 4520	8604		LN	X 4573	8592		LN
X 4414	8558		MZ	X 4522	8419		LN	X 4574	8412		LN
X 4415	8586		MZ	X 4523	8360		MB	X 4575	8594		LN
X 4416	8361		MZ	X 4524	8534		SO	X 4576	8308		LN
X 4417	8382		MZ	X 4525	8535		RS	X 4577	8596		MB
X 4418	8383		MZ	X 4526	8364		LN	X 4578	8417		LN
X 4420	8552		MZ	X 4527	8537		LN	X 4579	8338		LN
X 4421	8526		MZ	X 4528	8538		SO	X 4580	8599		LN
X 4422	8387		MZ	X 4529	8371		LN	X 4581	8600		LN
X 4424	8386		MZ	X 4530	8416		LN	X 4582	8373		MB
X 4426	8391		TP	X 4531	8529		MB	X 4584	8375		LN
X 4427	8392		MZ	X 4532	8546		SO	X 4585	8376		MB
X 4428	8393		MZ	X 4533	8547		LN	X 4586	8377		LN
X 4429	8394		MZ	X 4534	8548		LN	X 4587	8616		LN
X 4430	8395		TP	X 4536	8530		LN	X 4589	8618		LN
X 4432	8593	B r	MZ	X 4538	8508		SO	X 4590	8619	B r	SO
X 4433	8584	B r	MZ	X 4539	8510		SO	X 4591	8620		MB
X 4434	8523	B r	MZ	X 4540	8550		RS	X 4592	8305	G	RS
X 4435	8632	B r	TP	X 4541	8566		MB	X 4593	8641	B r	SO
X 4436	8541	B r	MZ	X 4542	8333	G r	RS	X 4594	8627	B r	SO
X 4437	8597	B r	TP	X 4543	8562		RS	X 4595	8624	G	RS
X 4438	8418	B r	TP	X 4544	8335		MB	X 4597	8397	B r	SO
X 4439	8531	B r	MZ	X 4545	8601		LN	X 4599	8399		LN
X 4440	8420	B r	TP	X 4546	8385	G r	RS	X 4600	8667	G r	RS
X 4441	8421	B r	TP	X 4547	8379		LN	X 4601	8505		LN
X 4442	8422	B r	TP	X 4548	8561		LN	X 4602	8402		LN
X 4443	8423	B r	MZ	X 4549	8353		MB	X 4603	8323		LN
X 4444	8424	B r	TP	X 4550	8563	G r	RS	X 4604	8404		LN
X 4445	8425		MZ	X 4551	8553	B r	SO	X 4605	8405		LN
X 4446	8426		MZ	X 4552	8334		MB	X 4606	8406	G r	RS
X 4447	8427		MZ	X 4553	8565		LN	X 4607	8415		LN
X 4448	8428		MZ	X 4554	8564		NV	X 4610	8635		MB
X 4449	8429		MZ	X 4555	8567		LN	X 4611	8636		LN
X 4450	8430		MZ	X 4556	8551	G r	RS	X 4612	8637		MB
X 4451	8431		MZ	X 4557	8571		LN	X 4613	8638		LN
X 4501	8503		SO	X 4558	8572		LN	X 4614	8639		NV
X 4503	8509		RS	X 4559	8372	G	RS	X 4615	8640	G r	RS
X 4504	8304		LN	X 4560	8622		LN	X 4616	8516	G r	RS
X 4505	8511		LN	X 4561	8575	B r	SO	X 4617	8407		LN
X 4506	8615		LN	X 4563	8341		LN	X 4618	8358		LN
X 4509	8512		NV	X 4564	8630		LN	X 4619	8409		LN
X 4510	8514		SO	X 4565	8583		LN	X 4620	8410	G	RS
X 4512	8432		LN	X 4566	8585		LN	X 4621	8411		LN
X 4513	8522		LN	X 4567	8380		MB	X 4622	8574	G	RS
X 4514	8414		LN	X 4568	8384		LN	X 4623	8433		MB
X 4515	8332		MB	X 4569	8413		LN	X 4624	8336	G r	RS
X 4516	8525		MB	X 4570	8350		RS	X 4626	8408		LN

Name: X 4364 REVIN

CLASS X 4630   TWO-CAR UNITS

A development of the preceding classes but featuring hydraulic transmission. The trailers are interchangeable with those of Classes X 4300 and X 4500. The NB units in **W** livery received new seats without headrests and a white livery but retained their original cabs. Some are now being fully overhauled and the old seats are being used in "mini" overhauls on Class X 4500. Non-refurbished units are now being withdrawn.

Built: 1974–78.   **Builder:** ANF.
Engine: Saurer SDHR (330 kW).   **Transmission:** Hydraulic. Voith T420r.
Formation: XBD + XRABx.
Accommodation: –/60 1T + 24/49 1T (**W** –/52 1T + 24/48 1T, r –/52 1T + 20/59 1T or –/52 1T + 12/60 1T).

Weight: 39 + 24 tonnes. **Length**: 21.24 + 21.24 m.
Wheel Arrangement: B-2 + 2-2. **Max. Speed**: 120 km/h.

X 4743 + 8740 have been rebuilt from X 4609 + 8634 and X 4744 + 8744 is ex X 94630.

X 4630	8642	G r	LN	X 4668	8665	W	NB	X 4707	8704			LV
X 4631	8643	B r	NB	X 4669	8666	B	LV	X 4708	8705			LV
X 4632	8644		NV	X 4670	8556	G r	NB	X 4709	8706			LV
X 4633	8645		NV	X 4671	8648	G r	LN	X 4710	8707			LV
X 4634	8646	Y r	NV	X 4672	8595	B r	NB	X 4711	8708	G r		LN
X 4635	8647		LV	X 4673	8670	B r	NB	X 4712	8709			LV
X 4636	8669	B r	NB	X 4674	8671	W	NV	X 4713	8710			NV
X 4637	8649	G r	LN	X 4675	8672	G r	LN	X 4714	8711			NB
X 4638	8650	T	NV	X 4676	8673	G r	NB	X 4715	8712			NV
X 4639	8651		LV	X 4677	8674		LV	X 4716	8713	G r		LN
X 4640	8652		NV	X 4678	8675	B r	NB	X 4717	8714			NV
X 4641	8653		LV	X 4679	8676	B r	NB	X 4718	8715			LV
X 4642	8654	G r	LN	X 4680	8677	B r	NB	X 4719	8716	G r		LN
X 4643	8655	B r	NB	X 4681	8678	W	NB	X 4720	8717	G r		LN
X 4644	8656		NV	X 4682	8679	B r	NB	X 4721	8718	T		LV
X 4645	8434	G r	LN	X 4683	8680		LV	X 4722	8719			LV
X 4646	8435		NV	X 4684	8681	W	LV	X 4723	8720			LV
X 4647	8436	G r	LN	X 4685	8682		LV	X 4724	8721	T		NV
X 4648	8437	G r	LN	X 4687	8684		LV	X 4725	8722			LV
X 4649	8444	G r	LN	X 4688	8685	W	NB	X 4726	8723			LV
X 4650	8439		NV	X 4689	8686		LV	X 4727	8724			LV
X 4651	8440		NV	X 4690	8687	B r	NB	X 4728	8725			LV
X 4652	8441	Y r	NV	X 4691	8688		LV	X 4729	8726	G r		LN
X 4653	8442		NV	X 4692	8689		LV	X 4730	8727			LV
X 4654	8443	B r	NB	X 4693	8690	W	NB	X 4731	8728			NV
X 4655	8445	Y r	LV	X 4694	8691		LV	X 4732	8729			LV
X 4656	8661	W	LV	X 4695	8692		LV	X 4733	8730			NV
X 4657	8446	B r	NB	X 4696	8693		LV	X 4734	8731			NV
X 4658	8447	Y r	NV	X 4697	8694	W	NV	X 4735	8732			NV
X 4659	8448	G r	LN	X 4698	8695		LV	X 4736	8733			LV
X 4660	8657	Y r	NV	X 4699	8696	R r	LV	X 4737	8734			NV
X 4661	8658	Y r	NV	X 4700	8697		LV	X 4738	8735			LV
X 4662	8659		LV	X 4701	8698		LV	X 4739	8736			NV
X 4663	8660	Y r	NV	X 4702	8699		LV	X 4740	8737			LV
X 4664	8438	B r	NB	X 4703	8700		LV	X 4741	8738	G r		LN
X 4665	8662	G r	LN	X 4704	8701		LV	X 4742	8739			NV
X 4666	8663	G r	LN	X 4705	8702	R r	LV	X 4743	8740	B r		NB
X 4667	8664	G r	LN	X 4706	8703		LV	X 4744	8744	G r		LN

CLASS X 4750 — TWO-CAR UNITS

The last of the two car sets to appear were this series having a more powerful engine and a higher maximum speed. Further members of the class, numbered from X 4797, are now being created by combining equipment from withdrawn Class X 94750 postal DMUs and Class X 4300.

Built: 1977–78. **Builder**: ANF.
Engine: Saurer S1DHR (440 kW). **Transmission**: Hydraulic. Voith T420r.
Formation: XBD + XRABx. **Accommodation**: –/60 1T + 24/49 1T.
Weight: 39 + 25 tonnes. **Length**: 21.24 + 21.24 m.
Wheel Arrangement: B-2 + 2-2. **Max. Speed**: 140 km/h.

X 4750	8750	R r	SO	X 4759	8759		MZ	X 4768	8768			MZ
X 4751	8751	R r	SO	X 4760	8760		MZ	X 4769	8769			MZ
X 4752	8752	R r	SO	X 4761	8761		MZ	X 4770	8770			MZ
X 4753	8753	B r	SO	X 4762	8762	Y r	MZ	X 4771	8771	R r		SO
X 4754	8754	R r	SO	X 4763	8763		SO	X 4772	8772			MZ
X 4755	8755		MZ	X 4764	8764		MZ	X 4773	8773			MZ
X 4756	8756		SO	X 4765	8765		MZ	X 4774	8774			MZ
X 4757	8757	R r	SO	X 4766	8766		MZ	X 4775	8775			SO
X 4758	8758		SO	X 4767	8767	R r	SO	X 4776	8776	R r		SO

X 4777	8777		SO	X 4784	8784	R r	MZ	X 4798	8798	Y r	MZ
X 4778	8778		MZ	X 4785	8785	Y r	MZ	X 4799	8799	Y r	MZ
X 4779	8779		SO	X 4786	8786	Y r	MZ	X 4800	8800	Y r	MZ
X 4780	8780		MZ	X 4787	8787	Y r	MZ	X 4801	8801	Y r	MZ
X 4781	8781		MZ	X 4788	8788	Y r	MZ	X 4802	8802	Y r	MZ
X 4782	8782	R r	MZ	X 4789	8789		MZ	X 4803	8803	Y r	MZ
X 4783	8783		SO	X 4797	8797	Y r	MZ				

Former Numbers.

X 4797	(X 4338)	X 4801	(X 4379)	X 8798	(X 8504)	X 8801	(X 8613)
X 4798	(X 4306)	X 4802	(X 4315)	X 8799	(X 8324)	X 8802	(X 8311)
X 4799	(X 4339)	X 4803	(X 4318)	X 8800	(X 8521)	X 8803	(X 8349)
X 4800	(X 4321)	X 8797	(X 8538)				

CLASS X 4790   TWO-CAR UNITS

These units are similar to Class X 4750 but have lower density seating. They used to carry orange/grey livery and work the Paris–Granville service. However this service is now loco-hauled and the units are used on other services in the Basse-Normandie region. All have now been refurbished with the new front ends.

Built: 1980–81.
Engine: Saurer S1DHR (440 kW).
Formation: XBD + XRABx.
Weight: 40 + 25 tonnes.
Wheel Arrangement: B-2 + 2-2.

Builder: ANF.
Transmission: Hydraulic. Voith T420r.
Accommodation: –/47 1T + 24/36 1T.
Length: 21.74 + 21.74 m.
Max. Speed: 140 km/h.

X 4790	8790	B	SO	BAGNOLES-DE-L'ORNE
X 4791	8791	B	SO	GRANVILLE
X 4792	8792	B	SO	VILLEDIEU-LES-POÊLES
X 4793	8793	B	SO	VIRE
X 4794	8794	B	SO	L'AIGLE
X 4795	8795	B	SO	FLERS
X 4796	8796	B	SO	ARGENTAN

CLASS X 4900   THREE-CAR UNITS

These are 3-car versions of Class X 4630 low density units and, like Class X 4790, are intended for long distance work as a higher standard of comfort is provided. They are known as EATs ("Éléments automoteurs triples") and are used mainly on Rouen–Caen–Rennes and Caen–Tours. X 4901–12 have snowploughs.

Built: 1975–77.
Engine: Saurer SHDR (320 kW).
Formation: XBD + XRAB + XBD.
Weight: 39 + 25 + 39 tonnes.
Wheel Arrangement: B-2 + 2-2 + 2-B.

Builder: ANF.
Transmission: Hydraulic. Voith T420r.
Accommodation: –/47 1T + 32/28 1T + –/47 1T.
Length: 21.24 + 20.75 + 21.24 m.
Max. Speed: 140 km/h.

X 4901	8901	X 4902	M	SO	VEYNES
X 4903	8902	X 4904	M	SO	MONOSQUE
X 4905	8903	X 4906	M	SO	
X 4907	8904	X 4908	M	SO	
X 4909	8905	X 4910	M	SO	
X 4911	8906	X 4912	M	SO	
X 4913	8907	X 4914	M	SO	
X 4915	8908	X 4916	M	SO	
X 4917	8909	X 4918	M	SO	
X 4919	8910	X 4920	M	SO	SOTTEVILLE-LÈS-ROUEN
X 4921	8911	X 4922	M	SO	
X 4923	8912	X 4924	M	SO	
X 4925	8913	X 4926	M	SO	

CLASS XR 6000   TRAILERS

Trailers constructed to work with Class X 2100. 96004 was formerly 6057.

Built: 1978–87.   **Builder:** ANF.

Type: XRAB. **Accommodation:** 16/60 1T.
Weight: 24 tonnes. **Length:** 24.04 m.
Max. Speed: 140 km/h.

No.			No.			No.			No.		
6001	M	LV	6040	M	LG	6088	M	LV	6139	R	LG
6002	M	LG	6041	M	CF	6089	M	LV	6140	R	LV
6003	M	LG	6042	M	CF	6091	M	LV	6141	R	MB
6004	M	LG	6043	M	CF	6095	M	LV	6142	R	MB
6005	M	LG	6044	M	CF	6098	M	LV	6143	R	LG
6006	M	LG	6045	M	LV	6100	M	LV	6144	R	LV
6007	M	LV	6046	M	LV	6101	G	CF	6145	R	LV
6008	M	LV	6047	M	LV	6102	G	CF	6146	R	MB
6009	M	CF	6048	M	LV	6103	G	CF	6147	R	BD
6010	M	LG	6049	M	LV	6104	G	RS	6148	R	BD
6011	M	LG	6050	M	LV	6105	G	RS	6149	R	BD
6012	M	LG	6051	M	LV	6106	G	RS	6150	R	LG
6013	M	CF	6052	M	LV	6107	G	RS	6151	R	BD
6014	M	CF	6053	M	LV	6108	G	RS	6152	R	BD
6015	M	CF	6054	M	LG	6109	G	RS	6153	R	BD
6016	M	CF	6055	M	LG	6110	G	RS	6154	R	BD
6017	M	CF	6056	M	LG	6111	R	LV	6155	R	LG
6018	M	CF	6058	M	LG	6112	R	MB	6156	R	LG
6019	M	CF	6059	M	TL	6113	R	LV	6157	R	LG
6020	M	CF	6060	M	TL	6114	R	LV	6158	A	BD
6021	M	TL	6061	M	TL	6115	R	LV	6159	A	BD
6022	M	TL	6062	M	TL	6116	R	LV	6160	A	BD
6023	M	TL	6063	M	TL	6117	R	LG	6161	R	BD
6024	M	LG	6064	M	TL	6118	R	LG	6162	R	BD
6025	M	LV	6065	M	TL	6120	R	LG	6163	G	RS
6026	M	CF	6066	M	TL	6121	R	LG	6164	G	RS
6027	M	CF	6067	M	TL	6122	R	BD	6165	G	RS
6028	M	LG	6068	B	TL	6123	R	LG	6166	G	RS
6029	M	CF	6070	M	LG	6127	R	LG	6167	G	RS
6030	M	CF	6071	M	LG	6128	R	LG	6168	G	RS
6031	M	CF	6072	M	LG	6129	R	LG	6169	G	RS
6032	M	CF	6073	M	LG	6130	R	LG	6170	G	RS
6033	M	TL	6074	M	LG	6131	R	LG	96001	B	NB
6034	M	CF	6075	M	LG	6132	A	BD	96002	B	NB
6035	M	CF	6076	M	LG	6133	R	BD	96003	B	NB
6036	M	CF	6077	M	LG	6134	R	BD	96004	M	TL
6037	M	CF	6085	M	LG	6136	R	MB	96005	G	SO
6038	M	TL	6086	M	LG	6137	R	LG	96006	M	TL
6039	M	CF	6087	M	LG						

CLASS XR 6200 TRAILERS

These trailers are similar to Class XR 6000, but have Class X 2200-style interiors.

Built: 1988–90. **Builder:** ANF.
Type: XRAB. **Accommodation:** 16/60 1T.
Weight: 24 tonnes. **Length:** 24.04 m.
Max. Speed: 140 km/h.

No.			No.			No.			No.		
6201	G	RS	6213	R	DV	6225	R	BD	6237	R	BD
6202	G	RS	6214	R	DV	6226	R	BD	6238	R	BD
6203	R	DV	6215	R	DV	6227	R	BD	6239	R	LG
6204	R	DV	6216	B	TP	6228	R	BD	6240	R	LG
6205	A	BD	6217	B	TP	6229	R	BD	6241	R	LV
6206	A	BD	6218	B	TP	6230	R	BD	6242	R	LV
6207	R	LG	6219	B	TP	6231	A	BD	6243	R	LV
6208	R	LG	6220	B	TP	6232	R	BD	6244	R	LV
6209	R	LV	6221	B	TP	6233	A	BD	6245	R	LV
6210	R	DV	6222	B	TP	6234	A	BD	6246	R	DV
6211	R	DV	6223	B	TP	6235	R	BD	6247	R	DV
6212	R	DV	6224	B	TP	6236	R	BD	6248	R	DV

6249	R	DV	96202	M	TL	96210	M	TL	96218	M	TL
6250	R	BD	96203	M	TL	96211	M	TL	96219	M	TL
6251	A	BD	96204	M	TL	96212	M	TL	96220	M	TL
6252	A	BD	96205	M	TL	96213	M	TL	96221	M	TL
6253	R	BD	96206	M	TL	96214	M	TL	96222	M	TL
6254	R	BD	96207	M	TL	96215	M	TL	96223	M	TL
6255	R	BD	96208	M	TL	96216	M	TL	96224	M	TL
96201	M	TL	96209	M	TL	96217	M	TL	96225	M	TL

CLASS X 72500 TWO- OR THREE-CAR UNITS

Class X 72500 is SNCF's "Automoteur TER", a new "wonder DMU" with a profile similar to the TGV and new standards of air-conditioned comfort inside. The units have automatic couplings under their streamlined nose. Large windows are better than in the TGV. Class X 72500 mainly operate Paris Austerlitz–Châteaudun–Vendôme–Tours, Nantes–Les Sables d'Olonne, Toulouse–Rodez, Lyon–Roanne, Dijon–Nevers, Nevers–Tours, Marseille–Aix-en-Provence and Nîmes–Mende. They are also likely to be used on semi-fast services around Bordeaux, Limoges, Montluçon, Clermont-Ferrand and Grenoble.

Built: 1997–.   **Builder:** GEC Alsthom.
Engines: Two MAN D2866 LUE 602 6-cylinder in line (258 kW) per car.
Transmission: Hydraulic. Voith T211 rzz.
Formation: XB (+ XRB) + XB.   **Accommodation:** -/78 (+ -/78 1T) + 22/50 1T.
Weight: 58 (+ 45) + 58 tonnes.   **Length:** 26.45 (+ 25.60) + 26.45 m.
Wheel Arrangement: 1A-A1 (+ 2-2) + 1A-A1.   **Maximum speed:** 160 km/h.

* Fitted with prototype tilt system.

X 72501	X 72502	T	TP	X 72571		X 72572	T	MB
X 72503	X 72504	T	LG	X 72573		X 72574	T	LG
X 72505	X 72506	T	TP	X 72575		X 72576	T	LG
X 72507	X 72508	T	TP	X 72577		X 72578	T	MB
X 72509	X 72510	T	TP	X 72579		X 72580	T	LV
X 72511	X 72512	T	NB	X 72581		X 72582	T	LV
X 72513	X 72514	T	LG	X 72583		X 72584	T	LG
X 72515	X 72516	T	LG	X 72585		X 72586	T	LG
X 72517	X 72518	T	LG	X 72587		X 72588	T	LG
X 72519	X 72520	T	NB	X 72589	721589	X 72590	T	TP
X 72521	X 72522	T	LG	X 72591		X 72592	T	TP
X 72523	X 72524	T	LG	X 72593		X 72594	T	LG
X 72525	X 72526	T	MB	X 72595		X 72596	T	LG
X 72527	X 72528	T	TP	X 72597		X 72598	T	LG
X 72529	X 72530	T	TP	X 72599		X 72600	T	NB
X 72531	X 72532	T	LV	X 72601		X 72602	T	LG
X 72533	X 72534	T	MB	X 72603		X 72604	T	LV
X 72535	X 72536	T	NB	X 72605		X 72606	T	LG
X 72537	X 72538	T	LG	X 72607		X 72608	T	LV
X 72539	X 72540	T	LG	X 72609		X 72610	T	MB
X 72541	X 72542	T	LV	X 72611		X 72612	T	LG
X 72543	X 72544	T	TP	X 72613		X 72614	T	LG
X 72545	X 72546	T	LG	X 72615		X 72616	T	LV
X 72547	X 72548	T	* LG	X 72617		X 72618	T	LG
X 72549	X 72550	T	TP	X 72619	721619	X 72620	T	TP
X 72551	X 72552	T	LG	X 72621		X 72622	T	NB
X 72553	X 72554	T	MB	X 72623	721623	X 72624	T	TP
X 72555	X 72556	T	TP	X 72625		X 72626	T	MB
X 72557	X 72558	T	NB	X 72627	721627	X 72628	T	TP
X 72559	X 72560	T	LG	X 72629		X 72630	T	LV
X 72561	X 72562	T	LG	X 72631	721631	X 72632	T	
X 72563	X 72564	T	LG	X 72633		X 72634	T	
X 72565	X 72566	T	LV	X 72635	721635	X 72636	T	
X 72567	X 72568	T	MB	X 72637		X 72638	T	
X 72569	X 72570	T	LG	X 72639	721639	X 72640	T	

X 72641		X 72642	T	X 72677		X 72678	T
X 72643	721643	X 72644	T	X 72679		X 72680	T
X 72645		X 72646	T	X 72681		X 72682	T
X 72647	721647	X 72648	T	X 72683		X 72684	T
X 72649		X 72650	T	X 72685		X 72686	T
X 72651	721651	X 72652	T	X 72687		X 72688	T
X 72653		X 72654	T	X 72689		X 72690	T
X 72655	721655	X 72656	T	X 72691		X 72692	T
X 72657		X 72658	T	X 72693		X 72694	T
X 72659	721659	X 72660	T	X 72695		X 72696	T
X 72661		X 72662	T	X 72697		X 72698	T
X 72663	721663	X 72664	T	X 72699		X 72700	T
X 72665		X 72666	T	X 72701		X 72702	T
X 72667	721667	X 72668	T	X 72703		X 72704	T
X 72669		X 72670	T	X 72705		X 72706	T
X 72671	721671	X 72672	T	X 72707		X 72708	T
X 72673		X 72674	T	X 72709		X 72710	T
X 72675		X 72676	T				

CLASS X 73500   SINGLE UNITS

Class X 73500 is the third part of SNCF's modernisation of regional (TER) services. This is a low cost single railcar for one person operation on lightly-used lines, known by SNCF as the "Autorail TER". The centre section will be low floor (550 mm). The initial order was unique in having been organised jointly by SNCF and German Railways (DB) (Class 641) who took 40 each. The French regions are now keen on the idea and have put in their own orders so that 139 vehicles will be delivered as follows: Alsace 38 (SB), Auvergne 2 (LV), Bourgogne 2 (LV), Bretagne 15 (RS), Centre 15 (TP), Franche-Comté 3 (LV), Haute Normandie 5 (SO), Languedoc-Roussillon 7 (TL), Midi-Pyrénées 7 (TL), Pays de la Loire 10 (NB), Picardie 5 (LN) and Rhône-Alpes 30 (LV). The railcars are likely to work all stations services while Class X 72500 take over limited stop trains. The first services earmarked for the railcars are Colmar-Metzeral and Tour-Loches. These railcars will have autmatic couplings and will not operate with trailers, thus ending an SNCF tradition of shunting trailers around country stations at great expense.

Built: 1999–.   **Builders:** De Dietrich/LHB.
Engines: Two MAN D2866 LUE 602 6-cylinder in line (258 kW) per car.
Transmission: Hydraulic. Voith T211 rzz.
Type: XB.   **Accommodation:** –/61 1T & 18 tip-up.
Weight: 49 tonnes.   **Length:** 28.90 m.
Wheel Arrangement: 1A-A1.   **Maximum Speed:** 140 km/h.

X 73501	T	X 73525	T	X 73549	T	X 73573	T
X 73502	T	X 73526	T	X 73550	T	X 73574	T
X 73503	T	X 73527	T	X 73551	T	X 73575	T
X 73504	T	X 73528	T	X 73552	T	X 73576	T
X 73505	T	X 73529	T	X 73553	T	X 73577	T
X 73506	T	X 73530	T	X 73554	T	X 73578	T
X 73507	T	X 73531	T	X 73555	T	X 73579	T
X 73508	T	X 73532	T	X 73556	T	X 73580	T
X 73509	T	X 73533	T	X 73557	T	X 73581	T
X 73510	T	X 73534	T	X 73558	T	X 73582	T
X 73511	T	X 73535	T	X 73559	T	X 73583	T
X 73512	T	X 73536	T	X 73560	T	X 73584	T
X 73513	T	X 73537	T	X 73561	T	X 73585	T
X 73514	T	X 73538	T	X 73562	T	X 73586	T
X 73515	T	X 73539	T	X 73563	T	X 73587	T
X 73516	T	X 73540	T	X 73564	T	X 73588	T
X 73517	T	X 73541	T	X 73565	T	X 73589	T
X 73518	T	X 73542	T	X 73566	T	X 73590	T
X 73519	T	X 73543	T	X 73567	T	X 73591	T
X 73520	T	X 73544	T	X 73568	T	X 73592	T
X 73521	T	X 73545	T	X 73569	T	X 73593	T
X 73522	T	X 73546	T	X 73570	T	X 73594	T
X 73523	T	X 73547	T	X 73571	T	X 73595	T
X 73524	T	X 73548	T	X 73572	T	X 73596	T

X 73597 T	X 73608 T	X 73619 T	X 73630 T
X 73598 T	X 73609 T	X 73620 T	X 73631 T
X 73599 T	X 73610 T	X 73621 T	X 73632 T
X 73600 T	X 73611 T	X 73622 T	X 73633 T
X 73601 T	X 73612 T	X 73623 T	X 73634 T
X 73602 T	X 73613 T	X 73624 T	X 73635 T
X 73603 T	X 73614 T	X 73625 T	X 73636 T
X 73604 T	X 73615 T	X 73626 T	X 73637 T
X 73605 T	X 73616 T	X 73627 T	X 73638 T
X 73606 T	X 73617 T	X 73628 T	X 73639 T
X 73607 T	X 73618 T	X 73629 T	

1.5. DIESEL SHUNTERS

Small diesel shunters are known as "locotracteurs" in France and can be operated by station staff as well as loco drivers.

All diesel shunters are in livery **V** unless otherwise shown.

CLASS Y 7100   **B**

The Y 6xxx series were built after World War Two and virtually continued pre-war designs. The Y 7100 series was a completely fresh design and featured hydraulic transmission. However this form of transmission was dropped for future classes after Y 7192 had been converted to mechanical transmission and renumbered Y 7001. Used on light shunting duties. Y 7118/28 have been sold to industrial users.

Built: 1958–62.
Builder: Billard (7101–7230), Decauville (7231–7310).
Engine: Poyaud 6PYT (150 kW).   **Transmission:** Hydraulic. Voith.
Weight: 32 tonnes.
Max. T.E.: 73 kN.   **Length:** 8.94 m.
Wheel Dia.: 1050 mm.   **Max. Speed:** 54 km/h.

No.	J	Code	No.	J	Code	No.	J	Code	No.	J	Code	No.	J	Code
Y 7101		MZ	Y 7145	J	DP	Y 7187	J	LG	Y 7229		AV	Y 7270		LV
Y 7102		MZ	Y 7146		SO	Y 7188	J	LE	Y 7230	J	NV	Y 7271	J	PV
Y 7103		MZ	Y 7147		LN	Y 7189	J	AC	Y 7231		MZ	Y 7272		LE
Y 7104	J	MZ	Y 7148		DP	Y 7190		MZ	Y 7232		MZ	Y 7273		VG
Y 7105		BZ	Y 7149	J	SO	Y 7191		LE	Y 7233	J	MZ	Y 7274		LE
Y 7106	J	BZ	Y 7150		LN	Y 7193	J	LN	Y 7234	J	DP	Y 7275	J	MB
Y 7107	J	LE	Y 7151	J	NV	Y 7194		MZ	Y 7235	J	LV	Y 7276	J	LV
Y 7108		SB	Y 7152		PV	Y 7195		MZ	Y 7236	J	LE	Y 7277		AV
Y 7109	J	SO	Y 7153	J	TP	Y 7196		MZ	Y 7237	J	LE	Y 7278	J	AV
Y 7110		AC	Y 7154		HE	Y 7197		LV	Y 7238	J	LE	Y 7279		CB
Y 7111	J	MZ	Y 7155		LN	Y 7198		SO	Y 7239	J	HE	Y 7280		VG
Y 7112	J	MZ	Y 7156	J	LV	Y 7199	J	PV	Y 7240	J	LG	Y 7281		VG
Y 7113	J	MZ	Y 7157	J	BZ	Y 7200	J	MZ	Y 7241	J	HE	Y 7282		SO
Y 7114	J	MZ	Y 7158		MZ	Y 7201		NV	Y 7242	J	BZ	Y 7283	J	LE
Y 7115		MZ	Y 7159	J	NV	Y 7202		VG	Y 7243		AV	Y 7284		TP
Y 7116	J	MZ	Y 7160	J	TP	Y 7203	J	SO	Y 7244	J	AV	Y 7285		LE
Y 7117	J	MZ	Y 7161		LE	Y 7204		MZ	Y 7245		MZ	Y 7286		PV
Y 7119	J	MB	Y 7162	J	AC	Y 7205	J	MZ	Y 7246	J	AV	Y 7287		MB
Y 7120		BZ	Y 7163	J	TP	Y 7206	J	VG	Y 7247		MZ	Y 7288	J	MB
Y 7121		BZ	Y 7164		BD	Y 7207	J	LE	Y 7248		MZ	Y 7289	J	LV
Y 7122	J	LE	Y 7165		AC	Y 7208	J	BZ	Y 7249		VG	Y 7290	J	PV
Y 7123		PV	Y 7166		DP	Y 7209	*	BZ	Y 7250	J	DP	Y 7291		PV
Y 7124		AC	Y 7167		LV	Y 7210	J	LN	Y 7251	J	LN	Y 7292		SO
Y 7125		MZ	Y 7168	J	TP	Y 7211		TP	Y 7252		LE	Y 7293		AC
Y 7126	J	LN	Y 7169	J	HE	Y 7212	J	BD	Y 7253	J	LN	Y 7294	J	SO
Y 7127		MZ	Y 7170	J	SO	Y 7213		BD	Y 7254		NV	Y 7295		AC
Y 7129		AC	Y 7171		HE	Y 7214	J	NV	Y 7255	J	HE	Y 7296	J	LE
Y 7130	J	SO	Y 7172		MZ	Y 7215		LV	Y 7256	J	NV	Y 7297	J	LE
Y 7131	J	AV	Y 7173		BZ	Y 7216	J	LE	Y 7257	J	TP	Y 7298	J	LN
Y 7132		MZ	Y 7174	J	LE	Y 7217	J	LE	Y 7258	J	BZ	Y 7299		LN
Y 7133		MZ	Y 7175		BZ	Y 7218		SO	Y 7259	J	MB	Y 7300		VG
Y 7134	J	MZ	Y 7176	J	BZ	Y 7219	J	TP	Y 7260		MB	Y 7301	J	MB
Y 7135	J	MZ	Y 7177	J	MB	Y 7220	J	NV	Y 7261	J	MB	Y 7302		VG
Y 7136	J	PV	Y 7178	J	SO	Y 7221		NV	Y 7262	J	MZ	Y 7303	J	MB
Y 7137	J	MB	Y 7179		DP	Y 7222		NV	Y 7263		MZ	Y 7304	J	MB
Y 7138	J	MB	Y 7180	J	PO	Y 7223		NV	Y 7264		MZ	Y 7305	J	BZ
Y 7139		BZ	Y 7181		AV	Y 7224		MZ	Y 7265		BD	Y 7306	J	BZ
Y 7140		AV	Y 7182		MB	Y 7225	J	LN	Y 7266	J	TP	Y 7307	J	MB
Y 7141		CB	Y 7183		LG	Y 7226		SO	Y 7267		BD	Y 7308	J	VG
Y 7142	J	MB	Y 7184	J	LE	Y 7227		AC	Y 7268	J	BZ	Y 7309	J	DP
Y 7143		BD	Y 7185	J	AC	Y 7228	J	MB	Y 7269	J	AC	Y 7310	J	VG
Y 7144	J	MZ	Y 7186	J	BD									

CLASS Y 7400 B

After succesful trials the mechanical transmission applied to 7001 became standard and the production run lasted nearly 10 years. They are found all over the network on a variety of shunting and trip duties.

Built: 1959 (7001), 1963–72 (others).
Builder: Billard (7001), Decauville (7401-7520), De Dietrich (7521-7625), Moyse (7626-7888).
Engine: Poyaud 6PYT (150 kW).   **Transmission:** Mechanical.
Weight: 32 tonnes.
Max. T.E.: 73 kN.   **Length:** 8.94 m.
Wheel Dia.: 1050 mm.   **Max. Speed:** 60 km/h.

* Béziers Works.

No.	J	Cl.	No.	J	Cl.	No.	J	Cl.	No.	J	Cl.	No.	J	Cl.
Y 7001		LE	Y 7450		TP	Y 7500		LE	Y 7550		DP	Y 7600		SB
Y 7401		PV	Y 7451	J	LV	Y 7501	J	LN	Y 7551		LN	Y 7601	J	RS
Y 7402		LN	Y 7452	J	LV	Y 7502		DP	Y 7552	J	TP	Y 7602		PV
Y 7403		TP	Y 7453		LV	Y 7503		CB	Y 7553	J	CB	Y 7603	J	RS
Y 7404		PV	Y 7454	J	NV	Y 7504		CB	Y 7554		DP	Y 7604	J	PO
Y 7405		PV	Y 7455	J	LN	Y 7505		PV	Y 7555	J	MB	Y 7605	J	NB
Y 7406		LN	Y 7456		LN	Y 7506	J	VG	Y 7556	J	CB	Y 7606	J	LE
Y 7407		TP	Y 7457		AC	Y 7507		LE	Y 7557		CB	Y 7607	J	LN
Y 7408	J	TP	Y 7458		PV	Y 7508	J	BZ	Y 7558	J	LE	Y 7608	J	LN
Y 7409		LG	Y 7459	J	LV	Y 7509		SO	Y 7559		SB	Y 7609	J	LV
Y 7410		DP	Y 7460		MB	Y 7510	J	VG	Y 7560	J	AC	Y 7610	J	LV
Y 7411		AC	Y 7461		LV	Y 7511	J	LN	Y 7561	J	DP	Y 7611	J	DP
Y 7412	J	TP	Y 7462	J	MB	Y 7512		LV	Y 7562	J	VG	Y 7612	J	BD
Y 7413	J	BD	Y 7463		LV	Y 7513		AC	Y 7563	J	VG	Y 7613	J	BD
Y 7414		CB	Y 7464		PV	Y 7514		LN	Y 7564	J	SB	Y 7614		BD
Y 7415	J	SO	Y 7465		LV	Y 7515	J	PO	Y 7565	J	SB	Y 7615	J	BD
Y 7416		LV	Y 7466		AV	Y 7516	J	AC	Y 7566	J	CY	Y 7616	J	VG
Y 7417		DP	Y 7467	J	PV	Y 7517		AC	Y 7567		CY	Y 7617	J	VG
Y 7418		DP	Y 7468		BD	Y 7518		SB	Y 7568		TP	Y 7618	J	VG
Y 7419	J	VG	Y 7469	J	VG	Y 7519		LE	Y 7569	J	DP	Y 7619	J	NV
Y 7420	J	NV	Y 7470	J	AC	Y 7520		LE	Y 7570	J	TL	Y 7620	J	PV
Y 7421	J	DP	Y 7471	J	PV	Y 7521		DP	Y 7571		PV	Y 7621	J	CY
Y 7422		VG	Y 7472	J	VG	Y 7522		CY	Y 7572	J	VG	Y 7622	J	VG
Y 7423		VG	Y 7473	J	LN	Y 7523	J	CY	Y 7573		BD	Y 7623		PV
Y 7424		AV	Y 7474		LN	Y 7524		DP	Y 7574		BD	Y 7624		SB
Y 7425		MB	Y 7475	J	LE	Y 7525		PV	Y 7575		CB	Y 7625	J	BD
Y 7426		AV	Y 7476		BD	Y 7526		CB	Y 7576	J	DP	Y 7626	J	LG
Y 7427	J	BZ	Y 7477	J	CB	Y 7527	J	TP	Y 7577		CY	Y 7627	J	DP
Y 7428		AV	Y 7478		DP	Y 7528		BD	Y 7578		SB	Y 7628	J	PO
Y 7429		BZ	Y 7479	J	BZ	Y 7529	J	CB	Y 7579		DP	Y 7629	J	PO
Y 7430	J	NV	Y 7480		AV	Y 7530	J	VG	Y 7580	J	SB	Y 7630	J	RS
Y 7431	J	MB	Y 7481	J	PO	Y 7531		NV	Y 7581		VG	Y 7631		BD
Y 7432		PV	Y 7482		DP	Y 7532		DP	Y 7582		SO	Y 7632		BD
Y 7433		VG	Y 7483	J	LN	Y 7533		DP	Y 7583	J	AC	Y 7633	J	CY
Y 7434	J	NV	Y 7484		LE	Y 7534	J	CY	Y 7584		SO	Y 7634	J	SB
Y 7435	J	DP	Y 7485	J	BD	Y 7535		LE	Y 7585		LN	Y 7635	J	LE
Y 7436	J	VG	Y 7486		BD	Y 7536		DP	Y 7586		DP	Y 7636	J	LE
Y 7437		PV	Y 7487		NV	Y 7537		PV	Y 7587	J	LE	Y 7637	J	LN
Y 7438		PV	Y 7488	J	VG	Y 7538	J	LE	Y 7588		LV	Y 7638	J	RS
Y 7439		LE	Y 7489		MB	Y 7539	J	LN	Y 7589		AV	Y 7639	J	AC
Y 7440	J	TP	Y 7490	J	BZ	Y 7540	J	DP	Y 7590	J	BZ	Y 7640	J	NV
Y 7441		TP	Y 7491		DP	Y 7541	J	TP	Y 7591	J	CB	Y 7641	J	VG
Y 7442		TP	Y 7492	J	PV	Y 7542		CB	Y 7592	J	BD	Y 7642	J	LV
Y 7443		BD	Y 7493	J	PO	Y 7543		LV	Y 7593	J	LG	Y 7643	J	NV
Y 7444		TP	Y 7494		VG	Y 7544		MB	Y 7594	J	TP	Y 7644	J	LV
Y 7445	J	LN	Y 7495	J	BD	Y 7545		CB	Y 7595	J	AC	Y 7645		LE
Y 7446		CB	Y 7496		DP	Y 7546	J	DP	Y 7596		DP	Y 7646	J	NV
Y 7447		DP	Y 7497		DP	Y 7547	J	PV	Y 7597		DP	Y 7647	J	LG
Y 7448		DP	Y 7498	J	CB	Y 7548		SB	Y 7598	J	CB	Y 7648	J	TP
Y 7449		LM	Y 7499	J	MB	Y 7549		PV	Y 7599		CY	Y 7649	J	PO

Y No.	J	Code	Y No.	J	Code	Y No.	J	Code	Y No.	J	Code	Y No.	J	Code
Y 7650		PO	Y 7698	J	LG	Y 7746	J	PO	Y 7794	J	CY	Y 7842	J	TL
Y 7651	J	TP	Y 7699	J	LG	Y 7747	J	BD	Y 7795	J	TP	Y 7843	J	VG
Y 7652	J	CY	Y 7700	J	PO	Y 7748	J	DP	Y 7796	J	SB	Y 7844	J	PO
Y 7653	J	NB	Y 7701	J	NB	Y 7749	J	SB	Y 7797	J	SB	Y 7845	J	LG
Y 7654	J	LV	Y 7702	J	RS	Y 7750	J	SO	Y 7798	J	SB	Y 7846	J	BD
Y 7655	J	VG	Y 7703	J	CY	Y 7751	J	LV	Y 7799	J	PV	Y 7847		CB
Y 7656	J	LE	Y 7704	J	NV	Y 7752	J	LN	Y 7800	J	LE	Y 7848	J	DP
Y 7657		PV	Y 7705	J	RS	Y 7753	J	LN	Y 7801	J	NB	Y 7849	J	VG
Y 7658	J	LE	Y 7706	J	PO	Y 7754	J	RS	Y 7802	J	TL	Y 7850	J	VG
Y 7659	J	AC	Y 7707	J	SB	Y 7755	J	NB	Y 7803	J	NB	Y 7851	J	LV
Y 7660	J	AC	Y 7708	J	CY	Y 7756	J	NB	Y 7804	J	BZ	Y 7852	J	CY
Y 7661		TL	Y 7709	J	CY	Y 7757	J	BD	Y 7805		CB	Y 7853	J	CY
Y 7662		DP	Y 7710	J	DP	Y 7758	J	PO	Y 7806	J	NV	Y 7854	J	LN
Y 7663	J	DP	Y 7711	J	TL	Y 7759	J	PO	Y 7807	J	PO	Y 7855	J	SO
Y 7664	J	NV	Y 7712	J	LN	Y 7760	J	LV	Y 7808	J	PO	Y 7856	J	NB
Y 7665		TL	Y 7713	J	AC	Y 7761		VG	Y 7809	J	NB	Y 7857	J	BD
Y 7666	J	BZ	Y 7714	J	LE	Y 7762	J	LV	Y 7810	J	BD	Y 7858	J	AC
Y 7667		MB	Y 7715	J	NB	Y 7763	J	MB	Y 7811	J	SB	Y 7859	J	SO
Y 7668	J	BZ	Y 7716	J	TP	Y 7764	J	BZ	Y 7812	J	NB	Y 7860	J	VG
Y 7669	J	LN	Y 7717	J	TP	Y 7765	J	LV	Y 7813	J	NB	Y 7861		CB
Y 7670	J	PO	Y 7718	J	TL	Y 7766	J	NV	Y 7814	J	RS	Y 7862	J	LV
Y 7671	J	PO	Y 7719	J	CB	Y 7767	J	LG	Y 7815	J	CY	Y 7863	J	BD
Y 7672	J	BD	Y 7720	J	VG	Y 7768	J	BD	Y 7816	J	SB	Y 7864	J	SO
Y 7673		LM	Y 7721	J	VG	Y 7769	J	LN	Y 7817	J	CY	Y 7865	J	SO
Y 7674	J	PV	Y 7722	J	LV	Y 7770	J	CY	Y 7818	J	LE	Y 7866	J	NB
Y 7675	J	CY	Y 7723	J	BZ	Y 7771	J	NB	Y 7819	J	LN	Y 7867	J	LM
Y 7676	J	AC	Y 7724	J	AV	Y 7772	J	LE	Y 7820	J	BZ	Y 7868	J	PO
Y 7677	J	LN	Y 7725	J	LG	Y 7773	J	DP	Y 7821	J	SB	Y 7869	J	TP
Y 7678	J	LN	Y 7726	J	LE	Y 7774	J	LE	Y 7822	J	RS	Y 7870	J	SO
Y 7679	J	LN	Y 7727	J	TL	Y 7775	J	NB	Y 7823	J	RS	Y 7871	J	NB
Y 7680	J	RS	Y 7728	J	BD	Y 7776	J	PO	Y 7824	J	SO	Y 7872	J	RS
Y 7681	J	LM	Y 7729		SB	Y 7777	J	NB	Y 7825	J	BD	Y 7873	J	RS
Y 7682	J	AC	Y 7730	J	CY	Y 7778	J	LG	Y 7826	J	TP	Y 7874	J	SB
Y 7683	J	AC	Y 7731	J	LN	Y 7779	J	LG	Y 7827		BD	Y 7875	J	SB
Y 7684	J	LG	Y 7732	J	DP	Y 7780	J	TL	Y 7828	J	LN	Y 7876	J	SB
Y 7685	J	TL	Y 7733	J	LN	Y 7781	J	NV	Y 7829	J	TL	Y 7877		VG
Y 7686	J	TP	Y 7734	J	RS	Y 7782	J	DP	Y 7830	J	VG	Y 7878	J	PV
Y 7687	J	LN	Y 7735	J	RS	Y 7783	J	CB	Y 7831	J	NV	Y 7879	J	RS
Y 7688	J	NV	Y 7736	J	TL	Y 7784	J	AV	Y 7832	J	NV	Y 7880	J	RS
Y 7689	J	LV	Y 7737	J	TL	Y 7785	J	LV	Y 7833		DP	Y 7881	J	LN
Y 7690		VG	Y 7738	J	TL	Y 7786	J	MB	Y 7834	J	CY	Y 7882	J	AC
Y 7691	J	CB	Y 7739	J	VG	Y 7787	J	LG	Y 7835	J	CY	Y 7883	J	DP
Y 7692	J	MB	Y 7740	J	CY	Y 7788	J	PO	Y 7836	J	LE	Y 7884	J	DP
Y 7693	J	LV	Y 7741	J	NV	Y 7789	J	LG	Y 7837	J	DP	Y 7885	J	LV
Y 7694	J	BZ	Y 7742		LE	Y 7790	J	TP	Y 7838	J	RS	Y 7886		NV
Y 7695	J	LV	Y 7743	J	AV	Y 7791	J	BD	Y 7839	J	SO	Y 7887		CB
Y 7696	J	DP	Y 7744	J	TL	Y 7792	J	TL	Y 7840	J	TL	Y 7888	J	LV
Y 7697	J	TL	Y 7745	J	TP	Y 7793	J	CY	Y 7841	J	TL			

CLASS Y 8000   B

This is the new standard hydraulic shunter in the new yellow livery. Being more powerful and with a higher speed than previous designs the class sees more main line use on trip workings and they are allocated to fewer depots. Those at AV are maintained by MB, those at CB by LV and those at VG by NV. Some are radio fitted for use in stations. Y 8300 was tested with remote control as a prototype for the Y 8400 series. Certain later locos were used to test Renault and Unidiesel engines, the latter being adopted for Y 8491-8550.

Built: 1977–90.
Builder: Moyse (8001-8090), Fauvet Girel (8091-8375).
Engine: Poyaud V12-520NS (224kW) (* Renault MIDR 063540 (219 kW), + Unidiesel UD18L6R3 (219 kW), § Renault MIDR 62045 (219 kW) - 50 locos will be fitted with this type of engine).
Transmission: Hydraulic. Voith LZr4SU2. (+ Electric).
Weight: 36 tonnes.

80

Max. T.E.: 118/62 kN. **Length**: 10.14 m.
Wheel Dia.: 1050 mm. **Max. Speed**: 30/60 km/h.

r Remote control fitted. Prototype loco for Class Y 8400.

Y 8001	J	TP	Y 8061	J	MB	Y 8121	J	RS	Y 8181	J	CY	Y 8241	J	LE
Y 8002	J	MZ	Y 8062	J	BZ	Y 8122	J	AC	Y 8182	J	DP	Y 8242	J	LE
Y 8003	J	CY	Y 8063	J	MB	Y 8123	J	MZ	Y 8183	J	PV	Y 8243	J	PV
Y 8004	J	MZ	Y 8064	J	DP	Y 8124	J	MZ	Y 8184	J	SB	Y 8244	J	CY
Y 8005	J	CY	Y 8065	J	NV	Y 8125	J	BZ	Y 8185	J	SB	Y 8245	J	RS
Y 8006	J	CY	Y 8066	J	DP	Y 8126	J	LN	Y 8186	J	CY	Y 8246	J	NB
Y 8007	J	PV	Y 8067	J	TP	Y 8127	J	LN	Y 8187	J	AC	Y 8247	J	SO
Y 8008	J	SB	Y 8068	J	TP	Y 8128	J	PV	Y 8188	J	SO	Y 8248	J	RS
Y 8009	J	MZ	Y 8069	J	TP	Y 8129	J	PV	Y 8189	J	BD	Y 8249	J	RS
Y 8010	J	MZ	Y 8070	J	LE	Y 8130	J	LG	Y 8190	J	TP	Y 8250	J	SO
Y 8011	J	LN	Y 8071	J	LN	Y 8131	J	TP	Y 8191	J	TP	Y 8251	J	RS
Y 8012	J	SO	Y 8072	J	BD	Y 8132	J	TP	Y 8192	J	BZ	Y 8252	J	AC
Y 8013	J	MZ	Y 8073	J	BD	Y 8133	J	TP	Y 8193	J	LG	Y 8253	J	SO
Y 8014	J	SB	Y 8074	J	SB	Y 8134	J	CY	Y 8194	J	BD	Y 8254	J	AC
Y 8015	J	MZ	Y 8075	J	LE	Y 8135	J	PV	Y 8195	J	BD	Y 8255	J	SO
Y 8016	J	MB	Y 8076	J	TP	Y 8136	J	LG	Y 8196	J	TP	Y 8256	J	CB
Y 8017	J	MB	Y 8077	J	TP	Y 8137	J	NV	Y 8197	J	TL	Y 8257	J	DP
Y 8018	J	MB	Y 8078	J	MB	Y 8138	J	NV	Y 8198	J	LG	Y 8258	J	CB
Y 8019	J	MB	Y 8079	J	PV	Y 8139	J	CB	Y 8199	J	TP	Y 8259	J	BD
Y 8020	J	TP	Y 8080	J	TL	Y 8140	J	LV	Y 8200	J	LE	Y 8260	J*	NV
Y 8021	J	BD	Y 8081	J	TP	Y 8141	J	NV	Y 8201	J	PV	Y 8261	J	LE
Y 8022	J	LN	Y 8082	J	LN	Y 8142	J	LV	Y 8202	J	PV	Y 8262	J	LE
Y 8023	J	RS	Y 8083	J	LN	Y 8143	J	RS	Y 8203	J	LN	Y 8263	J	TP
Y 8024	J	SO	Y 8084	J	TL	Y 8144	J	SO	Y 8204	J	NB	Y 8264	J	MZ
Y 8025	J	SO	Y 8085	J	TL	Y 8145	J	SB	Y 8205	J	SO	Y 8265	J	BD
Y 8026	J	BZ	Y 8086	J	LN	Y 8146	J	AC	Y 8206	J	NV	Y 8266	J	NV
Y 8027	J	DP	Y 8087	J	LE	Y 8147	J	MB	Y 8207	J	NV	Y 8267	J	LE
Y 8028	J	LV	Y 8088	J	LE	Y 8148	J	BZ	Y 8208	J	NV	Y 8268	J	PV
Y 8029	J	LV	Y 8089	J	BD	Y 8149	J	PV	Y 8209	J	CB	Y 8269	J	TP
Y 8030	J	RS	Y 8090	J	+rLG	Y 8150	J	PV	Y 8210	J	MB	Y 8270	J	LG
Y 8031	J	RS	Y 8091	J	LN	Y 8151	J	LN	Y 8211	J	CY	Y 8271	J	TL
Y 8032	J	NB	Y 8092	J	CY	Y 8152	J	MZ	Y 8212	J	SB	Y 8272	J	LG
Y 8033	J	RS	Y 8093	J	SO	Y 8153	J	PV	Y 8213	J	SB	Y 8273	J	NV
Y 8034	J	NV	Y 8094	J	PV	Y 8154	J	BD	Y 8214	J	SO	Y 8274	J	NV
Y 8035	J	NV	Y 8095	J	NV	Y 8155	J	CY	Y 8215	J	LG	Y 8275	J	PV
Y 8036	J	NV	Y 8096	J	BZ	Y 8156	J	LG	Y 8216	J	SB	Y 8276	J	PV
Y 8037	J	PV	Y 8097	J	NB	Y 8157	J	LG	Y 8217	J	TP	Y 8277	J	CY
Y 8038	J	PV	Y 8098	J	BZ	Y 8158	J	TP	Y 8218	J	TP	Y 8278	J	LE
Y 8039	J	SO	Y 8099	J	TL	Y 8159	J	TP	Y 8219	J	TP	Y 8279	J	LV
Y 8040	J	AC	Y 8100	J	NB	Y 8160	J	RS	Y 8220	J	TL	Y 8280	J	LE
Y 8041	J	MB	Y 8101	J	NB	Y 8161	J	RS	Y 8221	J	PV	Y 8281	J	LE
Y 8042	J	MB	Y 8102	J	AC	Y 8162	J	SO	Y 8222	J	LE	Y 8282	J	PV
Y 8043	J	MB	Y 8103	J	BZ	Y 8163	J	AC	Y 8223	J	LN	Y 8283	J	BZ
Y 8044	J	MB	Y 8104	J	MB	Y 8164	J	SO	Y 8224	J	LN	Y 8284	J	BZ
Y 8045	J	BZ	Y 8105	J	BZ	Y 8165	J	SO	Y 8225	J	BD	Y 8285	J	NB
Y 8046	J	LN	Y 8106	J	DP	Y 8166	J	TL	Y 8226	J	NB	Y 8286	J	LE
Y 8047	J	DP	Y 8107	J	RS	Y 8167	J	BD	Y 8227	J	RS	Y 8287	J	BZ
Y 8048	J	NB	Y 8108	J	PV	Y 8168	J	TL	Y 8228	J	NB	Y 8288	J	PV
Y 8049	J	TL	Y 8109	J	CY	Y 8169	J	LE	Y 8229	J	AC	Y 8289	J	LG
Y 8050	J	BZ	Y 8110	J	MZ	Y 8170	J	SB	Y 8230	J	AC	Y 8290	J	LE
Y 8051	J	SO	Y 8111	J	MB	Y 8171	J	RS	Y 8231	J	MB	Y 8291	J	NV
Y 8052	J	LN	Y 8112	J	SB	Y 8172	J	MB	Y 8232	J	CB	Y 8292	J	LG
Y 8053	J	LV	Y 8113	J	PV	Y 8173	J	MB	Y 8233	J	BZ	Y 8293	J	CB
Y 8054	J	LV	Y 8114	J	CB	Y 8174	J	BZ	Y 8234	J	MB	Y 8294	J	LV
Y 8055	J	LV	Y 8115	J	LN	Y 8175	J	SB	Y 8235	J	NV	Y 8295	J	MB
Y 8056	J	PV	Y 8116	J	SB	Y 8176	J	SB	Y 8236	J	NV	Y 8296	J	TP
Y 8057	J	SO	Y 8117	J	SB	Y 8177	J	NV	Y 8237	J	BZ	Y 8297	J	SB
Y 8058	J	DP	Y 8118	J	MZ	Y 8178	J	MB	Y 8238	J	BD	Y 8298	J	LG
Y 8059	J	SO	Y 8119	J	DP	Y 8179	J	MB	Y 8239	J	MB	Y 8299	J	NV
Y 8060	J	SO	Y 8120	J	CB	Y 8180	J	DP	Y 8240	J	CB	Y 8300	J +	LN

Y 8301	J	MB	Y 8316	J	TP	Y 8331	J	LE	Y 8346	J	MZ	Y 8361	J	TP
Y 8302	J	MB	Y 8317	J	RS	Y 8332	J	CY	Y 8347	J	CB	Y 8362	J	BD
Y 8303	J	LV	Y 8318	J	TP	Y 8333	J	TP	Y 8348	J*	NV	Y 8363	J +	LV
Y 8304	J	BD	Y 8319	J	AC	Y 8334	J	PV	Y 8349	J*	NV	Y 8364	J	LV
Y 8305	J	LE	Y 8320	J	TP	Y 8335	J	PV	Y 8350	J*	NV	Y 8365	J	LV
Y 8306	J	AC	Y 8321	J	SO	Y 8336	J	BD	Y 8351	J*	NV	Y 8366	J +	NV
Y 8307	J	RS	Y 8322	J	LE	Y 8337	J	LE	Y 8352	J*	NV	Y 8367	J +	LV
Y 8308	J	AC	Y 8323	J	LE	Y 8338	J	MB	Y 8353	J*	NV	Y 8368	J	BD
Y 8309	J	RS	Y 8324	J	CB	Y 8339	J	LV	Y 8354	J*	NV	Y 8369	J	LE
Y 8310	J	AC	Y 8325	J	LG	Y 8340	J	MZ	Y 8355	J*	NV	Y 8370	J	AC
Y 8311	J	LG	Y 8326	J	PV	Y 8341	J	CB	Y 8356	J*	NV	Y 8371	J	CB
Y 8312	J	TL	Y 8327	J	MZ	Y 8342	J§	PV	Y 8357	J*	NV	Y 8372	J	CB
Y 8313	J	TP	Y 8328	J	LN	Y 8343	J	TP	Y 8358	J	TL	Y 8373	J	BD
Y 8314	J	AC	Y 8329	J	BZ	Y 8344	J	NV	Y 8359	J	TP	Y 8374	J	LE
Y 8315	J	TP	Y 8330	J	CY	Y 8345	J	LE	Y 8360	J	PV	Y 8375	J	BZ

CLASS Y 8400   B

After testing remote control on Y 8300, the SNCF decided to follow the DB and go for radio control on its new small shunters thus allowing the duties of driver and shunter to be combined. The loco can either be controlled from a portable radio, or from the cab. Externally the locos are similar to Class Y 8000, but there is an illuminated "TELE" sign at cab roof level and there are marker lights under the buffer beams at the four corners to indicate to staff that remote control is in operation.

Details as Class Y 8000 except:

Built: 1990–95.   **Builder:** Arbel Fauvet Rail.
Engine: Poyaud V12-520NS (224kW) (+ Unidiesel UD18L6R3 (219 kW)).
Transmission: Hydraulic. Voith LZr4SU2. (+ Electric).
Weight: 36 tonnes.
Max. T.E.: 118/62 kN.   **Length:** 10.14 m.
Wheel Dia.: 1050 mm.   **Max. Speed:** 30/60 km/h.

Y 8401	J	AC	Y 8431	J	MB	Y 8461	J	SO	Y 8491	J +	LV	Y 8521	J +	PV
Y 8402	J	PV	Y 8432	J	SO	Y 8462	J	BD	Y 8492	J +	NV	Y 8522	J +	BD
Y 8403	J	AC	Y 8433	J	BZ	Y 8463	J	PV	Y 8493	J +	PV	Y 8523	J +	DP
Y 8404	J	PV	Y 8434	J	BZ	Y 8464	J	CB	Y 8494	J +	BD	Y 8524	J +	MZ
Y 8405	J	AC	Y 8435	J	BZ	Y 8465	J	AC	Y 8495	J +	BD	Y 8525	J +	MZ
Y 8406	J	AC	Y 8436	J	NV	Y 8466	J	MB	Y 8496	J +	SB	Y 8526	J +	MZ
Y 8407	J	MZ	Y 8437	J	DP	Y 8467	J	BD	Y 8497	J +	LE	Y 8527	J +	AC
Y 8408	J	MZ	Y 8438	J	SO	Y 8468	J	CB	Y 8498	J +	MZ	Y 8528	J +	NB
Y 8409	J	SO	Y 8439	J	SO	Y 8469	J	NV	Y 8499	J +	MB	Y 8529	J +	MZ
Y 8410	J	MZ	Y 8440	J	MB	Y 8470	J	LE	Y 8500	J +	MZ	Y 8530	J +	SB
Y 8411	J	AC	Y 8441	J	MB	Y 8471	J	AC	Y 8501	J +	BD	Y 8531	J +	MZ
Y 8412	J	PV	Y 8442	J	MB	Y 8472	J	MZ	Y 8502	J +	CB	Y 8532	J +	MZ
Y 8413	J	AC	Y 8443	J	MB	Y 8473	J	MB	Y 8503	J +	BD	Y 8533	J +	SB
Y 8414	J	LE	Y 8444	J	BZ	Y 8474	J	CB	Y 8504	J +	MZ	Y 8534	J +	PV
Y 8415	J	PV	Y 8445	J	BD	Y 8475	J	BD	Y 8505	J +	CB	Y 8535	J +	LV
Y 8416	J	LE	Y 8446	J	BZ	Y 8476	J	NV	Y 8506	J +	NB	Y 8536	J +	SB
Y 8417	J	SO	Y 8447	J	PV	Y 8477	J	LE	Y 8507	J +	CB	Y 8537	J +	SB
Y 8418	J	MB	Y 8448	J	DP	Y 8478	J	NB	Y 8508	J +	NB	Y 8538	J +	MZ
Y 8419	J	MB	Y 8449	J	CB	Y 8479	J	CB	Y 8509	J +	NB	Y 8539	J +	MZ
Y 8420	J	LE	Y 8450	J	MB	Y 8480	J	NB	Y 8510	J +	MZ	Y 8540	J +	SB
Y 8421	J	LE	Y 8451	J	DP	Y 8481	J	LE	Y 8511	J +	BZ	Y 8541	J +	AC
Y 8422	J	SB	Y 8452	J	DP	Y 8482	J	DP	Y 8512	J +	NB	Y 8542	J +	AC
Y 8423	J	PV	Y 8453	J	BD	Y 8483	J	MZ	Y 8513	J +	MZ	Y 8543	J +	AC
Y 8424	J	PV	Y 8454	J	DP	Y 8484	J	NB	Y 8514	J +	CB	Y 8544	J +	TL
Y 8425	J	PV	Y 8455	J	DP	Y 8485	J	TL	Y 8515	J +	AC	Y 8545	J +	TL
Y 8426	J	LE	Y 8456	J	PV	Y 8486	J	TL	Y 8516	J +	NV	Y 8546	J +	LV
Y 8427	J	LE	Y 8457	J	DP	Y 8487	J	LV	Y 8517	J +	BZ	Y 8547	J +	LV
Y 8428	J	LE	Y 8458	J	DP	Y 8488	J	NB	Y 8518	J +	NV	Y 8548	J +	LE
Y 8429	J	MB	Y 8459	J	NV	Y 8489	J	CB	Y 8519	J +	BZ	Y 8549	J +	TL
Y 8430	J	MB	Y 8460	J	DP	Y 8490	J	CB	Y 8520	J +	DP	Y 8550	J +	LV

LOCMAs

Since the last edition, Classes Y 2200, 2400, 5100, 6200 and 6400 have all been either withdrawn or are now considered as "machine tools", being maintained by the depot or works concerned. These locos are known as LOCMAs ("LOComotive de MAnoeuvres") and are numbered 0001 upwards. Many carry their old number or no number and have been painted in special liveries by the depots. Please note that our information on these locos is incomplete. We thank Eric Dunkling for his help in compiling this information.

CLASS Y 2200   B

Built: 1956–60.
Builders: Moyse (2201–2249), Decauville (2250–2340).
Engine: Poyaud 2PDT (44 kW) (* Agrom (40 kW)).
Transmission: Mechanical.
Weight: 16 tonnes.   **Length:** 5.79 m.
Wheel Dia.: 1050 mm.   **Max. Speed:** 14/50 km/h.

Old No.	LOCMA	Location	Old No	LOCMA	Location
Y 2203	21	Saulon p.w. depot	Y 2285	0030	TV "TEF"
Y 2208	0033	Chalons-sur-Marne wagon works	Y 2298	0034	CB
Y 2215	0001	CY	Y 2301		Nice St. Roch
Y 2237	0006	NV	Y 2310	0004	VE
Y 2243	0035	TV	Y 2317	0005	VE
Y 2255	0025	Béziers works	Y 2321		Romilly carriage works
Y 2260	0009	CB	Y 2322	0003	Metz Sablon
Y 2266	0007	NV	Y 2330	0045	NB
Y 2282	0013	TP			

CLASS Y 2400   B

Built: 1962–69.   **Builder:** Decauville.
Engine: Agrom 6r (45 kW).   **Transmission:** Mechanical.
Weight: 17 tonnes.   **Length:** 7.18 m.
Wheel Dia.: 1050 mm.   **Max. Speed:** 15/58 km/h.

Old No.	LOCMA	Location	Old No	LOCMA	Location
Y 2401		Granville	Y 2464	0109	MB
Y 2404	0084	LG	Y 2465		Les Laumes-Alésia depot
Y 2409		St Dizier p.w. depot	Y 2471	0027	Oullins works
Y 2410	0046	Troyes wagon works	Y 2474	0036	CB
Y 2414	0042	Ambérieu wagon works	Y 2476	0119	CB
Y 2416		Brive works	Y 2479	0031	DP
Y 2417		Nîmes depot	Y 2480	0065	NV
Y 2420	0017	Paris Masséna carriage sdgs.	Y 2481	0095	PS
Y 2424	0063	BZ	Y 2482		Toulouse Raynal
Y 2425		BZ	Y 2483	0122	Laroche-Migennes depot
Y 2427		Moulins p.w. depot	Y 2484	0028	AV
Y 2428	22	Saulon p.w. depot	Y 2490	0064	Quimper
Y 2433	0018	PO	Y 2493	0115	BD
Y 2436	0022	TP	Y 2495	0105	Clermont Ferrand wagon works
Y 2439	0062	EMM Cerbère	Y 2499		Lamure-sur-Azergues
Y 2441	0048	DP	Y 2500	0118	Avignon Champfleury works
Y 2443	0026	Sotteville wagon works	Y 2502	0038	TP
Y 2444	0113	AV	Y 2506	0057	VG
Y 2447	0099	MB	Y 2507	0058	VG
Y 2448	0016	Marseille St. Charles car. wks.	Y 2510		Périgueux wagon works
Y 2451	0108	MB	Y 2511		EIMM Béziers
Y 2453	0126	Miramas depot	Y 2514		Vichy
Y 2456	0125	Nice St. Roch	Y 2519	57001	CB
Y 2460	0059	Paris Charolais depot			

CLASS Y 5100   B

Built: 1960–63.
Engine: Poyaud 4PYT (81 kW).
Weight: 20 tonnes.
Wheel Dia.: 1050 mm.

Builder: De Dietrich.
Transmission: Hydromechanical.
Length: 7.18 m.
Max. Speed: 18 km/h.

Old No.	LOCMA	Location	Old No	LOCMA	Location
Y 5103	0101	Le Mans works	Y 5137		Bretenoux-Biars p.w. depot
Y 5104	0052	Nantes carriage works	Y 5138	0102	Le Mans works
Y 5105	0091	MR	Y 5140	0079	Villeneuve St Georges wheel shop
Y 5106	0097	PO	Y 5142	0077	CF
Y 5107	0081	Les Aubrais depot	Y 5143	0078	PV (named 'MILLAU')
Y 5108	0086	TL	Y 5144	0089	LE
Y 5109	0096	PO	Y 5145	0071	CY
Y 5116	0076	NV	Y 5147	0055	LN
Y 5117	0112	LN	Y 5148	0093	CY
Y 5119	0098	LN	Y 5150	0104	Le Mans works
Y 5121	0068	SO	Y 5151	0056	VG
Y 5123	0069	BD	Y 5155	0073	PL
Y 5124	0047	LG	Y 5159	0094	TV
Y 5125	0114	Les Aubrais wagon works	Y 5161	0029	AV
Y 5126	0087	TL	Y 5201	0092	AC
Y 5127	0037	PO	Y 5205		Bretenoux-Biars p.w. depot
Y 5129	0066	MZ	Y 5210	0070	CY
Y 5131	0041	SB	Y 5211	0061	Le Mans works
Y 5132	0032	TV	Y 5212		Moulin Neuf p.w. works
Y 5133	0085	Chalons-sur-Marne wagon works	Y 5213	0067	TP
Y 5136	0044	Tours S.P. p.w. works	Y 5214	0039	CY

CLASS Y 6200   B

Built: 1949–55.
Builders: BDR (6201–6230), St. Lilloise (6231–6259), Moyse (6260–6297).
Engine: Poyaud 6PDT (132 kW).
Weight: 32 tonnes.
Wheel Dia.: 1050 mm.

Transmission: Electric. Oerlikon.
Length: 8.90 m.
Max. Speed: 20/60 km/h.

Old No.	LOCMA	Location	Old No	LOCMA	Location
Y 6207	0021	Nevers Works	Y 6266	0106	MB
Y 6220		Nevers Works	Y 6276	0075	TL
Y 6230		Calais carriage depot	Y 6281	0074	TP

CLASS Y 6400   B

Built: 1954–58.
Builders: BDR (6301–6330), De Dietrich (6401–6430, 6501–6625), Decauville (6431–6500).
Engine: Poyaud 6PDT (132 kW).
Weight: 32 tonnes.
Wheel Dia.: 1050 mm.

Transmission: Electric. Oerlikon.
Length: 8.90 m.
Max. Speed: 20/60 km/h.

Old No.	LOCMA	Location	Old No	LOCMA	Location
Y 6410	0019	Somain wagon works	Y 6565	0123	VG
Y 6423	0049	VG	Y 6569	0124	Chalons-sur-Marne wagon works
Y 6429	0080	VE	Y 6571		Romilly carriage works
Y 6432	0043	Lumes wagon works	Y 6575	0072	PL
Y 6490	61	Saulon p.w. depot	Y 6585		EMM Sotteville
Y 6493	62	Saulon p.w. depot	Y 6591	0082	Les Aubrais wagon works
Y 6510		TV	Y 6605		RS
Y 6513	0051	VG	Y 6612	0121	Bordeaux wagon shop
Y 6520	0107	MB	Y 6617	0083	Les Aubrais depot
Y 6522	0117	Le Havre Soquence	Y 6621		RS
Y 6531	0053	Sotteville Quatre Mares works	Y 6622	0012	RS
Y 6539	0116	TL	Y 6623		Somain yard

1.6. ELECTRIC MULTIPLE UNITS

Many EMUs carry set numbers on the front ends. Where applicable, these are listed in the first column followed by the individual vehicle numbers.

CLASS Z 5300   3/4-CAR UNITS

With suburban traffic increasing these 4-car units were delivered and again features stainless steel bodywork. For years they have worked out of Paris Austerlitz and Lyon stations on suburban trains but the development of the Paris RER services and the introduction of double-deck EMUs has seen more congregating on Paris Montparnasse and Paris Lyon services. A number have gone to TP depot for stopping services around Orléans and Tours. For this, one of the centre cars is removed. From 5367, units have headcode panels for Paris RER services. Unit numbers are the last three numerals of the power car except that to distinguish MR units not equipped for one-person-operation, the unit numbers are now in the 500 series although individual car numbers are unchanged.

Built: 1965–68 (5301–5361), 1972–75 (5362–5445).
System: 1500 V d.c.
Builders: Carel & Fouché/MTE/TCO.
Traction Motors: Four Oerlikon EMW 510 (245 kW).
Formation: ZBD + ZRB + ZRB + ZRABx.
Accommodation: –/87 1T + –/112 + –/106 1T + 44/40.
Weight: 62 + 30 + 30 + 42 tonnes.
Length: 25.925 (25.80*) + 25.60 (25.85*) + 25.60 (25.85*) + 25.925 (25.80*) m.
Wheel Arrangement: Bo-Bo + 2-2 + 2-2 + 2-2.
Max. Speed: 130 km/h.

5301–5361 are non-gangwayed. 5362–5445 have gangways for staff use only.

302	Z 5302	25304	25303	15302	U	*	VG	337	Z 5337	25374	25373	15337	U	* VG
303	Z 5303	25306	25305	15303	U	*	VG	338	Z 5338	25376	25375	15338	U	* VG
303	Z 5304	25308	25307	15304	U	*	VG	339	Z 5339	25378	25377	15339	U	* VG
305	Z 5305	25310	25309	15305	U	*	MR	340	Z 5340	25380	25379	15340	U	* VG
306	Z 5306	25312	25311	15306	U	*	VG	341	Z 5341	25382	25381	15341	U	* VG
307	Z 5307	25314	25313	15307	U	*	MR	342	Z 5342	25384	25383	15301	U	* VG
308	Z 5308	25316	25315	15308	U	*	VG	343	Z 5343	25386	25385	15343	U	* MR
309	Z 5309	25318	25317	15309	U	*	VG	344	Z 5344	25388	25387	15344	U	* VG
310	Z 5310	25320	25319	15310	U	*	VG	345	Z 5345	25390	25389	15345	U	* VG
311	Z 5311	25322	25321	15311	U	*	VG	346	Z 5346	25392	25391	15346	U	* VG
312	Z 5312	25324	25323	15312	U	*	MR	347	Z 5347	25394	25393	15347	U	* MR
313	Z 5313	25326	25325	15313	U	*	VG	348	Z 5348	25396	25395	15348	U	* VG
314	Z 5314	25328	25327	15314	U	*	MR	349	Z 5349	25398	25397	15349	U	* MR
315	Z 5315	25330	25329	15315	U	*	MR	350	Z 5350	25400	25399	15350	U	* VG
316	Z 5316	25332	25591	15316	U	*	VG	351	Z 5351	25402	25401	15351	U	* MR
317	Z 5317	25334	25333	15317	U	*	MR	352	Z 5352	25404	25403	15352	U	* MR
318	Z 5318	25336	25335	15318	U	*	MR	353	Z 5353	25406	25405	15353	U	* MR
319	Z 5319	25338	25337	15319	U	*	VG	354	Z 5354	25408	25407	15354	U	* MR
320	Z 5320	25340	25339	15320	U	*	MR	355	Z 5355	25410	25409	15355	U	* MR
321	Z 5321	25342	25341	15321	U	*	VG	356	Z 5356	25412	25411	15356	U	* VG
322	Z 5322	25344	25343	15322	U	*	MR	357	Z 5357	25414	25413	15357	U	* VG
323	Z 5323	25346	25345	15323	U	*	MR	358	Z 5358	25416	25415	15358	U	* VG
324	Z 5324	25348	25347	15324	U	*	MR	359	Z 5359	25592	25593	15359	U	* VG
326	Z 5326	25352	25351	15326	U	*	VG	360	Z 5360	25594	25595	15360	U	* VG
327	Z 5327	25354	25353	15327	U	*	MR	361	Z 5361	25596	25597	15361	U	* VG
328	Z 5328	25356	25355	15328	U	*	VG	362	Z 5362	25424	25423	15362	U	VG
329	Z 5329	25358	25357	15329	U	*	MR	363	Z 5363	25426	25425	15363	U	VG
330	Z 5330	25360	25359	15330	U	*	MR	364	Z 5364	25428	25427	15364	U	VG
331	Z 5331	25362	25361	15331	U	*	VG	365	Z 5365	25430	25429	15365	U	VG
332	Z 5332	25364	25363	15332	U	*	VG	366	Z 5366	25432	25331	15366	U	VG
333	Z 5333	25366	25415	15333	U	*	VG	367	Z 5367	25434	25433	15367	U	VG
334	Z 5334	25368	25367	15334	U	*	VG	368	Z 5368	25436	25435	15368	U	VG
335	Z 5335	25370	25369	15335	U	*	VG	369	Z 5369	25438	25437	15369	U	VG
336	Z 5336	25372	25371	15336	U	*	VG	370	Z 5370	25440	25439	15370	U	VG

371	Z 5371	25442	25441	15371	U	MR	409	Z 5409	25518	25517	15409	U	PA
372	Z 5372	25444	25443	15372	U	MR	410	Z 5410	25520	25519	15410	U	PA
373	Z 5373		25445	15373	U	TP	411	Z 5411	25522	25521	15411	U	PA
374	Z 5374		25447	15374	U	TP	412	Z 5412	25431	25523	15412	U	PA
375	Z 5375	25450	25449	15375	U	PA	413	Z 5413	25526	25525	15413	U	PA
376	Z 5376	25452	25451	15376	U	PA	414	Z 5414	25528	25527	15414	U	PA
577	Z 5377	25454	25453	15377	U	MR	415	Z 5415	25530	25529	15415	U	PA
378	Z 5378		25455	15378	U	TP	416	Z 5416	25532	25531	15416	U	PA
579	Z 5379	25458	25457	15379	U	MR	417	Z 5417	25534	25533	15417	U	PA
380	Z 5380		25459	15380	U	TP	418	Z 5418	25536	25535	15418	U	PA
581	Z 5381	25462	25461	15381	U	MR	419	Z 5419	25538	25537	15419	U	PA
582	Z 5382	25464	25463	15382	U	MR	420	Z 5420	25540	25539	15420	U	PA
383	Z 5383		25465	15383	U	TP	421	Z 5421	25542	25541	15421	U	PA
584	Z 5384	25468	25467	15384	U	MR	522	Z 5422	25544	25543	15422	U	MR
385	Z 5385		25469	15385	U	TP	423	Z 5423		25545	15423	U	TP
386	Z 5386	25472	25471	15386	U	PA	424	Z 5424		25547	15424	U	TP
387	Z 5387	25474	25473	15387	U	PA	425	Z 5425		25549	15425	U	TP
588	Z 5388	25476	25475	15388	U	MR	426	Z 5426	25552	25551	15426	U	MR
389	Z 5389		25477	15389	U	TP	427	Z 5427		25553	15427	U	TP
590	Z 5390	25480	25479	15390	U	MR	428	Z 5428		25555	15428	U	TP
591	Z 5391	25482	25481	15391	U	MR	429	Z 5429		25557	15429	U	TP
392	Z 5392	25484	25483	15392	U	PA	430	Z 5430		25559	15430	U	TP
393	Z 5393	25486	25485	15393	U	TP	431	Z 5431		25561	15431	U	TP
594	Z 5394	25488	25487	15394	U	MR	432	Z 5432		25563	15432	U	TP
395	Z 5395	25490	25489	15395	U	MR	433	Z 5433		25565	15433	U	TP
396	Z 5396	25492	25491	15396	U	PA	434	Z 5434	25568	25567	15434	U	PA
397	Z 5397	25494	25493	15397	U	PA	535	Z 5435	25570	25569	15435	U	MR
598	Z 5398	25496	25495	15398	U	MR	436	Z 5436	25572	25571	15436	U	PA
399	Z 5399	25498	25497	15399	U	PA	437	Z 5437	25574	25573	15437	U	PA
400	Z 5400	25500	25499	15400	U	PA	438	Z 5438	25554	25575	15438	U	PA
401	Z 5401	25502	25501	15401	U	PA	439	Z 5439	25578	25577	15439	U	PA
402	Z 5402	25504	25503	15402	U	PA	440	Z 5440	25580	25579	15440	U	PA
403	Z 5403	25506	25505	15403	U	PA	441	Z 5441	25582	25581	15441	U	PA
404	Z 5404	25508	25507	15404	U	PA	442	Z 5442	25584	25583	15442	U	PA
405	Z 5405	25510	25509	15405	U	PA	443	Z 5443	25586	25585	15443	U	PA
406	Z 5406	25512	25511	15406	U	PA	444	Z 5444	25588	25587	15444	U	PA
407	Z 5407	25514	25513	15407	U	PA	445	Z 5445	25590	25589	15445	U	PA
408	Z 5408	25516	25515	15408	U	PA							

Spare trailers:

25446	TP	25466	TP	25548	TP	25558	TP	25564	TP
25448	TP	25478	TP	25550	TP	25560	TP	25566	TP
25456	TP	25546	TP	25556	TP	25562	TP		

Name: 5395 ISSY-LES-MOULINEAUX

CLASS Z 5600   4/6-CAR DOUBLE-DECK UNITS

These were the first double-deck EMUs to operate in France and together with dual-voltage version Class Z 8800 are generically known as Z2N sets. The six-car sets now operate on Paris Gare de Lyon–Laroche Migennes outer suburban services whilst the four-car sets operate on RER line C. Trailer cars are numbered ZRB 25601-25742 and ZRAB 35601-35710. This gives one second and one composite per four-car set plus an extra two seconds for six-car sets. Additional cars ZRB 25801-25821 and ZRABs 35801-35821 were built for Class Z 20500. Trailers are shared with Class Z 8800 and formations are non-sequential and have been changed regularly, especially as toilets have been retro-fitted to VG sets.

Built: 1983–85.   **System:** 1500 V d.c.
Builders-Mech. Parts: ANF/CIMT.   **Builders-Elec. Parts:** Alsthom/TCO.
Traction Motors: Four TCO 4 FHO 3262 (350 kW) per power car.

Formation: ZB + ZRB + (+ZRB) + ZRAB + (+ZRB) + ZB.
Accommodation: -/118 1T + -/164 1T (+ -/164 1T) + 62/91 1T (+ -/164 1T) + -/118 1T.
Weight: 66 + 41 (+ 41) + 42 (+ 41) + 66 tonnes.
Length: 25.10 + 24.28 (+ 24.28) + 24.28 (+ 24.28) + 25.10 m.
Wheel Arrangement: Bo-Bo + 2-2 (+ 2-2) + 2-2 + (+ 2-2) + Bo-Bo.
Max. Speed: 140 km/h.

Some VG units have VDUs in the cabs which display the view along the platform at certain stations for one-man operation.

Six-Car units.

01C	Z 5601	25605	25663	35695	25732	Z 5602	I	VG
02C	Z 5603	25603	25656	35666	25741	Z 5634	I	VG
03C	Z 5605	25650	25623	35687	25730	Z 5606	I	VG
04C	Z 5607	25665	35668	25621	25737	Z 5608	I	VG
05C	Z 5609	25660	25619	35678	25739	Z 5610	I	VG
06C	Z 5611	25624	25657	35697	25738	Z 5612	I	VG
07C	Z 5613	25637	25729	35676	25733	Z 5614	I	VG
08C	Z 5615	25669	25659	35670	25735	Z 5616	I	VG
09C	Z 5617	25658	25648	35686	25736	Z 5618	I	VG
10C	Z 5619	25662	25610	35677	25731	Z 5620	I	VG
11C	Z 5621	25661	25654	35674	25740	Z 5622	I	VG
12C	Z 5623	25625	25645	35669	25742	Z 5624	I	VG
13C	Z 5625	25622	25644	35681	25651	Z 5626	I	VG
14C	Z 5627	25652	25666	35667	25727	Z 5628	I	VG
15C	Z 5629	25667	25647	35665	25728	Z 5630	I	VG
16C	Z 5631	25734	35671	25649	25631	Z 5632	I	VG

Four-Car units.

17C	Z 5633	25628	35619	Z 5634	I	PA	35C	Z 5669	25613	35692	Z 5670	I PA
18C	Z 5635	25678	35615	Z 5636	I	PA	36C	Z 5671	25633	35623	Z 5672	I PA
19C	Z 5637	25641	35628	Z 5638	I	PA	37C	Z 5673	25636	35679	Z 5674	I PA
20C	Z 5639	25635	35654	Z 5640	I	PA	38C	Z 5675	25609	35682	Z 5676	I PA
21C	Z 5641	25632	35629	Z 5642	I	PA	39C	Z 5677	25604	35672	Z 5678	I PA
22C	Z 5643	25612	35683	Z 5645	I	PA	40C	Z 5679	25673	35625	Z 5680	I PA
23C	Z 5645	25601	35696	Z 5646	I	PA	41C	Z 5681	25606	35680	Z 5682	I PA
24C	Z 5647	25671	35624	Z 5648	I	PA	42C	Z 5683	25615	35675	Z 5684	I PA
25C	Z 5649	25608	35605	Z 5650	I	PA	43C	Z 5685	25682	35688	Z 5686	I PA
26C	Z 5651	25683	35608	Z 5652	I	PA	44C	Z 5687	25646	35616	Z 5688	I PA
27C	Z 5653	25607	35700	Z 5654	I	PA	45C	Z 5689	25614	35699	Z 5690	I PA
28C	Z 5655	25679	35673	Z 5656	I	PA	46C	Z 5691	25675	35632	Z 5692	I PA
29C	Z 5657	25617	35622	Z 5658	I	PA	47C	Z 5693	25674	35689	Z 5694	I PA
30C	Z 5659	25620	35621	Z 5660	I	PA	48C	Z 5695	25670	35685	Z 5696	I PA
31C	Z 5661	25677	35690	Z 5662	I	PA	49C	Z 5697	25680	35698	Z 5698	I PA
32C	Z 5663	25672	35694	Z 5664	I	PA	50C	Z 5699	25681	35693	Z 5700	I PA
33C	Z 5665	25653	35626	Z 5666	I	PA	51C	Z 5701	25616	35627	Z 5702	I PA
34C	Z 5667	25634	35691	Z 5668	I	PA	52C	Z 5703	25684	35684	Z 5704	I PA

Names:

5601/5602	SAVIGNY-LE-TEMPLE	5697/5698	BRÉTIGNY-SUR-ORGE
5633/5634	ATHIS-MONS	5699/5700	ÉTAMPES
5635/5636	VIROFLAY		

CLASS Z 6100   3-CAR UNITS

Like the early d.c. units these are finished off in stainless steel. They operate suburban services out of Paris Nord as far north as Amiens. The last three digits of the running number also appear on cabsides and in cab windows as set numbers. 6168/9 have been sold to Luxembourg where they operate as CFL 262/1 respectively. These units have a monomotor bogie, which is the same type as on Class BB 67000/67300 up to 6120. From 6121, the bogie is similar to those on Class BB 67400.

Built: 1965–71.
Builders-Mech. Parts: Carel & Fouché/Schneider/De Dietrich.
Builders-Elec. Parts: CEM/Siemens/Alsthom.
Traction Motor: 690 kW.
Formation: ZBD + ZRB + ZRABx.
Weight: 51 + 28 + 31 tonnes.
Wheel Arrangement: 2-B + 2-2 + 2-2.

System: 25 kV a.c.

Accommodation: –/86 1T + –/107 1T + 36/51 1T.
Length: 25.50 + 23.80 + 25.15 m.
Max. Speed: 120 km/h.

101	Z 6101	26101 16101	U	PL
102	Z 6102	26102 16102	U	PL
104	Z 6104	26104 16104	U	PL
106	Z 6106	26106 16106	U	PL
107	Z 6107	26107 16107	U	PL
108	Z 6108	26108 16108	U	PL
109	Z 6109	26109 16109	U	PL
111	Z 6111	26111 16111	U	PL
112	Z 6112	26112 16112	U	PL
113	Z 6113	26113 16113	U	PL
114	Z 6114	26114 16114	U	PL
115	Z 6115	26115 16115	U	PL
116	Z 6116	26116 16116	U	PL
117	Z 6117	26117 16117	U	PL
118	Z 6118	26118 16118	U	PL
119	Z 6119	26119 16119	U	PL
120	Z 6120	26120 16120	U	PL
121	Z 6121	26121 16121	U	PL
122	Z 6122	26122 16122	U	PL
123	Z 6123	26123 16123	U	PL
125	Z 6125	26125 16125	U	PL
126	Z 6126	26126 16126	U	PL
127	Z 6127	26127 16127	U	PL
128	Z 6128	26128 16128	U	PL
129	Z 6129	26129 16129	U	PL
130	Z 6130	26130 16130	U	PL
131	Z 6131	26131 16131	U	PL
132	Z 6132	26132 16132	U	PL
133	Z 6133	26133 16133	U	PL
134	Z 6134	26134 16134	U	PL
135	Z 6135	26135 16135	U	PL
136	Z 6136	26136 16136	U	PL
137	Z 6137	26137 16137	U	PL
139	Z 6139	26139 16139	U	PL
140	Z 6140	26140 16140	U	PL
141	Z 6141	26141 16141	U	PL
142	Z 6142	26142 16142	U	PL
143	Z 6143	26143 16143	U	PL
144	Z 6144	26144 16144	U	PL
145	Z 6145	26145 16145	U	PL
146	Z 6146	26146 16146	U	PL
147	Z 6147	26147 16147	U	PL
148	Z 6148	26148 16148	U	PL
149	Z 6149	26149 16149	U	PL
150	Z 6150	26150 16150	U	PL
151	Z 6151	26151 16151	U	PL
152	Z 6152	26152 16152	U	PL
153	Z 6153	26153 16153	U	PL
154	Z 6154	26154 16154	U	PL
155	Z 6155	26155 16155	U	PL
156	Z 6156	26156 16156	U	PL
157	Z 6157	26157 16157	U	PL
158	Z 6158	26158 16158	U	PL
159	Z 6159	26159 16159	U	PL
160	Z 6160	26160 16160	U	PL
161	Z 6161	26161 16161	U	PL
162	Z 6162	26162 16162	U	PL
163	Z 6163	26163 16163	U	PL
164	Z 6164	26164 16164	U	PL
165	Z 6165	26165 16165	U	PL
166	Z 6166	26166 16179	U	PL
167	Z 6167	26167 16167	U	PL
170	Z 6170	26170 16170	U	PL
171	Z 6171	26171 16171	U	PL
172	Z 6172	26172 16172	U	PL
173	Z 6173	26173 16173	U	PL
174	Z 6174	26174 16174	U	PL
175	Z 6175	26175 16175	U	PL
176	Z 6176	26176 16176	U	PL
177	Z 6177	26177 16177	U	PL
178	Z 6178	26178 16178	U	PL
180	Z 6180	26180 16180	U	PL
181	Z 6181	26181 16181	U	PL
182	Z 6182	26182 16182	U	PL
183	Z 6183	26140 16140	U	PL
184	Z 6184	26184 16184	U	PL

CLASS Z 6300   3-CAR UNITS

These units originally operated suburban services out of Paris St. Lazare but with the arrival of more modern types, around half have been transferred to local services around Metz, Reims and Amiens. Those at LN will be withdrawn or transferred away during 1999. These units have a monomotor bogie, which is the same type as on Class BB 67000/67300.

Built: 1967–70.
Builders-Mech. Parts: Carel & Fouché/Fives-Lille/De Dietrich.
Builders-Elec. Parts: CEM/Siemens/Alsthom.
Traction Motor: 615 kW.
Formation: ZBD + ZRAB + ZRBx. Non-gangwayed.
Accommodation: –/39 1T + 40/21 1T + –/67 1T.
Weight: 52 + 26 + 28 tonnes.
Wheel Arrangement: 2-B + 2-2 + 2-2.

System: 25 kV a.c.
Length: 20.75 + 18.825 + 20.525 m.
Max. Speed: 120 km/h.

301	Z 6301	26301	16301	U	TV
302	Z 6302	26302	16302	U	PS
303	Z 6303	26303	16303	U	TV
304	Z 6304	26304	16304	U	TV
305	Z 6305	26305	16305	U	TV
306	Z 6306	26306	16306	U	TV
307	Z 6307	26307	16307	U	PS
308	Z 6308	26308	16308	U	TV
309	Z 6309	26309	16309	U	TV
310	Z 6310	26310	16310	U	LN
311	Z 6311	26311	16311	U	PS
312	Z 6312	26312	16312	U	TV
313	Z 6313	26313	16313	U	TV
314	Z 6314	26314	16314	U	PS
315	Z 6315	26315	16315	U	TV
316	Z 6316	26316	16316	U	LN
317	Z 6317	26317	16317	U	TV
318	Z 6318	26318	16318	U	TV
319	Z 6319	26319	16319	U	TV
320	Z 6320	26320	16320	U	LN
321	Z 6321	26321	16321	U	PS
322	Z 6322	26322	16322	U	PS
323	Z 6323	26323	16323	U	PS
324	Z 6324	26324	16324	U	PS
325	Z 6325	26325	16325	U	PS
326	Z 6326	26326	16326	U	TV
327	Z 6327	26327	16327	U	PS
328	Z 6328	26328	16328	U	LN
329	Z 6329	26329	16329	U	PS
330	Z 6330	26330	16330	U	LN
331	Z 6331	26331	16331	U	TV
332	Z 6332	26332	16332	U	LN
333	Z 6333	26333	16333	U	LN
334	Z 6334	26334	16334	U	LN
335	Z 6335	26335	16335	U	TV

CLASS Z 6400   4-CAR UNITS

This was the last type of EMU to feature stainless steel bodywork. Introduced for services out of Paris St. Lazare some operated out of Paris Nord for a while. Part of the fleet has high platform steps for use on the "Group II" lines out of Paris St. Lazare (i.e. the lines to Versailles and Marly), whereas the rest has steps fitted for low platforms to serve the "Group III" line to Poissy. The last three digits of the power car number appear in the cab window, so that the first unit shows 401 at one end and 402 at the other. All units are to be refurbished and painted in a version of livery I.

Built: 1976–79.
Builder-Mech. Parts: Carel & Fouché.
Traction Motors: Four 295 kW per power car.
Formation: ZAD + ZRB + ZRB + ZBD.
Weight: 64 + 32 + 32 + 63 tonnes.
Wheel Arrangement: Bo-Bo + 2-2 + 2-2 + Bo-Bo.
Max. Speed: 120 km/h.
Class Specific Livery: S Stainless steel with blue around the windows.

System: 25 kV a.c.
Builders-Elec. Parts: Alsthom/TCO.

Accommodation: 72/– + –/102 + –/102 + –/84.
Length: 22.70 + 22.39 + 22.39 + 22.70 m.

h Fixed steps for high platform use only.

Z 6401	26401	26402	Z 6402	S		PS	Z 6443	26443	26444	Z 6444	S	h	PS
Z 6403	26403	26404	Z 6404	S		PS	Z 6445	26445	26446	Z 6446	S	h	PS
Z 6405	26405	26406	Z 6406	S		PS	Z 6447	26447	26448	Z 6448	S	h	PS
Z 6407	26407	26408	Z 6408	S		PS	Z 6449	26449	26450	Z 6450	S	h	PS
Z 6409	26409	26410	Z 6410	S		PS	Z 6451	26451	26452	Z 6452	S	h	PS
Z 6411	26411	26412	Z 6412	S		PS	Z 6453	26453	26454	Z 6454	S	h	PS
Z 6413	26413	26414	Z 6414	S		PS	Z 6455	26455	26456	Z 6456	S	h	PS
Z 6415	26415	26416	Z 6416	S		PS	Z 6457	26457	26458	Z 6458	S	h	PS
Z 6417	26417	26418	Z 6418	S		PS	Z 6459	26459	26460	Z 6460	S	h	PS
Z 6419	26419	26420	Z 6420	S		PS	Z 6461	26461	26462	Z 6462	S	h	PS
Z 6421	26421	26422	Z 6422	S		PS	Z 6463	26463	26464	Z 6464	S	h	PS
Z 6423	26423	26424	Z 6424	S		PS	Z 6465	26465	26466	Z 6466	S	h	PS
Z 6425	26425	26426	Z 6426	S		PS	Z 6467	26467	26468	Z 6468	S	h	PS
Z 6427	26427	26428	Z 6428	S		PS	Z 6469	26469	26470	Z 6470	S	h	PS
Z 6429	26429	26430	Z 6430	S		PS	Z 6471	26471	26472	Z 6472	S	h	PS
Z 6431	26431	26432	Z 6432	S		PS	Z 6473	26473	26474	Z 6474	S	h	PS
Z 6433	26433	26434	Z 6434	S		PS	Z 6475	26475	26476	Z 6476	S	h	PS
Z 6435	26435	26436	Z 6436	S		PS	Z 6477	26477	26478	Z 6478	S	h	PS
Z 6437	26437	26438	Z 6438	S		PS	Z 6479	26479	26480	Z 6480	S	h	PS
Z 6439	26439	26440	Z 6440	S		PS	Z 6481	26481	26482	Z 6482	S	h	PS
Z 6441	26441	26442	Z 6442	S	h	PS	Z 6483	26483	26484	Z 6484	S	h	PS

Z 6485	26485	26486	Z 6486	**S**	h	PS
Z 6487	26487	26488	Z 6488	**S**	h	PS
Z 6489	26489	26490	Z 6490	**S**	h	PS
Z 6491	26491	26492	Z 6492	**S**	h	PS
Z 6493	26493	26494	Z 6494	**S**	h	PS
Z 6495	26495	26496	Z 6496	**S**	h	PS
Z 6497	26497	26498	Z 6498	**S**	h	PS
Z 6499	26499	26500	Z 6500	**S**	h	PS
Z 6501	26501	26502	Z 6502	**S**	h	PS
Z 6503	26503	26504	Z 6504	**S**	h	PS
Z 6505	26505	26506	Z 6506	**S**	h	PS
Z 6507	26507	26508	Z 6508	**S**	h	PS
Z 6509	26509	26510	Z 6510	**S**	h	PS
Z 6511	26511	26512	Z 6512	**S**	h	PS
Z 6513	26513	26514	Z 6514	**S**	h	PS
Z 6515	26515	26516	Z 6516	**S**	h	PS
Z 6517	26517	26518	Z 6518	**S**	h	PS
Z 6519	26519	26520	Z 6520	**S**	h	PS
Z 6521	26521	26522	Z 6522	**S**	h	PS
Z 6523	26523	26524	Z 6524	**S**	h	PS
Z 6525	26525	26526	Z 6526	**S**		PS
Z 6527	26527	26528	Z 6528	**S**		PS
Z 6529	26529	26530	Z 6530	**S**		PS
Z 6531	26531	26532	Z 6532	**S**		PS
Z 6533	26533	26534	Z 6534	**S**		PS
Z 6535	26535	26536	Z 6536	**S**		PS
Z 6537	26537	26538	Z 6538	**S**		PS
Z 6539	26539	26540	Z 6540	**S**		PS
Z 6541	26541	26542	Z 6542	**S**		PS
Z 6543	26543	26544	Z 6544	**S**		PS
Z 6545	26545	26546	Z 6546	**S**		PS
Z 6547	26547	26548	Z 6548	**S**		PS
Z 6549	26549	26550	Z 6550	**S**		PS

Names:

6447/6448	CHAVILLE
6449/6450	COURBEVOIE
6457/6458	LOUVECIENNES
6471/6472	SAINT-NOM-LA-BRETÈCHE
6475/6476	L'ÉTANG-LA-VILLE
6485/6486	GARCHES
6505/6506	VAUCRESSON
6519/6520	LA CELLE-SAINT CLOUD
6523/6524	MARLY-LE-ROI
6549/6550	LA GARENNE-COLOMBES

CLASS Z 7100   2/4-CAR UNITS

This class carried on the diesel tradition of single power cars hauling loose trailers. They have now all been refurbished and formed into fixed two or four car formations. The trailer cars gained the number appropriate to the power car of the set which they happened to be in at the time of refurbishing. This was not necessarily their original number in the same series! After an accident, Z 7115 was transformed as tilting prototype Z 7001 and then withdrawn in 1981. Z 7102 was reformed in 1996 and for some reason renumbered Z 7150. Units are now being withdrawn as Z 23500 are delivered to Lyon.

Built: 1960–62.   **System:** 1500 V d.c.
Builders-Mech. Parts: Decauville/De Dietrich.   **Builder-Elec. Parts:** Oerlikon.
Traction Motors: 2 x 470 kW.
Formation: ZABD (+ ZRAB + ZRB) + ZRBDx. Non-gangwayed.
Accommodation: 12/46 1T (+ 12/62 1T + –/78 1T) + –/65 1T.
Weight: 56 + 26 + 26 + 27 tonnes.   **Length:** 26.13 (+ 22.68 + 22.68) + 22.68 mm.
Wheel Arrangement: 2-Bo (+ 2-2 + 2-2) + 2-2.   **Max. Speed:** 130 km/h.

* Rheostatic braking.

Z 7101	27201	27101	17101	**M**		VE		Z 7120	27220	27120	17120	**M**	VE
Z 7103	27203	27103	17103	**M**		VE		Z 7121			17121	**M** *	AV
Z 7104	27204	27104	17104	**M**		VE		Z 7122			17122	**M** *	AV
Z 7105	27205	27105	17105	**M**		VE		Z 7123			17123	**M** *	AV
Z 7106	27206	27106	17106	**M**		VE		Z 7124			17124	**M** *	AV
Z 7107	27207	27107	17107	**M**		VE		Z 7126			17126	**M** *	AV
Z 7108	27208	27108	17108	**M**		VE		Z 7127			17127	**M** *	AV
Z 7109	27209	27109	17109	**M**		VE		Z 7128			17128	**M** *	AV
Z 7111	27211	27111	17111	**M**		VE		Z 7129			17129	**M** *	AV
Z 7112	27212	27112	17112	**M**		VE		Z 7130			17130	**M** *	AV
Z 7113	27213	27113	17113	**M**		VE		Z 7131			17131	**M** *	AV
Z 7116	27216	27116	17116	**M**		VE		Z 7132			17132	**M** *	AV
Z 7117	27217	27117	17117	**M**		VE		Z 7133			17133	**M** *	AV
Z 7118	27218	27118	17118	**M**		VE		Z 7150			17150	**M** *	AV
Z 7119	27219	27119	17119	**M**		VE		Z 7125				**M** *	AV

CLASS Z 7300   2-CAR UNITS (Z2)

The first of a new generation of EMUs not intended for Paris suburban work and known as Z2 type. (Z1 being Z 7100). They are used on short and medium distance stopping trains all over the south-west of France and around Avignon. All are fitted with facing seats. They were originally turned out in dark blue and red, most have now been repainted in one of four regional liveries. Z 7351/2 never existed. They were built as Z 97383/4. The Centre region is financing the refurbishment of 15 sets (7347–50/53–56/58–63/73) with air conditionong which will appear in livery **T**.

Built: 1980–85.
Builders: Alsthom/Francorail-MTE.
Traction Motors: Four 305 kW.
Formation: ZABD + ZRBx.
Weight: 64 + 40 tonnes.
Wheel Arrangement: Bo-Bo + 2-2.

System: 1500 V d.c.

Accommodation: 24/43 2T + –/84 1T.
Length: 25.10 + 25.10 m.
Max. Speed: 160 km/h.

Z 7301	17301	B	BD	Z 7326	17326	R	BD	Z 7353	17353	B	BD
Z 7302	17302	B	BD	Z 7327	17327	R	BD	Z 7354	17354	B	BD
Z 7303	17303	B	BD	Z 7328	17328	R	BD	Z 7355	17355	B	BD
Z 7304	17304	B	BD	Z 7329	17329	R	BD	Z 7356	17356	Z	BD
Z 7305	17305	B	BD	Z 7330	17330	R	BD	Z 7357	17357	T	MB
Z 7306	17306	B	BD	Z 7331	17331	R	BD	Z 7358	17358	Z	BD
Z 7307	17307	B	BD	Z 7332	17332	R	BD	Z 7359	17359	Z	BD
Z 7308	17308	B	BD	Z 7333	17333	R	BD	Z 7360	17360	Z	BD
Z 7309	17309	B	BD	Z 7334	17334	R	BD	Z 7361	17361	Z	BD
Z 7310	17310	B	BD	Z 7335	17335	R	BD	Z 7362	17362	Z	BD
Z 7311	17311	B	BD	Z 7336	17336	R	BD	Z 7363	17363	Z	BD
Z 7312	17312	B	BD	Z 7337	17337	R	BD	Z 7364	17364	Y	MB
Z 7313	17313	B	BD	Z 7338	17338	R	BD	Z 7365	17365	Y	MB
Z 7314	17314	B	BD	Z 7339	17339	R	BD	Z 7366	17366	Y	MB
Z 7315	17315	R	BD	Z 7340	17340	R	BD	Z 7367	17367	Y	MB
Z 7316	17316	R	BD	Z 7341	17341	R	BD	Z 7368	17368	Y	MB
Z 7317	17317	R	BD	Z 7342	17342	R	BD	Z 7369	17369	Y	MB
Z 7318	17318	R	BD	Z 7343	17343	R	BD	Z 7370	17370	Y	MB
Z 7319	17319	R	BD	Z 7344	17344	R	BD	Z 7371	17371	Y	MB
Z 7320	17320	R	BD	Z 7345	17345	R	BD	Z 7372	17372	Y	MB
Z 7321	17321	R	BD	Z 7346	17346	R	BD	Z 7373	17373	Z	BD
Z 7322	17322	R	BD	Z 7347	17347	R	BD	Z 97381	917381	B	BD
Z 7323	17323	R	BD	Z 7348	17348	B	BD	Z 97382	917382	B	BD
Z 7324	17324	R	BD	Z 7349	17349	B	BD	Z 97383	917383	Y	MB
Z 7325	17325	R	BD	Z 7350	17350	B	BD	Z 97384	917384	Y	MB

Names:

7314	SOULAC-SUR-MER		97381	MIDI-PYRENÉES
7321	LESPARRE-MEDOC		97382	MIDI-PYRENÉES
7339	PESSAC		97383	LANGUEDOC-ROUSSILLON
7346	MARMANDE		97384	LANGUEDOC-ROUSSILLON
7370	MONTEUX			

CLASS Z 7500   2-CAR UNITS (Z2)

This class is similar to Class Z 7300 but has more first class and unidirectional seating. Mainly used around Avignon, most are now in Provence-Alpes-Côte d'Azur blue/white livery.

Built: 1982–83.
Builders: Alsthom/Francorail-MTE.
Traction Motors: Four 305 kW.
Formation: ZABD + ZRBx.
Weight: 64 + 40 tonnes.
Wheel Arrangement: Bo-Bo + 2-2.

System: 1500 V d.c.

Accommodation: 32/35 1T + –/84 1T.
Length: 25.10 + 25.10 m.
Max. Speed: 160 km/h.

Z 7501	17501	B	VE	Z 7506	17506	Z	VE	Z 7512	17512	B	VE
Z 7502	17502	B	VE	Z 7507	17507	B	VE	Z 7513	17513	B	VE
Z 7503	17503	B	VE	Z 7508	17508	Z	VE	Z 7514	17514	B	VE
Z 7504	17504	B	VE	Z 7510	17510	B	VE	Z 7515	17515	B	VE
Z 7505	17505	B	VE	Z 7511	17511	B	VE				

Names:

7502	CHATEAUNEUF DU PAPE	7515	ORANGE
7513	BARBENTANE		

CLASS Z 8100   4-CAR UNITS (MI 79/MI 84)

This Paris area suburban stock is known as MI 79 (Matériel Interconnection 79) stock and broke away from tradition by not using stainless steel bodywork. The units are made from aluminium alloy extrusions and have adjustable steps as the platforms on RER line B are at different levels on the RER and SNCF parts of the line. They are dual-voltage units for working over RER line B which incorporates SNCF lines to Roissy and Mitry Claye. From Z 8341 sets are known as MI 84 and are owned by RATP for use on RER line A. Ownership can be seen just behind the cabs where RER SNCF or RER RATP (RATP is the Paris transport authority) is marked. Although theoretically allocated to PL, all maintenance of SNCF sets is done at RATP's Massy depot. The "first class" seating is identical to second class! Two units were damaged by terrorist bombs in 1995 and 1996.

Built: 1980–84.   **System:** 1500 V d.c/25 kV a.c.
Builders-Mech. Parts: Alsthom/Franco-Belge, ANF.
Builders-Elec. Parts: Alsthom/TCO.
Traction Motors: Four 350 kW per power car.
Formation: ZBD + ZRB + ZRAB + ZBD.   **Accommodation:** –/72 + –/84 + 32/52 + –/72.
Weight: 56 + 48 + 48 + 56 tonnes.   **Length:** 26.08 + 26.00 + 26.00 + 26.08 m.
Wheel Arrangement: Bo-Bo + 2-2 + 2-2 + Bo-Bo.
Max. Speed: 140 km/h.

Z 8101	28101	28102	Z 8102 I	MY	
Z 8103	28103	28104	Z 8104 I	PL	
Z 8105	28105	28106	Z 8106 I	MY	
Z 8107	28107	28108	Z 8108 I	MY	
Z 8109	28109	28110	Z 8110 I	MY	
Z 8111	28111	28112	Z 8112 I	MY	
Z 8113	28113	28114	Z 8114 I	MY	
Z 8115	28115	28116	Z 8116 I	MY	
Z 8117	28117	28118	Z 8118 I	MY	
Z 8119	28119	28120	Z 8120 I	MY	
Z 8121	28121	28122	Z 8122 I	PL	
Z 8123	28123	28124	Z 8124 I	MY	
Z 8125	28125	28126	Z 8126 I	PL	
Z 8127	28127	28128	Z 8128 I	PL	
Z 8129	28129	28130	Z 8130 I	MY	
Z 8131	28131	28132	Z 8132 I	PL	
Z 8133	28133	28134	Z 8134 I	PL	
Z 8135	28135	28136	Z 8136 I	PL	
Z 8137	28137	28138	Z 8138 I	MY	
Z 8139	28139	28140	Z 8140 I	PL	
Z 8141	28141	28142	Z 8142 I	PL	
Z 8143	28143	28144	Z 8144 I	PL	
Z 8145	28145	28146	Z 8146 I	MY	
Z 8147	28147	28148	Z 8148 I	PL	
Z 8149	28149	28150	Z 8150 I	PL	
Z 8151	28151	28152	Z 8152 I	PL	
Z 8153	28153	28154	Z 8154 I	MY	
Z 8155	28155	28156	Z 8156 I	PL	
Z 8157	28157	28158	Z 8158 I	PL	
Z 8159	28159	28160	Z 8160 I	PL	
Z 8161	28161	28162	Z 8162 I	MY	
Z 8163	28163	28164	Z 8164 I	PL	
Z 8165	28165	28166	Z 8166 I	PL	
Z 8169	28169	28170	Z 8170 I	MY	
Z 8171	28171	28172	Z 8172 I	PL	
Z 8173	28173	28174	Z 8174 I	PL	
Z 8175	28175	28176	Z 8176 I	PL	
Z 8177	28177	28178	Z 8178 I	MY	
Z 8179	28179	28180	Z 8180 I	PL	
Z 8181	28181	28182	Z 8182 I	PL	
Z 8183	28183	28184	Z 8184 I	PL	
Z 8185	28185	28186	Z 8186 I	PL	
Z 8187	28187	28188	Z 8188 I	MY	
Z 8189	28189	28190	Z 8190 I	PL	
Z 8191	28191	28192	Z 8192 I	PL	
Z 8193	28193	28194	Z 8194 I	MY	
Z 8195	28195	28196	Z 8196 I	MY	
Z 8197	28197	28198	Z 8198 I	PL	
Z 8199	28199	28200	Z 8200 I	PL	
Z 8201	28201	28202	Z 8202 I	MY	
Z 8203	28203	28204	Z 8204 I	MY	
Z 8205	28205	28206	Z 8206 I	PL	
Z 8207	28207	28208	Z 8208 I	PL	
Z 8209	28209	28210	Z 8210 I	MY	
Z 8211	28211	28212	Z 8212 I	MY	
Z 8213	28213	28214	Z 8214 I	PL	
Z 8215	28215	28216	Z 8216 I	PL	
Z 8217	28217	28218	Z 8218 I	MY	
Z 8219	28219	28220	Z 8220 I	MY	
Z 8221	28221	28222	Z 8222 I	PL	
Z 8223	28223	28224	Z 8224 I	PL	
Z 8225	28225	28226	Z 8226 I	MY	
Z 8227	28227	28228	Z 8228 I	MY	
Z 8229	28229	28230	Z 8230 I	PL	
Z 8231	28231	28232	Z 8232 I	PL	
Z 8233	28233	28234	Z 8234 I	MY	

Z 8167	28167	28168	Z 8168	I	PL	Z 8235	28235	28236	Z 8236	I	MY
Z 8237	28237	28238	Z 8238	I	PL	Z 8363	28363	28364	Z 8364	I	BY
Z 8239	28239	28240	Z 8240	I	PL	Z 8365	28365	28366	Z 8366	I	BY
Z 8241	28241	28242	Z 8242	I	MY	Z 8367	28367	28368	Z 8368	I	BY
Z 8243	28243	28244	Z 8244	I	PL	Z 8369	28369	28370	Z 8370	I	BY
Z 8245	28245	28246	Z 8246	I	PL	Z 8371	28371	28372	Z 8372	I	BY
Z 8247	28247	28248	Z 8248	I	PL	Z 8373	28373	28374	Z 8374	I	BY
Z 8249	28249	28250	Z 8250	I	PL	Z 8375	28375	28376	Z 8376	I	BY
Z 8251	28251	28252	Z 8252	I	PL	Z 8377	28377	28378	Z 8378	I	BY
Z 8253	28253	28254	Z 8254	I	PL	Z 8379	28379	28380	Z 8380	I	BY
Z 8255	28255	28256	Z 8256	I	PL	Z 8381	28381	28382	Z 8382	I	BY
Z 8257	28257	28258	Z 8258	I	PL	Z 8383	28383	28384	Z 8384	I	BY
Z 8259	28259	28260	Z 8260	I	PL	Z 8385	28385	28386	Z 8386	I	BY
Z 8261	28261	28262	Z 8262	I	PL	Z 8387	28387	28388	Z 8388	I	BY
Z 8263	28263	28264	Z 8264	I	PL	Z 8389	28389	28390	Z 8390	I	BY
Z 8265	28265	28266	Z 8266	I	MY	Z 8391	28391	28392	Z 8392	I	BY
Z 8267	28267	28268	Z 8268	I	MY	Z 8393	28393	28394	Z 8394	I	BY
Z 8269	28269	28270	Z 8270	I	MY	Z 8395	28395	28396	Z 8396	I	BY
Z 8271	28271	28272	Z 8272	I	MY	Z 8397	28397	28398	Z 8398	I	BY
Z 8273	28273	28274	Z 8274	I	MY	Z 8399	28399	28400	Z 8400	I	BY
Z 8275	28275	28276	Z 8276	I	MY	Z 8401	28401	28402	Z 8402	I	BY
Z 8277	28277	28278	Z 8278	I	MY	Z 8403	28403	28404	Z 8404	I	BY
Z 8279	28279	28280	Z 8280	I	MY	Z 8405	28405	28406	Z 8406	I	BY
Z 8281	28281	28282	Z 8282	I	MY	Z 8407	28407	28408	Z 8408	I	BY
Z 8283	28283	28284	Z 8284	I	MY	Z 8409	28409	28410	Z 8410	I	BY
Z 8285	28285	28286	Z 8286	I	MY	Z 8411	28411	28412	Z 8412	I	BY
Z 8287	28287	28288	Z 8288	I	MY	Z 8413	28413	28414	Z 8414	I	BY
Z 8289	28289	28290	Z 8290	I	MY	Z 8415	28415	28416	Z 8416	I	BY
Z 8291	28291	28292	Z 8292	I	MY	Z 8417	28417	28418	Z 8418	I	BY
Z 8293	28293	28294	Z 8294	I	MY	Z 8419	28419	28420	Z 8420	I	BY
Z 8295	28295	28296	Z 8296	I	MY	Z 8421	28421	28422	Z 8422	I	BY
Z 8297	28297	28298	Z 8298	I	MY	Z 8423	28423	28424	Z 8424	I	BY
Z 8299	28299	28300	Z 8300	I	MY	Z 8425	28425	28426	Z 8426	I	BY
Z 8301	28301	28302	Z 8302	I	MY	Z 8427	28427	28428	Z 8428	I	BY
Z 8303	28303	28304	Z 8304	I	MY	Z 8429	28429	28430	Z 8430	I	BY
Z 8305	28305	28306	Z 8306	I	MY	Z 8431	28431	28432	Z 8432	I	BY
Z 8307	28307	28308	Z 8308	I	MY	Z 8433	28433	28434	Z 8434	I	BY
Z 8309	28309	28310	Z 8310	I	MY	Z 8435	28435	28436	Z 8436	I	BY
Z 8311	28311	28312	Z 8312	I	MY	Z 8437	28437	28438	Z 8438	I	BY
Z 8313	28313	28314	Z 8314	I	MY	Z 8439	28439	28440	Z 8440	I	BY
Z 8315	28315	28316	Z 8316	I	MY	Z 8441	28441	28442	Z 8442	I	BY
Z 8317	28317	28318	Z 8318	I	MY	Z 8443	28443	28444	Z 8444	I	BY
Z 8319	28319	28320	Z 8320	I	MY	Z 8445	28445	28446	Z 8446	I	BY
Z 8321	28321	28322	Z 8322	I	MY	Z 8447	28447	28448	Z 8448	I	BY
Z 8323	28323	28324	Z 8324	I	MY	Z 8449	28449	28450	Z 8450	I	BY
Z 8325	28325	28326	Z 8326	I	MY	Z 8451	28451	28452	Z 8452	I	BY
Z 8327	28327	28328	Z 8328	I	MY	Z 8453	28453	28454	Z 8454	I	BY
Z 8329	28329	28330	Z 8330	I	MY	Z 8455	28455	28456	Z 8456	I	BY
Z 8331	28331	28332	Z 8332	I	MY	Z 8457	28457	28458	Z 8458	I	BY
Z 8333	28333	28334	Z 8334	I	MY	Z 8459	28459	28460	Z 8460	I	BY
Z 8335	28335	28336	Z 8336	I	MY	Z 8461	28461	28462	Z 8462	I	BY
Z 8337	28337	28338	Z 8338	I	MY	Z 8463	28463	28464	Z 8464	I	BY
Z 8339	28339	28340	Z 8340	I	MY	Z 8465	28465	28466	Z 8466	I	BY
Z 8341	28341	28342	Z 8342	I	BY	Z 8467	28467	28468	Z 8468	I	BY
Z 8343	28343	28344	Z 8344	I	BY	Z 8469	28469	28470	Z 8470	I	BY
Z 8345	28345	28346	Z 8346	I	BY	Z 8471	28471	28472	Z 8472	I	BY
Z 8347	28347	28348	Z 8348	I	BY	Z 8473	28473	28474	Z 8474	I	BY
Z 8349	28349	28350	Z 8350	I	BY	Z 8475	28475	28476	Z 8476	I	BY
Z 8351	28351	28352	Z 8352	I	BY	Z 8477	28477	28478	Z 8478	I	BY
Z 8353	28353	28354	Z 8354	I	BY	Z 8479	28479	28480	Z 8480	I	BY
Z 8355	28355	28356	Z 8356	I	BY	Z 8481	28481	28482	Z 8482	I	BY
Z 8357	28357	28358	Z 8358	I	BY	Z 8483	28483	28484	Z 8484	I	BY
Z 8359	28359	28360	Z 8360	I	BY	Z 8485	28485	28486	Z 8486	I	BY
Z 8361	28361	28362	Z 8362	I	BY						

Names:

8121/8122	EPINAY-SUR-SEINE	8341/8342	BOISSY ST. LEGER
8257/8258	RAISMES	8413/8414	POISSY
8261/8262	MITRY-MORY	8441/8442	INTERLAKEN
8263/8264	PERSAN		

CLASS Z 8800   4-CAR DOUBLE-DECK UNITS

These are a dual voltage version of Class Z 5600 and are used on RER line C, particularly on the branch to Argenteuil and Martigny-Beauchamp. The trailer cars are common with the Z 5600 Class.

Built: 1986–88.
System: 1500 V d.c/25 kV a.c.
Builders-Mech. Parts: ANF/CIMT.
Builders-Elec. Parts: Alsthom/TCO.
Traction Motors: Four Alsthom TCO 4 FHO (350 kW) per power car.
Formation: ZB + ZRB + ZRAB + ZB.
Accommodation: -/107 1T + -/168 1T + 70/82 1T + -/107 1T.
Weight: 69 t + 41 t + 42 t + 69 t.
Length: 25.10 m + 24.28 m + 24.28 m + 25.10 m.
Wheel Arrangement: Bo-Bo + 2-2 + 2-2 + Bo-Bo.
Max. Speed: 140 km/h.

01B	Z 8801	25686	35631	Z 8802	I	PA	30B	Z 8859	25709 35647	Z 8860	I PA
02B	Z 8803	25687	35662	Z 8804	I	PA	31B	Z 8861	25706 35656	Z 8862	I PA
03B	Z 8805	25688	35618	Z 8806	I	PA	32B	Z 8863	25708 35644	Z 8864	I PA
04B	Z 8807	25685	35658	Z 8808	I	PA	33B	Z 8865	25707 35640	Z 8866	I PA
05B	Z 8809	25611	35607	Z 8810	I	PA	34B	Z 8867	25618 35710	Z 8868	I PA
06B	Z 8811	25689	35659	Z 8812	I	PA	35B	Z 8869	25710 35642	Z 8870	I PA
07B	Z 8813	25690	35660	Z 8814	I	PA	36B	Z 8871	25626 35704	Z 8872	I PA
08B	Z 8815	25602	35650	Z 8816	I	PA	37B	Z 8873	25711 35604	Z 8874	I PA
09B	Z 8817	25691	35612	Z 8818	I	PA	38B	Z 8875	25725 35652	Z 8876	I PA
10B	Z 8819	25640	35664	Z 8820	I	PA	39B	Z 8877	25639 35701	Z 8878	I PA
11B	Z 8821	25676	35653	Z 8822	I	PA	40B	Z 8879	25664 35614	Z 8880	I PA
12B	Z 8823	25668	35611	Z 8824	I	PA	41B	Z 8881	25713 35646	Z 8882	I PA
13B	Z 8825	25643	35707	Z 8826	I	PA	42B	Z 8883	25724 35634	Z 8884	I PA
14B	Z 8827	25698	35630	Z 8828	I	PA	43B	Z 8885	25714 35637	Z 8886	I PA
15B	Z 8829	25712	35649	Z 8830	I	PA	44B	Z 8887	25716 35603	Z 8888	I PA
16B	Z 8831	25692	35639	Z 8832	I	PA	45B	Z 8889	25715 35609	Z 8890	I PA
17B	Z 8833	25700	35651	Z 8834	I	PA	46B	Z 8891	25630 35706	Z 8892	I PA
18B	Z 8835	25694	35645	Z 8836	I	PA	47B	Z 8893	25695 35633	Z 8894	I PA
19B	Z 8837	25693	35657	Z 8838	I	PA	48B	Z 8895	25718 35648	Z 8896	I PA
20B	Z 8839	25719	35606	Z 8840	I	PA	49B	Z 8897	25717 35635	Z 8898	I PA
21B	Z 8841	25703	35638	Z 8842	I	PA	50B	Z 8899	25642 35702	Z 8900	I PA
22B	Z 8843	25697	35663	Z 8844	I	PA	51B	Z 8901	25629 35703	Z 8902	I PA
23B	Z 8845	25699	35613	Z 8846	I	PA	52B	Z 8903	25720 35655	Z 8904	I PA
24B	Z 8847	25705	35610	Z 8848	I	PA	53B	Z 8905	25627 35705	Z 8906	I PA
25B	Z 8849	25696	35601	Z 8850	I	PA	54B	Z 8907	25722 35620	Z 8908	I PA
26B	Z 8851	25701	35636	Z 8852	I	PA	55B	Z 8909	25723 35643	Z 8910	I PA
27B	Z 8853	25721	35602	Z 8854	I	PA	56B	Z 8911	25638 35708	Z 8912	I PA
28B	Z 8855	25702	35641	Z 8856	I	PA	57B	Z 8913	25655 35709	Z 8914	I PA
29B	Z 8857	25704	35617	Z 8858	I	PA	58B	Z 8915	25726 35661	Z 8916	I PA

Names:

8801/8802	SAINT GRATIEN	8809/8810	ERMONT-EAUBONNE
8803/8804	FRANCONVILLE	8811/8812	GENNEVILLIERS
8805/8806	GROSLAY	8813/8814	LE PLESSIS BOUCHARD
8807/8808	SANNOIS		

CLASS Z 9500   2-CAR UNITS (Z2)

This is a dual-voltage version of Class Z 7500 and has unidirectional seating. Used mainly in the Jura, east of Dijon and in the Alps, east of Lyon.

Built: 1982–83.
System: 1500 V d.c/25 kV a.c.
Builders: Alsthom/Francorail-MTE.
Traction Motors: Four 305 kW.

Formation: ZABD + ZRBx.
Weight: 66 + 50 tonnes.
Wheel Arrangement: Bo-Bo + 2-2.

Accommodation: 32/35 1T + –/84 1T.
Length: 25.10 + 25.10 m.
Max. Speed: 160 km/h.

Z 9501	19501	Z	VE	Z 9508	19508	Z	VE	Z 9515	19515	Z	VE
Z 9502	19502	B	VE	Z 9509	19509	Z	VE	Z 9516	19516	R	VE
Z 9503	19503	Z	VE	Z 9510	19510	Z	VE	Z 9517	19517	Z	VE
Z 9504	19504	B	VE	Z 9511	19511	Z	VE	Z 9518	19518	Z	VE
Z 9505	19505	R	VE	Z 9512	19512	Z	VE	Z 99581	919581	B	VE
Z 9506	19506	R	VE	Z 9513	19513	Z	VE	Z 99582	919582	B	VE
Z 9507	19507	Z	VE	Z 9514	19514	R	VE				

Names:

9502	ARLES	99581	FRANCHE-COMTÉ
9513	AMBÉRIEU-EN-BUGEY	99582	FRANCHE-COMTÉ
9517	SAINT-PRIEST		

CLASS Z 9600   2-CAR UNITS (Z2)

This is the dual-voltage version of Class Z 7300 and is used to the west of Le Mans and in the Alps.

Built: 1984–87.
Builders: Alsthom/Francorail-MTE.
Traction Motors: Four 305 kW.
Formation: ZABD + ZRBx.
Weight: 66 + 50 tonnes.
Wheel Arrangement: Bo-Bo + 2-2.

Systems: 1500 V d.c/25 kV a.c.

Accommodation: 24/43 1T + –/84 1T.
Length: 25.10 + 25.10 m.
Max. Speed: 160 km/h.

Z 9601	19601	Z		RS	Z 9613	19613	B	*	RS	Z 9625	19625	B * RS
Z 9602	19602	Z		RS	Z 9614	19614	Z		VE	Z 9626	19626	B * RS
Z 9603	19603	Z		RS	Z 9615	19615	Z		VE	Z 9627	19627	B * RS
Z 9604	19604	G		RS	Z 9616	19616	Z		VE	Z 9628	19628	Z RS
Z 9605	19605	Z		RS	Z 9617	19617	Z		VE	Z 9629	19629	Z RS
Z 9606	19606	Z		RS	Z 9618	19618	Z		VE	Z 9630	19630	B * RS
Z 9607	19607	Z	*	RS	Z 9619	19619	Z		VE	Z 9631	19631	Z VE
Z 9608	19608	B	*	RS	Z 9620	19620	Z		VE	Z 9632	19632	Z VE
Z 9609	19609	B	*	RS	Z 9621	19621	B	*	RS	Z 9633	19633	Z VE
Z 9610	19610	B	*	RS	Z 9622	19622	B	*	RS	Z 9634	19634	Z VE
Z 9611	19611	B	*	RS	Z 9623	19623	B	*	RS	Z 9635	19635	Z VE
Z 9612	19612	B	*	RS	Z 9624	19624	B	*	RS	Z 9636	19636	Z VE

Names:

9617	FIRMINY	9633	RIVES
9620	RUMILLY		

9635 has three names: These are: CHÊNE BOURG, CHÊNE BOURGERIES and THÔNEX!
9607–13/21–7/29/30 are all named 'LES PAYS DE LA LOIRE'.

CLASS Z 11500   2-CAR UNITS (Z2)

An a.c. only version of Class Z 7300 for use around Metz. Luxembourg Railways (CFL) have 22 Class 2000 units developed from this design. In order to optimise efficiency, SNCF units work some local services within Luxembourg and Class 2000 operate in multiple with SNCF sets through to Nancy.

Built: 1986–67.
Builders: Alsthom/Francorail-MTE.
Traction Motors: Four 305 kW.
Formation: ZABD + ZRBx.
Weight: 66 + 50 tonnes.
Wheel Arrangement: Bo-Bo + 2-2.

System: 25 kV a.c.

Accommodation: 24/43 1T + –/84 1T.
Length: 25.10 + 25.10 m.
Max. Speed: 160 km/h.

Z 11501	111501	Y	TV	Z 11504	111504	Y	TV	Z 11508	111508	Y	TV
Z 11502	111502	Y	TV	Z 11505	111505	Y	TV	Z 11509	111509	Y	TV
Z 11503	111503	Y	TV	Z 11506	111506	Y	TV				

Z 11510	111510	**Y**	TV	Z 11515	111515	**Y**	TV	Z 11519	111519	**Y**	TV
Z 11511	111511	**Y**	TV	Z 11516	111516	**Y**	TV	Z 11520	111520	**Y**	TV
Z 11512	111512	**Y**	TV	Z 11517	111517	**Y**	TV	Z 11521	111521	**Y**	TV
Z 11513	111513	**Y**	TV	Z 11518	111518	**Y**	TV	Z 11522	111522	**Y**	TV
Z 11514	111514	**Y**	TV								

Names:

11501 SCHILTIGHEIM		11521 WOIPPY
11517 ANCY-SUR-MOSELLE		11521 LONGUYON

CLASS Z 20500   4/5-CAR DOUBLE-DECK UNITS

These units are a further development of Class Z 8800 with a modified appearance and longer trailers. They have asynchronous motors. Vitry (Les Ardoines) units are four-car and operate in multiple with Classes Z 5600 and Z 8800 on RER line C. Villeneuve units are five-car and operate on RER line D. Noisy sets are four-car and work Paris Est–Meaux services. Les Joncherolles sets are divided between five-car sets which work RER line D and a few four-car sets which work St Lazare–Nanterre Université and Paris Nord services. An additional order will go to RER line C replacing Class Z 5300 completely. The new sets will be air-conditioned and will have security equipment for evening trains.

Built: 1988–97.
Builders-Mech. Parts: CIMT/ANF.
Systems: 1500 V d.c./25 kV a.c.
Builder-Elec. Parts: GEC Alsthom.
Traction Motors: Four Alsthom FHA 2870 asynchronous (350 kW) per power car.
Formation: ZB + ZRB + ZRAB (+ ZRB) + ZB.
Weight: 70 + 44 + 44 (+ 44) + 70 tonnes.
Length: 25.10 + 26.40 + 26.40 (+ 26.40) + 25.10 m.
Accommodation: –/110 + –/204 1T + 80/108 1T (+ –/204 1T) + –/110.
Wheel Arrangement: Bo-Bo + 2-2 + 2-2 (+ 2-2) + Bo-Bo.
Max. Speed: 140 km/h.

* Power cars have GEC Alsthom's new ONIX traction package incorporating IGBT technology.
† Trailer ZR 201579 has a stainless steel body.

01A	Z 20501	201501	202501		Z 20502	I	PA
02A	Z 20503	201503	202503		Z 20504	I	PA
03A	Z 20505	201505	202505		Z 20506	I	PA
04A	Z 20507	201507	202507		Z 20508	I	PJ
05P	Z 20509	201509	202509	203549	Z 20510	I	PJ
06A	Z 20511	25816	35811		Z 20512	I	PA
07A	Z 20513	201513	202513		Z 20514	I	PA
08P	Z 20515	201515	202515	203515	Z 20516	I	PJ
09P	Z 20517	201517	202517	203507	Z 20518	I	PJ
10P	Z 20519	201519	202519	203531	Z 20520	I	PJ
11A	Z 20521	201521	202521		Z 20522	I	PJ
12A	Z 20523	201523	202523		Z 20524	I	PJ
13A	Z 20525	201525	202525		Z 20526	I	PA
14A	Z 20527	201527	202527		Z 20528	I	PA
15A	Z 20529	201529	202529		Z 20530	I	PA
16A	Z 20531	201531	202531		Z 20532	I	PA
17A	Z 20533	201533	202533		Z 20534	I	PA
18P	Z 20535	201535	202535	203525	Z 20536	I	PJ
19P	Z 20537	201537	202537	203517	Z 20538	I	PJ
20J	Z 20539	201539	202539	203539	Z 20540	I	PJ
21A	Z 20541	201541	202541		Z 20542	I	PJ
22J	Z 20543	201543	202543	203551	Z 20544	I	PJ
23J	Z 20545	201545	202545	203545	Z 20546	I	PJ
24A	Z 20547	201547	202547		Z 20548	I	PA
25A	Z 20549	201549	202549		Z 20550	I	PA
26A	Z 20551	201551	202551		Z 20552	I	PJ
27A	Z 20553	201553	202553		Z 20554	I	PJ
28A	Z 20555	201555	202555		Z 20556	I	PJ
29A	Z 20557	201557	202557		Z 20558	I	PA
30A	Z 20559	201559	202559		Z 20560	I	PJ

31J	Z 20561	201561	202561	203511	Z 20562	I		PJ
32J	Z 20563	201563	202563	203541	Z 20564	I		PJ
33A	Z 20565	201565	202565		Z 20566	I		PA
34A	Z 20567	201567	202567		Z 20568	I		PA
35A	Z 20569	201569	202569		Z 20570	I		PJ
36A	Z 20571	201571	202571		Z 20572	I		PA
37A	Z 20573	201573	202573		Z 20574	I		PA
38A	Z 20575	201575	202575		Z 20576	I		PA
39J	Z 20577	201577	202577	203553	Z 20578	I		PJ
40A	Z 20579	25802	35803		Z 20580	I		PA
41A	Z 20581	201581	202581		Z 20582	I		PA
42A	Z 20583	201583	202583		Z 20584	I		PA
43A	Z 20585	25821	35808		Z 20586	I		PA
44A	Z 20587	25820	35812		Z 20588	I		PA
45A	Z 20589	201579	202579		Z 20590	I	†	PA
46A	Z 20591	25817	35806		Z 20592	I		PA
47A	Z 20593	25819	35810		Z 20594	I		PA
48A	Z 20595	25806	35802		Z 20596	I		PA
49A	Z 20597	25815	35815		Z 20598	I		PA
50A	Z 20599	25803	35814		Z 20600	I		PA
51A	Z 20601	25812	35805		Z 20602	I		PA
52A	Z 20603	201511	202511		Z 20604	I		PA
53A	Z 20605	25801	35804		Z 20606	I		PA
54A	Z 20607	25810	35801		Z 20608	I		PA
55A	Z 20609	25805	35816		Z 20610	I		PA
56A	Z 20611	25813	35813		Z 20612	I		PA
57A	Z 20613	25811	35807		Z 20614	I		PA
58A	Z 20615	25804	35820		Z 20616	I		PA
59A	Z 20617	25818	35817		Z 20618	I		PA
60A	Z 20619	25808	35818		Z 20620	I		PA
61A	Z 20621	25807	35809		Z 20622	I		PA
62A	Z 20623	25809	35821		Z 20624	I		PA
63A	Z 20625	25814	35819		Z 20626	I		PA
64V	Z 20627	201627	202627	203627	Z 20628	I		VG
65V	Z 20629	201629	202629	203629	Z 20630	I		VG
66V	Z 20631	201631	202631	203631	Z 20632	I		VG
67V	Z 20633	201633	202633	203633	Z 20634	I		VG
68V	Z 20635	201635	202635	203635	Z 20636	I		VG
69V	Z 20637	201637	202637	203637	Z 20638	I		VG
70V	Z 20639	201639	202639	203639	Z 20640	I		VG
71V	Z 20641	201641	202641	203641	Z 20642	I		VG
72V	Z 20643	201643	202643	203643	Z 20644	I		VG
73V	Z 20645	201645	202645	203645	Z 20646	I		VG
74V	Z 20647	201647	202647	203647	Z 20648	I		VG
75V	Z 20649	201649	202649	203649	Z 20650	I		VG
76V	Z 20651	201651	202651	203651	Z 20652	I		VG
77V	Z 20653	201653	202653	203653	Z 20654	I		VG
78V	Z 20655	201655	202655	203655	Z 20656	I		VG
79V	Z 20657	201657	202657	203657	Z 20658	I		VG
80V	Z 20659	201659	202659	203659	Z 20660	I		VG
81V	Z 20661	201661	202661	203661	Z 20662	I		VG
82V	Z 20663	201663	202663	203663	Z 20664	I		VG
83V	Z 20665	201665	202665	203665	Z 20666	I		VG
84V	Z 20667	201667	202667	203667	Z 20668	I		VG
85V	Z 20669	201669	202669	203669	Z 20670	I		VG
86V	Z 20671	201671	202671	203671	Z 20672	I		VG
87V	Z 20673	201673	202673	203673	Z 20674	I		VG
88V	Z 20675	201675	202675	203675	Z 20676	I		VG
89V	Z 20677	201677	202677	203677	Z 20678	I		VG
90V	Z 20679	201679	202679	203679	Z 20680	I		VG
91V	Z 20681	201681	202681	203681	Z 20682	I		VG
92V	Z 20683	201683	202683	203683	Z 20684	I		VG
93V	Z 20685	201685	202685	203685	Z 20686	I		VG
94V	Z 20687	201687	202687	203687	Z 20688	I		VG

99V	Z 20697	203565	202697	203697	Z 20698	I	VG
100V	Z 20699	201699	202699	203699	Z 20700	I	VG
101V	Z 20701	201701	202701	203701	Z 20702	I	VG
102V	Z 20703	201703	202703	203703	Z 20704	I	VG
103V	Z 20705	201705	202705	203705	Z 20706	I	VG
104V	Z 20707	201707	202707	203707	Z 20708	I	VG
105V	Z 20709	201709	202709	203709	Z 20710	I	VG
106V	Z 20711	201711	202711	203711	Z 20712	I	VG
107V	Z 20713	201713	202713	203713	Z 20714	I	VG
108V	Z 20715	201715	202715	203715	Z 20716	I	VG
109V	Z 20717	201717	202717	203717	Z 20718	I	VG
110J	Z 20719	201719	202719	203719	Z 20720	I	PJ
111J	Z 20721	201721	202721	203721	Z 20722	I	PJ
112J	Z 20723	201723	202723	203723	Z 20724	I	PJ
113J	Z 20725	201725	202725	203725	Z 20726	I	PJ
114J	Z 20727	201727	202727	203727	Z 20728	I	PJ
115J	Z 20729	201729	202729	203729	Z 20730	I	PJ
116J	Z 20731	201731	202731	203731	Z 20732	I	PJ
117J	Z 20733	201733	202733	203733	Z 20734	I	PJ
118J	Z 20735	201735	202735	203735	Z 20736	I	PJ
119J	Z 20737	201737	202737	203737	Z 20738	I	PJ
120J	Z 20739	201739	202739	203739	Z 20740	I	PJ
121J	Z 20741	201741	202741	203741	Z 20742	I	PJ
122J	Z 20743	201743	202743	203743	Z 20744	I	PJ
123J	Z 20745	201745	202745	203745	Z 20746	I	PJ
124J	Z 20747	201747	202747	203747	Z 20748	I	PJ
125J	Z 20749	201749	202749	203749	Z 20750	I	PJ
126J	Z 20751	201751	202751	203557	Z 20752	I	PJ
127J	Z 20753	201753	202753	203519	Z 20754	I	PJ
128V	Z 20755	201755	202755	203501	Z 20756	I	VG
129J	Z 20757	201757	202757	203543	Z 20758	I	PJ
130J	Z 20759	201759	202759	203547	Z 20760	I	PJ
131J	Z 20761	201761	202761	203527	Z 20762	I	PJ
132J	Z 20763	201763	202763	203559	Z 20764	I	PJ
133J	Z 20765	201765	202765	203505	Z 20766	I	PJ
134J	Z 20767	201767	202767	203529	Z 20768	I	PJ
135J	Z 20769	201769	202769	203523	Z 20770	I	PJ
136J	Z 20771	201771	202771	203503	Z 20772	I	PJ
137J	Z 20773	201773	202773	203521	Z 20774	I	PJ
138J	Z 20775	201775	202775	203555	Z 20776	I	PJ
139A	Z 20777	201777	202777		Z 20778	I	PN
140A	Z 20779	201779	202779		Z 20780	I	PN
141A	Z 20781	201781	202781		Z 20782	I	PN
142A	Z 20783	201783	202783		Z 20784	I	PN
143A	Z 20785	201785	202785		Z 20786	I	PN
144A	Z 20787	201787	202787		Z 20788	I	PN
145J	Z 20789	201789	202789	203535	Z 20790	I	PJ
146J	Z 20791	201791	202791	203537	Z 20792	I	PJ
147J	Z 20793	201793	202793	203509	Z 20794	I	PJ
148J	Z 20795	201795	202795	203513	Z 20796	I	PJ
149J	Z 20797	201797	202797	203533	Z 20798	I	PJ
150J	Z 20799	201799	202799	203561	Z 20800	I	PJ
151J	Z 20801	201801	202801	203563	Z 20802	I	PJ
152A	Z 20803	201803	202803		Z 20804	I	PA
153A	Z 20805	201805	202805		Z 20806	I	PA
154A	Z 20807	201807	202807		Z 20808	I	PA
155A	Z 20809	201809	202809		Z 20810	I	PA
156A	Z 20811	201811	202811		Z 20812	I	PA
157A	Z 20813	201813	202813		Z 20814	I	PA
158A	Z 20815	201815	202815		Z 20816	I	PA
159A	Z 20817	201817	202817		Z 20818	I	PA
160A	Z 20819	201819	202819		Z 20820	I	PA
161A	Z 20821	201821	202821		Z 20822	I	PA
162A	Z 20823	201823	202823		Z 20824	I	PA

98

163A	Z 20825	201825	202825		Z 20826	I		PA
164A	Z 20827	201827	202827		Z 20828	I		PA
165A	Z 20829	201829	202829		Z 20830	I		PA
166A	Z 20831	201831	202831		Z 20832	I		PA
167A	Z 20833	201833	202833		Z 20834	I		PA
168A	Z 20835	201835	202835		Z 20836	I		PN
169A	Z 20837	201837	202837		Z 20838	I		PA
170A	Z 20839	201839	202839		Z 20840	I		PN
171A	Z 20841	201841	202841		Z 20842	I		PN
172A	Z 20843	201843	202843		Z 20844	I		PN
173A	Z 20845	201845	202845		Z 20846	I		PN
174V	Z 20847	201847	202847	203565	Z 20848	I		VG
175A	Z 20849	201849	202849		Z 20850	I		PA
176A	Z 20851	201851	202851		Z 20852	I		PA
177A	Z 20853	201853	202853		Z 20854	I		PA
178A	Z 20855	201855	202855		Z 20856	I		PA
179A	Z 20857	201857	202857		Z 20858	I		PN
180A	Z 20859	201859	202859		Z 20860	I		PA
181A	Z 20861	201861	202861		Z 20862	I		PA
182A	Z 20863	201863	202863		Z 20864	I		PA
183A	Z 20865	201865	202865		Z 20866	I		PA
184A	Z 20867	201867	202867		Z 20868	I		PA
185A	Z 20869	201869	202869		Z 20870	I		PA
186A	Z 20871	201871	202871		Z 20872	I		PA
187A	Z 20873	201873	202873		Z 20874	I		PA
188J	Z 20875	201875	202875	203875	Z 20876	I		PJ
189J	Z 20877	201877	202877	203877	Z 20878	I		PJ
190J	Z 20879	201879	202879	203879	Z 20880	I		PJ
191J	Z 20881	201881	202881	203881	Z 20882	I		PJ
192J	Z 20883	201883	202883	203883	Z 20884	I		PJ
193J	Z 20885	201885	202885	203885	Z 20886	I		PJ
194A	Z 20887	201887	202887		Z 20888	I	*	PA
	Z 20889	201889	202889		Z 20890	I	*	
	Z 20891	201891	202891		Z 20892	I	*	
	Z 20893	201893	202893		Z 20894	I	*	
	Z 20895	201895	202895		Z 20896	I	*	
	Z 20897	201897	202897		Z 20898	I	*	
	Z 20899	201899	202899		Z 20900	I	*	
	Z 20901	201901	202901		Z 20902	I	*	
	Z 20903	201903	202903		Z 20904	I	*	
	Z 20905	201905	202905		Z 20906	I	*	
	Z 20907	201907	202907		Z 20908	I	*	
	Z 20909	201909	202909		Z 20910	I	*	
	Z 20911	201911	202911		Z 20912	I	*	
	Z 20913	201913	202913		Z 20914	I	*	
	Z 20915	201915	202915		Z 20916	I	*	
	Z 20917	201917	202917		Z 20918	I	*	
	Z 20919	201919	202919		Z 20920	I	*	
	Z 20921	201921	202921		Z 20922	I	*	
	Z 20923	201923	202923		Z 20924	I	*	
	Z 20925	201925	202925		Z 20926	I	*	
	Z 20927	201927	202927		Z 20928	I	*	
	Z 20929	201929	202929		Z 20930	I	*	
	Z 20931	201931	202931		Z 20932	I	*	
	Z 20933	201933	202933		Z 20934	I	*	
	Z 20935	201935	202935		Z 20936	I	*	
	Z 20937	201937	202937		Z 20938	I	*	
	Z 20939	201939	202939		Z 20940	I	*	
	Z 20941	201941	202941		Z 20942	I	*	
	Z 20943	201943	202943		Z 20944	I	*	
	Z 20945	201945	202945		Z 20946	I	*	
	Z 20947	201947	202947		Z 20948	I	*	
	Z 20949	201949	202949		Z 20950	I	*	
	Z 20951	201951	202951		Z 20952	I	*	

Names:

20513/4   VILLIERS-LE-BEL | 20531/2   BEAUCHAMP

CLASS Z 22500   5-CAR DOUBLE-DECK UNITS

These double-deck units, though derived technically from Class Z 20500, are quite different, having been designed specifically for Paris RER services after experiments with a car inserted into an RATP set on RER line A. After this, it was decided to build the new class with three wide doors per side in order to allow fast boarding and alighting. In order to do this, electrical equipment has been spread throughout the train and the power bogies put under the second and fourth cars. It was impossible to design access to the upper decks from all three entrances so access is from the outer doors and the upper decks are closed at one end. The total effect has been to reduce seating capacity considerably although there is ample standing room. RATP has also ordered the design which it calls MI2N (Matériel Interconnection à deux Niveaux) for RER line A although these units have more axles powered. The SNCF units are all be allocated to a new depot at Noisy-le-Sec and will operate services on RER line E which will link Paris Est suburban services via a tunnel to St Lazare. This will later be extended to the western suburbs of Paris. For this, units will be shortened to four cars. 53 units are being delivered with an option for 50 more.

Built: 1996–
Builders-Mech. Parts: CIMT/ANF.
Traction Motors: Four Alsthom FHA 2870 asynchronous (375 kW) per power car.
Formation: ZRBx + ZB + ZRB + ZAB + ZRBx.
Accommodation: –/108 + –/110 + –/108 1T + 49/56 + –/108.
Weight: 277 tonnes total.   **Length:** 22.85 + 22.10 + 22.10 + 22.10 + 22.85 m.
Systems: 1500 V d.c./25 kV a.c.
Builder-Elec. Parts: GEC Alsthom.
Max. Speed: 140 km/h.
Wheel Arrangement: 2-2 + Bo-Bo + 2-2 + Bo-Bo + 2-2.
Class Specific Livery: S White with blue and red strips.

01E	221501	Z 22501	222501	Z 22502	221502	S	PN
02E	221503	Z 22503	222503	Z 22504	221504	S	PN
03E	221505	Z 22505	222505	Z 22506	221506	S	PN
04E	221507	Z 22507	222507	Z 22508	221508	S	PN
05E	221509	Z 22509	222509	Z 22510	221510	S	PN
06E	221511	Z 22511	222511	Z 22512	221512	S	PN
07E	221513	Z 22513	222513	Z 22514	221514	S	PN
08E	221515	Z 22515	222515	Z 22516	221516	S	PN
09E	221517	Z 22517	222517	Z 22518	221518	S	PN
10E	221519	Z 22519	222519	Z 22520	221520	S	PN
11E	221521	Z 22521	222521	Z 22522	221522	S	PS
12E	221523	Z 22523	222523	Z 22524	221524	S	PS
13E	221525	Z 22525	222525	Z 22526	221526	S	PS
14E	221527	Z 22527	222527	Z 22528	221528	S	PS
15E	221529	Z 22529	222529	Z 22530	221530	S	PS
16E	221531	Z 22531	222531	Z 22532	221532	S	PS
17E	221533	Z 22533	222533	Z 22534	221534	S	PS
18E	221535	Z 22535	222535	Z 22536	221536	S	PS
19E	221537	Z 22537	222537	Z 22538	221538	S	PS
20E	221539	Z 22539	222539	Z 22540	221540	S	PS
21E	221541	Z 22541	222541	Z 22542	221542	S	PS
22E	221543	Z 22543	222543	Z 22544	221544	S	PS
23E	221545	Z 22545	222545	Z 22546	221546	S	PN
24E	221547	Z 22547	222547	Z 22548	221548	S	PN
25E	221549	Z 22549	222549	Z 22550	221550	S	PN
26E	221551	Z 22551	222551	Z 22552	221552	S	PN
27E	221553	Z 22553	222553	Z 22554	221554	S	PN
28E	221555	Z 22555	222555	Z 22556	221556	S	PN
29E	221557	Z 22557	222557	Z 22558	221558	S	PN
30E	221559	Z 22559	222559	Z 22560	221560	S	PN
31E	221561	Z 22561	222561	Z 22562	221562	S	PN
32E	221563	Z 22563	222563	Z 22564	221564	S	PN
33E	221565	Z 22565	222565	Z 22566	221566	S	PN
34E	221567	Z 22567	222567	Z 22568	221568	S	PN
35E	221569	Z 22569	222569	Z 22570	221570	S	PN
36E	221571	Z 22571	222571	Z 22572	221572	S	PN

37E	221573	Z 22573	222573	Z 22574	221574	S	PN
38E	221575	Z 22575	222575	Z 22576	221576	S	PN
39E	221577	Z 22577	222577	Z 22578	221578	S	PN
40E	221579	Z 22579	222579	Z 22580	221580	S	PN
41E	221581	Z 22581	222581	Z 22582	221582	S	
42E	221583	Z 22583	222583	Z 22584	221584	S	
43E	221585	Z 22585	222585	Z 22586	221586	S	
44E	221587	Z 22587	222587	Z 22588	221588	S	
45E	221589	Z 22589	222589	Z 22590	221590	S	
46E	221591	Z 22591	222591	Z 22592	221592	S	
47E	221593	Z 22593	222593	Z 22594	221594	S	
48E	221595	Z 22595	222595	Z 22596	221596	S	
49E	221597	Z 22597	222597	Z 22598	221598	S	
50E	221599	Z 22599	222599	Z 22600	221600	S	
51E	221601	Z 22601	222601	Z 22602	221602	S	
52E	221603	Z 22603	222603	Z 22604	221604	S	
53E	221605	Z 22605	222605	Z 22606	221606	S	

CLASS Z 23500　　　2-CAR DOUBLE-DECK UNITS

These are two-car double-deck EMUs designed specifically for "regional" stopping services in conjunction with eight French regional councils as well as Luxembourg Railways (CFL). The new units represent a leap in quality for the passenger as they have air-conditioning, individual moquette-covered seats arranged 2 + 2, including in second class plus facilities for the handicapped. The units have been ordered by the Provence-Alpes-Côte d'Azur (34), Nord-Pas-de-Calais (30) and Rhône-Alpes (16) regions and were introduced at the beginning of 1998 on services such as Marseille–Toulon and Toulon–Vintimiglia plus from Lille to Maubeuge. As the cost is now low, all units are dual-voltage to allow flexibility in long-term use.

Built: 1997–　　　　　　　　　　　**Systems:** 1500 V d.c. / 25 kV a.c. 50 Hz.
Builder-Mech. Parts: CIMT/ANF.　　**Builder-Elec. Parts:** GEC-Alsthom.
Traction Motors: Four Alsthom FHA 2870 asynchronous (375 kW).
Formation: ZB + ZRABx　　　　　　**Accommodation:** –/75 + 19/96 1T.
Weight: 128.5 tonnes.　　　　　　　**Length:** 25.60 + 26.90 m.
Wheel Arrangement: Bo-Bo + 2-2.　**Max. Speed:** 140 km/h.

Z 23501	123501	T	MB	Z 23517	123517	T	LI	Z 23534	123534	T	LI
Z 23501	123501	T	MB	Z 23528	123528	T	MB	Z 23555	123555	T	
Z 23502	123502	T	LI	Z 23529	123529	T	MB	Z 23556	123556	T	
Z 23503	123503	T	VE	Z 23530	123530	T	LI	Z 23557	123557	T	
Z 23504	123504	T	MB	Z 23531	123531	T	VE	Z 23558	123558	T	
Z 23505	123505	T	MB	Z 23532	123532	T	MB	Z 23559	123559	T	
Z 23506	123506	T	LI	Z 23534	123534	T	LI	Z 23560	123560	T	
Z 23507	123507	T	MB	Z 23535	123535	T	VE	Z 23561	123561	T	
Z 23508	123508	T	MB	Z 23536	123536	T	MB	Z 23562	123562	T	
Z 23509	123509	T	MB	Z 23537	123537	T	MB	Z 23563	123563	T	
Z 23510	123510	T	MB	Z 23538	123538	T	MB	Z 23564	123564	T	
Z 23511	123511	T	MB	Z 23539	123539	T	VE	Z 23565	123565	T	
Z 23512	123512	T	VE	Z 23540	123540	T	MB	Z 23566	123566	T	
Z 23513	123513	T	MB	Z 23541	123541	T	MB	Z 23567	123567	T	
Z 23514	123514	T	LI	Z 23542	123542	T	LI	Z 23568	123568	T	
Z 23515	123515	T	VE	Z 23543	123543	T	LI	Z 23569	123569	T	
Z 23516	123516	T	VE	Z 23544	123544	T	MB	Z 23570	123570	T	
Z 23517	123517	T	LI	Z 23545	123545	T	MB	Z 23571	123571	T	
Z 23518	123518	T	LI	Z 23546	123546	T	LI	Z 23572	123572	T	
Z 23519	123519	T	MB	Z 23547	123547	T	MB	Z 23573	123573	T	
Z 23520	123520	T	MB	Z 23548	123548	T	VE	Z 23574	123574	T	
Z 23521	123521	T	MB	Z 23549	123549	T	MB	Z 23575	123575	T	
Z 23522	123522	T	LI	Z 23550	123550	T	MB	Z 23576	123576	T	
Z 23523	123523	T	VE	Z 23551	123551	T		Z 23577	123577	T	
Z 23524	123524	T	MB	Z 23552	123552	T		Z 23578	123578	T	
Z 23525	123525	T	MB	Z 23553	123553	T		Z 23579	123579	T	
Z 23526	123526	T	LI	Z 23554	123554	T	LI	Z 23580	123580	T	
Z 23527	123527	T	VE								

Name: 23526 AULNOYE AYMERIES UNE VILLE POUR TOUS

CLASS Z 92050   4-CAR DOUBLE-DECK UNITS

These are a special version of Class Z 20500 with lower density seating, with headrests, for services in the Nord-Pas-de-Calais around Lille, whose livery they are finished in. They are likely to be used mainly on the Lille–Jeumont route. They are the first powered rolling stock to be allocated to Lille depot which can be found south of Lille Flandres station, west of Champ de Mars yard.

Details as Class Z 20500 except:

Built: 1996.
Formation: ZB + ZRAB + ZRB + ZB.
Accommodation: –/82 1T + 38/126 1T + –/164 1T + –/82 1T.
Weight: 69 + 43 + 43 + 69 tonnes.
Class specific Livery: S White with dark blue band plus yellow doors and front end.

Z401	Z 92051	920151	920251	Z 92052	S	LI
Z402	Z 92053	920153	920253	Z 92054	S	LI
Z403	Z 92055	920155	920255	Z 92056	S	LI
Z404	Z 92057	920157	920257	Z 92058	S	LI
Z405	Z 92059	920159	920259	Z 92060	S	LI
Z406	Z 92061	920161	920261	Z 92062	S	LI

1.7. TRAINS À GRAND VITESSE (Tgvs)

The TGV is a modern day success story for SNCF. It is the fastest service train in the world.

TGV SUD-EST   8-CAR TWO-VOLTAGE SETS

Each TGV Sud-est set is a 10-car EMU with 1½ power cars at each end. It is not always appreciated that each TGV Sud-Est set has 6 motor bogies. There are two under each outer power car and the bogie next to the power car on the adjoining vehicles is also powered. The power cars are numbered as dual-voltage locomotives but with the prefix TGV. Each set also has a number set 01 has power cars 23001/2 etc.

Since their introduction, various modifications have been made. All sets have received new trailer bogies with better suspension. 64 sets have received TVM 430 signalling in order to operate over the Rhône-Alpes high-speed line to Avignon, Marseille and Nice or Montpellier and Perpignan. Other sets are now restricted to services north of St. Etienne, Lyon and Grenoble. Sets 33–37/100–2 which were first class only have been rebuilt in the normal configuration.

Normally the sets keep in formation but changes can take place following accidents, etc. Set 38 was converted into a postal set in 1995. Set 70 was partially destroyed in an accident and power car 23140 and four trailers are now spare. Set 88 was the TGV Atlantique prototype then became three-voltage set 118. Set 99 never existed. Set 101 became tilt prototype P01. Sets can occasionally be seen with a TGV Postal power car in extreme circumstances. Since their introduction, units have been fitted with new bogies with air suspension.

All set are now being refurbished with improved seating (as fitted to TGV-R) and fitted with TVM300 cab signalling to allow 300 km/h instead of the TVM 270 as built. They are being repainted in the standard grey-blue TGV livery. Sets without TVM 430 are restricted to services north of the Rhône-Alps LGV, i.e. to Dijon, Lyon, Genève, The Alps and Grenoble.

Electro-pneumatic brakes. Rheostatic brakes. Multiple working. Disc brakes on trailers in addition to blocks.

TGV + TGVZRADr + TGVRAr + TGVRA + TGVRBr + 3TGVRB + TGVZRB + TGV.
Systems: 1500 V d.c. + 25 kV a.c.
Built: 1978–86.
Builders: Alsthom/Francorail-MTE/De Dietrich.
Axle Arrangement: Bo-Bo + Bo-2-2-2-2-2-2-2-Bo + Bo-Bo.
Traction Motors: 12 x TAB676 per set of 525 kW each.
Weight: 65 + 43 + (6 x 28) + 44 + 65 tonnes.
Max. Speed: 280 km/h.
Livery: Orange with grey and white bands.
Accommodation:
0 + 35/– 1T + 38/– 1T + 38/– 1T + –/35 1T + –/60 2T + –/60 1T + –/60 2T+ –/60 1T + 0 .
(r 0 + 34/– 1T + 38/– 1T + 38/– 1T + –/16 1T + –/56 2T + –/54 1T + –/56 2T + –/56 1T + 0).
Length: 22.15 + 21.845 + (6 x 18.70) + 21.845 + 22.15 m.
Cab Signalling: TVM 270 (r TVM 300, [4] TVM 430).
Non-standard livery: N Metallic grey and dark blue with a red window band.

[4] TVM 430 cab signalling.
* Converted to prototype tilting TGV.

Non-driving motors and trailer cars are numbered in the sequence as follows:

Set *nnn:* 123*nnn*/223*nnn*/323*nnn*/423*nnn*/523*nnn*/623*nnn*/723*nnn*/823*nnn*.

01	TGV 23001	TGV 23002	Q	[4]	PE	CANNES
02	TGV 23003	TGV 23004	Q	[4]	PE	MARSEILLE
03	TGV 23005	TGV 23006	Q	[4]	PE	BELFORT
04	TGV 23007	TGV 23008	Q	[4]	PE	RAMBOUILLET
05	TGV 23009	TGV 23010	Q	[4]	PE	RIS-ORANGIS
06	TGV 23011	TGV 23012	Q	[4]	PE	FRASNE
07	TGV 23013	TGV 23014	Q	[4]	PE	CONFLANS-SAINTE-HONORINE
08	TGV 23015	TGV 23016	Q	[4]	PE	ROUEN
09	TGV 23017	TGV 23018	Q	[4]	PE	VINCENNES
10	TGV 23019	TGV 23020	Q		PE	HAYANGE
11	TGV 23021	TGV 23022	Q	[4]	PE	NÎMES
12	TGV 23023	TGV 23024	A	r[4]	PE	LE HAVRE

13	TGV 23025	TGV 23026	Q	^{4}	PE	ABLON-SUR-SEINE
14	TGV 23027	TGV 23028	A	r^4	PE	MONTPELLIER
15	TGV 23029	TGV 23030	Q	^{4}	PE	PAU
16	TGV 23031	TGV 23032	Q	^{4}	PE	LYON
17	TGV 23033	TGV 23034	Q	^{4}	PE	TERGNIER
18	TGV 23035	TGV 23036	Q	^{4}	PE	LE CREUSOT
19	TGV 23037	TGV 23038	Q	^{4}	PE	SAINT AMAND-LES-EAUX
20	TGV 23039	TGV 23040	Q	^{4}	PE	COLMAR
21	TGV 23041	TGV 23042	A	r	PE	DIJON
22	TGV 23043	TGV 23044	Q		PE	VALENCIENNES
23	TGV 23045	TGV 23046	Q	^{4}	PE	MONTBARD
24	TGV 23047	TGV 23048	A	r^4	PE	ALFORTVILLE
25	TGV 23049	TGV 23050	Q	^{4}	PE	BESANÇON
26	TGV 23051	TGV 23052	A	r^4	PE	SAINT ÉTIENNE
27	TGV 23053	TGV 23054	Q	^{4}	PE	MÂCON
28	TGV 23055	TGV 23056	A	^{4}	PE	MONTÉLIMAR
29	TGV 23057	TGV 23058	Q	^{4}	PE	VILLENEUVE-SAINT-GEORGES
30	TGV 23059	TGV 23060	A	r^4	PE	LILLE
31	TGV 23061	TGV 23062	A	r^4	PE	COMBS-LA-VILLE
32	TGV 23063	TGV 23064	A	r^4	PE	MAISONS-ALFORT
33	TGV 23065	TGV 23066	A	r	PE	FÉCAMP
34	TGV 23067	TGV 23068	A	r	PE	DUNKERQUE
35	TGV 23069	TGV 23070	A	r	PE	GRENOBLE
36	TGV 23071	TGV 23072	A	r	PE	SEINE SAINT-DENIS
37	TGV 23073	TGV 23074	A	r	PE	SAINT GERMAIN-EN-LAYE
39	TGV 23077	TGV 23078	Q	^{4}	PE	EVIAN + THONON-LES-BAINS
40	TGV 23079	TGV 23080	A	r^4	PE	VERSAILLES
41	TGV 23081	TGV 23082	A	r^4	PE	VILLIERS-LE-BEL
42	TGV 23083	TGV 23084	A	r^4	PE	CHAMBÉRY
43	TGV 23085	TGV 23086	A	r^4	PE	AIX-LES-BAINS
44	TGV 23087	TGV 23088	A	r^4	PE	CLERMONT-FERRAND
45	TGV 23089	TGV 23090	Q	^{4}	PE	VALENCE
46	TGV 23091	TGV 23092	A	r^4	PE	CONTREXÉVILLE
47	TGV 23093	TGV 23094	A	r^4	PE	NANCY
48	TGV 23095	TGV 23096	A	r	PE	COMTÉ-DE-NICE
49	TGV 23097	TGV 23098	A	r	PE	RENNES
50	TGV 23099	TGV 23100	Q	^{4}	PE	BEAUVAIS
51	TGV 23101	TGV 23102	Q	^{4}	PE	GIVORS/GRIGNY-BADAN
52	TGV 23103	TGV 23104	A	r	PE	GENÈVE
53	TGV 23105	TGV 23106	A	r^4	PE	LE PUY-EN-VELAY
54	TGV 23107	TGV 23108	A	r	PE	CHAGNY
55	TGV 23109	TGV 23110	A	r	PE	DENAIN
56	TGV 23111	TGV 23112	Q	^{4}	PE	ANNECY
57	TGV 23113	TGV 23114	Q		PE	BOURG-EN-BRESSE
58	TGV 23115	TGV 23116	A	r	PE	OULLINS
59	TGV 23117	TGV 23118	A	r^4	PE	HAUTMONT
60	TGV 23119	TGV 23120	A	r	PE	LANGÉAC
61	TGV 23121	TGV 23122	A	r	PE	FONTAINEBLEAU
62	TGV 23123	TGV 23124	A	r	PE	TOULOUSE
63	TGV 23125	TGV 23126	Q	^{4}	PE	VILLEURBANNE
64	TGV 23127	TGV 23128	A	r^4	PE	DOLE
65	TGV 23129	TGV 23130	Q	^{4}	PE	SÈTE
66	TGV 23131	TGV 23132	A	r^4	PE	AVIGNON
67	TGV 23133	TGV 23134	Q	^{4}	PE	BELLEGARDE-SUR-VALSERINE
68	TGV 23135	TGV 23136	Q		PE	MODANE
69	TGV 23137	TGV 23138	A	r	PE	VICHY
71	TGV 23141	TGV 23142	Q		PE	BRUNOY
72	TGV 23143	TGV 23144	Q		PE	CAHORS
73	TGV 23145	TGV 23146	A	r	PE	CHARENTON-LE-PONT
74	TGV 23147	TGV 23148	A	r^4	PE	ARBOIS/MOUCHARD/PORT-LESNEY
75	TGV 23149	TGV 23150	Q		PE	VITTEL
76	TGV 23151	TGV 23152	Q	^{4}	PE	PONTARLIER
77	TGV 23153	TGV 23154	Q	^{4}	PE	NUITS-SAINT-GEORGES
78	TGV 23155	TGV 23156	Q	^{4}	PE	CULOZ

79	TGV 23157	TGV 23158	Q	4	PE	ANNEMASSE
80	TGV 23159	TGV 23160	Q		PE	TOULON
81	TGV 23161	TGV 23162	Q		PE	TONNERRE
82	TGV 23163	TGV 23164	Q	4	PE	TRAPPES
83	TGV 23165	TGV 23166	Q		PE	MOISSY CRAMAYEL
84	TGV 23167	TGV 23168	Q		PE	DIEPPE
85	TGV 23169	TGV 23170	Q		PE	BEAUNE
86	TGV 23171	TGV 23172	Q	4	PE	MONTLUÇON
87	TGV 23173	TGV 23174	A	r4	PE	MONTCHANIN
89	TGV 23177	TGV 23178	Q	4	PE	LONS-LE-SAUNIER
90	TGV 23179	TGV 23180	Q	4	PE	EPINAL
91	TGV 23181	TGV 23182	Q	4	PE	MULHOUSE
92	TGV 23183	TGV 23184	Q	4	PE	NOYON
93	TGV 23185	TGV 23186	Q	4	PE	SENS
94	TGV 23187	TGV 23188	Q	4	PE	LES ARCS EN PROVENCE
95	TGV 23189	TGV 23190	Q		PE	SAINT RAPHAËL
96	TGV 23191	TGV 23192	Q	4	PE	MONTE CARLO
97	TGV 23193	TGV 23194	Q	4	PE	CORBEIL-ESSONNES
98	TGV 23195	TGV 23196	A	4	PE	ALBERTVILLE
100	TGV 23199	TGV 23200	A	r	PE	SAINT GERVAIS-LES-BAINS
P01	TGV 23201	TGV 23202	N	*	PE	
102	TGV 23203	TGV 23204	A	r	PE	VIGNEUX-SUR-SEINE
Spare		TGV 23140		4	PE	MELUN

Note: Trailers 323070–823070 also exist.

TGV SUD-EST   8-CAR THREE-VOLTAGE SETS

These sets are identical to sets 01–102 except that they are additionally equipped to operate under 15 kV a.c. 16²/₃ Hz in Switzerland. They operate from Paris via Dijon to Lausanne and Zürich via Bern and also to Brig in winter. The sets are now managed by an SNCF/SBB joint venture and were to be refurbished, with a special livery from 1997. As part of the deal, set 112 became property of SBB. Details and notes as for sets 01–102 except:

Systems: 1500 V d.c. + 25 kV 50 Hz + 15 kV 16²/₃ Hz a.c.
Non-standard Livery: As **A**, but with red stripe and "Ligne de Coeur" branding.

110	TGV 33001	TGV 33002	N	4	PE	PAYS DE VAUD
111	TGV 33003	TGV 33004	N	4	PE	SURESNES
112	TGV 33005	TGV 33006	N	4	PE	LAUSANNE
113	TGV 33007	TGV 33008	N	4	PE	NEUCHÂTEL
114	TGV 33009	TGV 33010	N	4	PE	CLUSES
115	TGV 33011	TGV 33012	N	4	PE	ZÜRICH
116	TGV 33013	TGV 33014	N	4	PE	VALAIS
117	TGV 33015	TGV 33016			PE	BERN/BERNE
118	TGV 33017	TGV 33018			PE	BISCHHEIM
	(ex 23175)	(ex 23176)				

TGV POSTES

These sets have 8 trailers like the TGV Sud-Est sets, but the trailers are postal vans. Numbers 1 to 5 are half sets. Numbers 6 and 7 were converted from TGV Sud-Est set 38 and are a complete set. Postal sets operate from Charolais sorting depot next to Paris Gare de Lyon to depots at Macon and Cavaillon.

Class Specific Livery: Yellow with grey and white bands.

Non-driving motors and trailer cars are numbered in the sequence as follows:

Set n: 91230n/92230n/93230n/94230n.

1	923001		S	PE
2	923002		S	PE
3	923003		S	PE
4	923004		S	PE
5	923005		S	PE
6 + 7	923006	923007	S	PE

TGV DUPLEX   8-CAR DOUBLE-DECK SETS

TGV Duplex sets were designed to address the problem of traffic growth on the Paris–Lyon route where it will not be possible to increase train frequencies. The result is a double-deck high-speed train, carrying 40% more passengers than a TGV-Réseau within the same weight limit and for a cost of only 24% more. Power cars are of the new generation with a central driving position and disc brakes although other details are broadly the same as TGV-Réseau.

TGV Duplex sets now operate all Paris–Lyon trains and certain Paris–Toulon and Montpellier services. Sets can operate in multiple with each other and with TGV-Réseau units. Further units of this type may be ordered shortly.

Systems: 1500 V d.c. / 25 kV a.c.
Maximum Speed: 300 km/h
Builder-Mech. Parts: GEC-Alsthom/De Dietrich
Builder-Elec. Parts: Francorail-MTE
Built: 1995–98
Livery: A
Continuous rating: 25 kV a.c. 8800 kW; 1500 V d.c. 3680 kW
Traction Motors : 8 x FM 47 synchronous of 1100 kW
Axle arrangement: Bo-Bo + 2-2-2-2-2-2-2-2 + Bo-Bo
Accommodation: 0 + 69/– 1T + 65/– 1T + 65/– 1T + –/16 bar + –/84 2T + –/84 2T + –/84 1T + –/96 2T + 0
Weight: 65 + 43 + 28 + 28 + 28 + 28 + 28 + 43 + 65 tonnes
Length: 22.15 + 21.845 + 18.7 + 18.7 + 18.7 + 18.7 + 18.7 + 21.845 + 22.15 m.
Cab Signalling: TVM 430.

Trailer cars are numbered in the sequence as follows:

Set *nnn:* 129*nnn*/229*nnn*/329*nnn*/429*nnn*/529*nnn*/629*nnn*/729*nnn*/829*nnn*.

201	TGV 29001	TGV 29002	A	PE	
202	TGV 29003	TGV 29004	A	PE	
203	TGV 29005	TGV 29006	A	PE	
204	TGV 29007	TGV 29008	A	PE	
205	TGV 29009	TGV 29010	A	PE	
206	TGV 29011	TGV 29013	A	PE	
207	TGV 29013	TGV 29014	A	PE	
208	TGV 29015	TGV 29016	A	PE	
209	TGV 29017	TGV 29018	A	PE	
210	TGV 29019	TGV 29020	A	PE	
211	TGV 29021	TGV 29022	A	PE	
212	TGV 29023	TGV 29024	A	PE	
213	TGV 29025	TGV 29026	A	PE	
214	TGV 29027	TGV 29028	A	PE	
215	TGV 29029	TGV 29030	A	PE	
216	TGV 29031	TGV 29032	A	PE	
217	TGV 29033	TGV 29034	A	PE	
218	TGV 29035	TGV 29036	A	PE	
219	TGV 29037	TGV 29038	A	PE	
220	TGV 29039	TGV 29040	A	PE	
221	TGV 29041	TGV 29042	A	PE	
222	TGV 29043	TGV 29044	A	PE	
223	TGV 29045	TGV 29046	A	PE	
224	TGV 29047	TGV 29048	A	PE	
225	TGV 29049	TGV 29050	A	PE	
226	TGV 29051	TGV 29052	A	PE	
227	TGV 29053	TGV 29054	A	PE	L'YONNE
228	TGV 29055	TGV 29056	A	PE	
229	TGV 29057	TGV 29058	A	PE	
230	TGV 29059	TGV 29060	A	PE	

TGV ATLANTIQUE 10-CAR TWO-VOLTAGE SETS

These sets are longer, more powerful and faster than the TGV Sud-Est sets. Trailer 2 has unidirectional seating with trailers 3 and 4 having facing seating including 6 ¬club" compartments with four seats in each. Trailer 1 has a wheelchair space and suitable toilet. Trailers 2,4 and 6 have a telephone. Trailers 8 and 9 include 4 family semi-compartments of 4 seats and trailer 9 also includes facilities for nursing mothers. Trailer 10 has a special 17 seat childrens compartment at the end. On 18th May 1990, set 325 attained a world record of 515.3 km/h.

TGV + TGVRADr + TGVRAr + TGVRA + TGVRBr + 6TGVRB + TGV.
Systems: 1500 V d.c. + 25 kV a.c.
Built: 1988–91.
Builders: Alsthom/Francorail-MTE/De Dietrich.
Axle Arrangement: Bo-Bo + 2-2-2-2-2-2-2-2-2-2-2-2 + Bo-Bo.
Traction Motors: 8 x 1100 kW synchronous per set.
Accommodation: 0 + 44/– 1T + 36/– 1T + 36/– 1T + Bar + –/60 2T + –/60 1T + –/60 2T + –/56 1T + –/56S 1T + –/77 2T + 0.
Weight: 444 tonnes.
Length: 22.15 + 21.845 + (8 x 18.70) + 21.845 + 22.15 m.
Max. Speed: 300 km/h
Non-standard Livery: White with a blue band.
Cab Signalling: TVM 300 ([4] TVM 430).

Trailer cars are numbered in the following sequence:

Set nnn: 241nnn/242nnn/243nnn/244nnn/245nnn/246nnn/247nnn/248nnn/249nnn/240nnn.

301	TGV 24001	TGV 24002	N	PC	
302	TGV 24003	TGV 24004	N	PC	
303	TGV 24005	TGV 24006	A	PC	
304	TGV 24007	TGV 24008	A	PC	LE MANS
305	TGV 24009	TGV 24010	A	PC	SAINT BRIEUC
306	TGV 24011	TGV 24012	A	PC	
307	TGV 24013	TGV 24014	A	PC	
308	TGV 24015	TGV 24016	A	PC	
309	TGV 24017	TGV 24018	A	PC	
310	TGV 24019	TGV 24020	A	PC	
311	TGV 24021	TGV 24022	A	PC	
312	TGV 24023	TGV 24024	A	PC	PAYS D'AURAY
313	TGV 24025	TGV 24026	A	PC	VILLEBON-SUR-YVETTE
314	TGV 24027	TGV 24028	A	PC	
315	TGV 24029	TGV 24030	A	PC	
316	TGV 24031	TGV 24032	A	PC	ANGOULÊME
317	TGV 24033	TGV 24034	A	PC	
318	TGV 24035	TGV 24036	A	PC	
319	TGV 24037	TGV 24038	A	PC	MARCOUSSIS
320	TGV 24039	TGV 24040	A	PC	
321	TGV 24041	TGV 24042	A	PC	ORTHEZ
322	TGV 24043	TGV 24044	A	PC	LAMBALLE Côtes d'armor
323	TGV 24045	TGV 24046	A	PC	
324	TGV 24047	TGV 24048	A	PC	
325	TGV 24049	TGV 24050	A	PC	VENDÔME
326	TGV 24051	TGV 24052	A	PC	
327	TGV 24053	TGV 24054	A	PC	
328	TGV 24055	TGV 24056	A	PC	
329	TGV 24057	TGV 24058	A	PC	MORLAIX
330	TGV 24059	TGV 24060	A	PC	CHINON
331	TGV 24061	TGV 24062	A	PC	
332	TGV 24063	TGV 24064	A	PC	LIBOURNE
333	TGV 24065	TGV 24066	A	PC	BORDEAUX
334	TGV 24067	TGV 24068	A	PC	VILLEJUST
335	TGV 24069	TGV 24070	A	PC	
336	TGV 24071	TGV 24072	A	PC	TOURS
337	TGV 24073	TGV 24074	A	PC	SAINT-PIERRE-DES-CORPS
338	TGV 24075	TGV 24076	A	PC	VOUVRAY

339	TGV 24077	TGV 24078	A		PC	MONTLOUIS-SUR-LOIRE
340	TGV 24079	TGV 24080	A		PC	DOURDAN
341	TGV 24081	TGV 24082	A		PC	ANGERS
342	TGV 24083	TGV 24084	A		PC	
343	TGV 24085	TGV 24086	A		PC	SAINT-NAZAIRE
344	TGV 24087	TGV 24088	A		PC	NANTES
345	TGV 24089	TGV 24090	A		PC	RÉGION CENTRE LE COEUR DE FRANCE
346	TGV 24091	TGV 24092	A		PC	
347	TGV 24093	TGV 24094	A		PC	
348	TGV 24095	TGV 24096	A		PC	POITIERS
349	TGV 24097	TGV 24098	A		PC	LA BAULE
350	TGV 24099	TGV 24100	A		PC	
351	TGV 24101	TGV 24102	A		PC	
352	TGV 24103	TGV 24104	A		PC	
353	TGV 24105	TGV 24106	A		PC	LAVAL
354	TGV 24107	TGV 24108	A		PC	
355	TGV 24109	TGV 24110	A		PC	LE CROISIC
356	TGV 24111	TGV 24112	A		PC	Pays de Vannes
357	TGV 24113	TGV 24114	A		PC	
358	TGV 24115	TGV 24116	A		PC	
359	TGV 24117	TGV 24118	A		PC	CHÂTELLERAULT
360	TGV 24119	TGV 24120	A		PC	
361	TGV 24121	TGV 24122	A		PC	ALENÇON
362	TGV 24123	TGV 24124	A		PC	ST. JEAN-DE-LUZ
363	TGV 24125	TGV 24126	A		PC	
364	TGV 24127	TGV 24128	A		PC	BAYONNE
365	TGV 24129	TGV 24130	A		PC	TARBES
366	TGV 24131	TGV 24132	A		PC	
367	TGV 24133	TGV 24134	A		PC	
368	TGV 24135	TGV 24136	A		PC	
369	TGV 24137	TGV 24138	A		PC	LOURDES
370	TGV 24139	TGV 24140	A		PC	HENDAYE
371	TGV 24141	TGV 24142	A		PC	LORIENT
372	TGV 24143	TGV 24144	A		PC	
373	TGV 24145	TGV 24146	A		PC	
374	TGV 24147	TGV 24148	A		PC	
375	TGV 24149	TGV 24150	A		PC	
376	TGV 24151	TGV 24152	A		PC	
377	TGV 24153	TGV 24154	A		PC	
378	TGV 24155	TGV 24156	A		PC	
379	TGV 24157	TGV 24158	A		PC	
380	TGV 24159	TGV 24160	A		PC	
381	TGV 24161	TGV 24162	A		PC	
382	TGV 24163	TGV 24164	A		PC	
383	TGV 24165	TGV 24166	A		PC	
384	TGV 24167	TGV 24168	A		PC	
385	TGV 24169	TGV 24170	A		PC	
386	TGV 24171	TGV 24172	A		PC	
387	TGV 24173	TGV 24174	A		PC	
388	TGV 24175	TGV 24176	A		PC	
389	TGV 24177	TGV 24178	A		PC	LE POULIGUEN
390	TGV 24179	TGV 24180	A		PC	ANCENIS
391	TGV 24181	TGV 24182	A		PC	MASSY
392	TGV 24183	TGV 24184	A		PC	
393	TGV 24185	TGV 24186	A	4	PC	PORNICHET
394	TGV 24187	TGV 24188	A	4	PC	
395	TGV 24189	TGV 24190	A	4	PC	
396	TGV 24191	TGV 24192	A	4	PC	LOCHES
397	TGV 24193	TGV 24194	A	4	PC	
398	TGV 24195	TGV 24196	A	4	PC	LANGEIS
399	TGV 24197	TGV 24198	A	4	PC	
400	TGV 24199	TGV 24200	A	4	PC	QUIMPER
401	TGV 24201	TGV 24202	A	4	PC	
402	TGV 24203	TGV 24204	A	4	PC	

403	TGV 24205	TGV 24206	A	4	PC	
404	TGV 24207	TGV 24208	A	4	PC	
405	TGV 24209	TGV 24210	A	4	PC	AYTRÉ
Spare	TGX 24211					

TGV RÉSEAU (TGV-R)   8-CAR TWO-VOLTAGE SETS

TGV-Réseau is basically an eight-car version of TGV-Atlantique with very similar power cars. Trailers differ in that all have an open layout and none have the "semi-compartments" found in TGV-A first class. The bar vehicle has been completely transformed. Another difference is slightly lower density seating in second class as TGV-R sets, as their names suggest, are designed for work over the whole TGV network, often on long distance services.

Dual-voltage units first went into service in 1993 on TGV-Nord Europe services from Paris Nord to Lille, Valenciennes, Dunkerque and Calais/Boulogne. In 1994 they were then introduced on the Lille–Lyon–Marseille–Nice route, via the Jonction high-speed line avoiding Paris. From 1996, they spread to Lille–Rennes, Nantes and Bordeaux services.

TGV 502 was involved in a crash at Bergues on 25th September 1997 which destroyed power car 28004 and damaged trailers R7 and R8. The other trailers were used to repair Thalys PBKA set 4342.

Systems: 1500 V d.c. / 25 kV a.c.
Maximum Speed: 300 km/h.
Builder-Mech. Parts : GEC-Alsthom/De Dietrich
Builder-Elec. Parts : Francorail-MTE
Built : 1992-94
Livery : A
Continuous rating: 25 kV a.c. 8800 kW; 3000 V d.c. and 1500 V d.c. 3680 kW
Traction Motors : 8 x FM 47 synchronous of 1100 kW each
Axle arrangement: Bo-Bo + 2-2-2-2-2-2-2-2-2 + Bo-Bo
Accommodation: 0 + 42/- 1T + 39/- 1T + 39/- 1T + -/16 bar + -/56 2T + -/56 2T + - /56 1T + -/ 73 2T + 0
Weight: 65 + 43 + 28 + 28 + 28 + 28 + 28 + 43 + 65 tonnes
Length: 22.15 + 21.845 + 18.7 + 18.7 + 18.7 + 18.7 + 18.7 + 18.7 + 21.845 + 22.15 m.
Cab Signalling: TVM 430).

Trailer cars are numbered in the following sequence, prefixed TGVR:

Set nnn: 281nnn + 282nnn + 283nnn + 284nnn + 285nnn + 286nnn + 287nnn + 288nnn

501	TGV 28001	TGV 28002	A	LY	
503	TGV 28005	TGV 28006	A	LY	
504	TGV 28007	TGV 28008	A	LY	
505	TGV 28009	TGV 28010	A	LY	
506	TGV 28011	TGV 28013	A	LY	
507	TGV 28013	TGV 28014	A	LY	
508	TGV 28015	TGV 28016	A	LY	
509	TGV 28017	TGV 28018	A	LY	
510	TGV 28019	TGV 28020	A	LY	
511	TGV 28021	TGV 28022	A	LY	
512	TGV 28023	TGV 28024	A	LY	
513	TGV 28025	TGV 28026	A	LY	
514	TGV 28027	TGV 28028	A	LY	LA MADELEINE
515	TGV 28029	TGV 28030	A	LY	
516	TGV 28031	TGV 28032	A	LY	DOUAI CITÉ DES GEANTS
517	TGV 28033	TGV 28034	A	LY	
518	TGV 28035	TGV 28036	A	LY	
519	TGV 28037	TGV 28038	A	LY	
520	TGV 28039	TGV 28040	A	LY	
521	TGV 28041	TGV 28042	A	LY	TOURCOING La Creative
522	TGV 28043	TGV 28044	A	LY	
523	TGV 28045	TGV 28046	A	LY	
524	TGV 28047	TGV 28048	A	LY	ARNOUVILLE-LES-GONNESSE
525	TGV 28049	TGV 28050	A	LY	
526	TGV 28051	TGV 28052	A	LY	CHESSY
527	TGV 28053	TGV 28054	A	LY	SAINT OMER AUDOMAROIS

528	TGV 28055	TGV 28056	A	LY	CAMBRAI
529	TGV 28057	TGV 28058	A	LY	
530	TGV 28059	TGV 28060	A	LY	
531	TGV 28061	TGV 28062	A	LP	
532	TGV 28063	TGV 28064	A	LY	CONSEIL GÉNÉRAL DU VAL D'OISE
533	TGV 28065	TGV 28066	A	LY	TOURNAN-EN-BRIE
534	TGV 28067	TGV 28068	A	LY	Ville de Dunkerque
535	TGV 28069	TGV 28070	A	LY	
536	TGV 28071	TGV 28072	A	LY	
537	TGV 28073	TGV 28074	A	LY	
538	TGV 28075	TGV 28076	A	LY	
539	TGV 28077	TGV 28078	A	LY	
540	TGV 28079	TGV 28080	A	LY	
541	TGV 28081	TGV 28082	A	LY	
542	TGV 28083	TGV 28084	A	LY	
543	TGV 28085	TGV 28086	A	LY	
544	TGV 28087	TGV 28088	A	LY	
545	TGV 28089	TGV 28090	A	LY	
546	TGV 28091	TGV 28092	A	LY	
547	TGV 28093	TGV 28094	A	LY	
548	TGV 28095	TGV 28096	A	LY	
549	TGV 28097	TGV 28098	A	LY	
550	TGV 28099	TGV 28100	A	LY	
Spare	TGV 28003		A	LY	

EUROSTAR   9-CAR "THREE CAPITALS" SETS

Eurostar sets work services through the Channel Tunnel between London and Paris and Brussels. The four-voltage sets also work London–Bourg St. Maurice ski trains in winter. 3225–8 are not used on Channel Tunnel services. They have just started working the Brussels–Nice service. Eurostars are based on the French TGV design concept, and the individual cars are numbered like French TGVs. Each train consists of two 9-coach sets back-to-back with a power car at the outer end. All sets are articulated with an extra motor bogie on the coach next to the power car. Coaches are also referred to by their position in the set viz. R1–R9 (and in traffic R10–R18 in the second set). Coaches R18–R10 are identical to R1–R9.

TGV + TGVZBD + 4 TGVRB + TGVRr + 2TGVRA + TGVRAD.
Systems: 750 V (3rd rail) + 3000 V d.c. + 25 kV a.c (v + 1500 V d.c.).
Built: 1992–93.
Builders: GEC-Alsthom/Brush/ANF/De Dietrich/BN Construction/ACEC.
Axle Arrangement: Bo-Bo + Bo-2-2-2-2-2-2-2-2-2.
Accommodation: 0 + –/48 1T + –/58 1T + –/58 2T + –/58 1T + –/58 2T + bar/kitchen + 39/– 1T + 39/– 1T + 25/– 1T.
Length: 22.15 + 21.845 + (7 x 18.70) + 21.845 m.
Max. Speed: 300 km/h.
Cab Signalling: TVM 430.
Class Specific Livery: S White with dark blue window band roof and yellow bodysides with Eurostar branding.
Non-standard Livery: N As above, but Eurostar branding removed.
Trailer cars are numbered in the following sequence.

Set nnnn: 37nnnn1/37nnnn2/37nnnn3/37nnnn4/37nnnn5/37nnnn6/37nnnn7/37nnnn8/37nnnn9.

Set	Owner	Power Car			Set	Owner	Power Car		
3001	EU	3730010	S	NP	3011	EU	3730110	S	NP
3002	EU	3730020	S	NP	3012	EU	3730120	S	NP
3003	EU	3730030	S	NP	3013	EU	3730130	S	NP
3004	EU	3730040	S	NP	3014	EU	3730140	S	NP
3005	EU	3730050	S	NP	3015	EU	3730150	S	NP
3006	EU	3730060	S	NP	3016	EU	3730160	S	NP
3007	EU	3730070	S	NP	3017	EU	3730170	S	NP
3008	EU	3730080	S	NP	3018	EU	3730180	S	NP
3009	EU	3730090	S	NP	3019	EU	3730190	S	NP
3010	EU	3730100	S	NP	3020	EU	3730200	S	NP

3021	EU	3730210	S		NP	3210	SNCF	3732100	S		LY
3022	EU	3730220	S		NP	3211	SNCF	3732110	S		LY
3023	EU	3730230	S		NP	3212	SNCF	3732120	S		LY
3024	EU	3730240	S		NP	3213	SNCF	3732130	S		LY
3025	EU	3730250	S		NP	3214	SNCF	3732140	S		LY
3026	EU	3730260	S		NP	3215	SNCF	3732150	S	v	LY
3027	EU	3730270	S		NP	3216	SNCF	3732160	S	v	LY
3028	EU	3730280	S		NP	3217	SNCF	3732170	S		LY
3101	SNCB	3731010	S		FF	3218	SNCF	3732180	S		LY
3102	SNCB	3731020	S		FF	3219	SNCF	3732190	S		LY
3103	SNCB	3731030	S		FF	3220	SNCF	3732200	S		LY
3104	SNCB	3731040	S		FF	3221	SNCF	3732210	S		LY
3105	SNCB	3731050	S		FF	3222	SNCF	3732220	S		LY
3106	SNCB	3731060	S		FF	3223	SNCF	3732230	S	v	LY
3201	SNCF	3732010	S	v	LY	3224	SNCF	3732240	S	v	LY
3202	SNCF	3732020	S	v	LY	3225	SNCF	3732250	S	v	LY
3203	SNCF	3732030	S	v	LY	3226	SNCF	3732260	S	v	LY
3204	SNCF	3732040	S	v	LY	3227	SNCF	3732270	S	v	LY
3205	SNCF	3732050	S		LY	3228	SNCF	3732280	S	v	LY
3206	SNCF	3732060	S		LY	3229	SNCF	3732290	S	v	LY
3207	SNCF	3732070	S	v	LY	3230	SNCF	3732300	S	v	LY
3208	SNCF	3732080	S	v	LY	3231	SNCF	3732310	S		LY
3209	SNCF	3732090	S		LY	3232	SNCF	3732320	S		LY

Spare Power Car

3999	LCR	3739990	S		NP

EUROSTAR 7-CAR REGIONAL SETS

These sets are similar to the "three capitals" sets except that they only have seven trailers. They are designed for operation north of London, but as yet these services have not materialised. They consist of a power car plus trailers type R1/3/2/5/6/7/9 in that order.

TGV + TGVZBD + 4 TGVRB + TGVRr + 2TGVRA + TGVRAD.
Systems: 750 V (3rd rail)/3000 V d.c. + 25 kV a.c.
Built: 1992–93.
Builders: GEC-Alsthom/Brush Electrical Machines/ANF/De Dietrich/BN Construction/ACEC.
Axle Arrangement: Bo-Bo + Bo-2-2-2-2-2-2-2.
Accommodation: 0 + –/48 1T + –/58 1T + –/58 1T + –/58 2T + bar/kitchen + 39/– 1T + 25/– 1T.
Length: 22.15 + 21.845 + (5 x 18.70) + 21.845 m.
Max. Speed: 300 km/h.
Cab Signalling: TVM 430.
Class Specific Livery: S White with dark blue window band roof and yellow bodysides with Eurostar branding.

Trailer cars are numbered in the following sequence.

Set nnnn: 37nnnn1/37nnnn3/37nnnn2/3nnnn5/37nnnn6/37nnnn737nnnn9.

3301	EU	3733010	S	NP	3308	EU	3733080	S	NP
3302	EU	3733020	S	NP	3309	EU	3733090	S	NP
3303	EU	3733030	S	NP	3310	EU	3733100	S	NP
3304	EU	3733040	S	NP	3311	EU	3733110	S	NP
3305	EU	3733050	S	NP	3312	EU	3733120	S	NP
3306	EU	3733060	S	NP	3313	EU	3733130	S	NP
3307	EU	3733070	S	NP	3314	EU	3733140	S	NP

THALYS 8-CAR FOUR-VOLTAGE SETS

This is basically a four-voltage version of TGV-Réseau but with the new generation of power car with a central driving position as first seen with TGV Duplex. Trailer cars are exactly the same as TGV-Réseau PBA sets 4531–4540 (see below). The power car includes all equipment necessary for operation in France, Belgium, the Netherlands and Germany including German Indusi and LZB cab signalling. With all this extra equipment, it was necessary to design a lighter transformer in order to keep the power car weight to 68 tonnes because of the 17 tonne axle load limit on French high-speed lines.

These sets entered service on Paris–Brussels–Liège services in 1997 then on Paris–Brussels–Köln/Amsterdam when the Belgian high-speed line opened in December 1997. Sets can operate in multiple with TGV-Réseau sets. The sets belong to the four railways concerned but will be based and maintained at Paris Le Landy or Brussels Forest.

Systems: 1500 V d.c. / 25 kV a.c. 50 Hz / 3000 V d.c. / 15 kV a.c. $^2/_3$ Hz
Built : 1996–98
Builder-Mech. Parts: GEC-Alsthom/De Dietrich/Bombardier Eurorail
Builder-Elec. Parts: GEC-Alsthom/ACEC/Holec
Axle arrangement: Bo-Bo + 2-2-2-2-2-2-2-2 + Bo-Bo
Weight: 67 + 43 + 28 + 28 + 28 + 28 + 28 + 43 + 67 tonnes
Length: 22.15 + 21.845 + 18.7 + 18.7 + 18.7 + 18.7 + 18.7 + 18.7 + 21.845 + 22.15 metres
Accommodation: 0 + 42/– 1T + 39/– 1T + 39/– 1T + –/16 bar + –/56 2T + –/56 2T + –/56 1T + –/73 2T + 0
Continuous Rating: 25 kV 8800 kW; 3000 V d.c. 5120 kW ; 1500 V d.c. and 15 kV a.c.3680 kW
Maximum Speed: 300 km/h
Cab Signalling: TVM 430.
Class-specific Livery: S Metallic grey with red front end and roof.

Trailer cars are numbered in the following sequence, prefixed TGVR:

Set nnnn: nnnn1 + nnnn2 + nnnn3 + nnnn4 + nnnn5 + nnnn6 + nnnn7 + nnnn8

Set	Owner	Power Car 1	Power Car 2	Liv	Depot
4301	SNCB	TGV 43010	TGV 43019	S	FF
4302	SNCB	TGV 43020	TGV 43029	S	FF
4303	SNCB	TGV 43030	TGV 43039	S	FF
4304	SNCB	TGV 43040	TGV 43049	S	FF
4305	SNCB	TGV 43050	TGV 43059	S	FF
4306	SNCB	TGV 43060	TGV 43069	S	FF
4307	SNCB	TGV 43070	TGV 43079	S	FF
4321	DB	TGV 43210	TGV 43219	S	FF
4322	DB	TGV 43220	TGV 43229	S	FF
4331	NS	TGV 43310	TGV 43319	S	FF
4332	NS	TGV 43320	TGV 43329	S	FF
4341	SNCF	TGV 43410	TGV 43419	S	LY
4342	SNCF	TGV 43420	TGV 43429	S	LY
4343	SNCF	TGV 43430	TGV 43439	S	LY
4344	SNCF	TGV 43440	TGV 43449	S	LY
4345	SNCF	TGV 43450	TGV 43459	S	LY
4346	SNCF	TGV 43460	TGV 43469	S	LY

TGV RESEAU (TGV-R)   8-CAR THREE-VOLTAGE SETS

Apart from three-voltage capabilities, these sets are otherwise identical to TGV-Réseau two-voltage sets and are designed to operate Belgium–south of France services. They were first infiltrated onto TGV Nord Europe services which they still work. From January 1995, they replaced certain Paris–Brussels services then in June 1995, operated a Brussels–Nice service via Lille. From 1996, there were more Brussels–south of France services and the sets also started operation on Paris–Brussels services in common with Thalys PBA sets. They no longer operate these.

The final 10 three-voltage sets have been equipped with a special pantograph and Dutch ATB automatic train protection in order to operate Paris–Brussels–Amsterdam services. Because of this they are known as PBA sets. These units also have a completely different "Thalys" livery and improved interiors with red moquette seats throughout. Initially, they interworked with sets 4501–4530 but the latter were replaced by the "real" Thalys sets from 1997.

The sets equipped to work into Italy started operating Paris–Torino–Milano services from September 1996.

Details as two-voltage sets except:

Systems: 1500 V d.c./25 kV a.c./3000 V d.c.
Built : 1994–96
Non-standard Livery: N 4530 is in advertising livery, whilst 4531–40 are in "Thalys" livery of metallic grey with red front ends and roof.

i = Equipped to operate into Italy under 3000 V d.c.

Trailers are numbered in the following sequence, prefixed TGVR:

Set nnnn: 38nnnn1 + 38nnnn2 + 38nnnn3 + 38nnnn4 + 38nnnn5 + 38nnnn6 + 38nnnn7 + 38nnnn8

4501	TGV 380001	TGV 380002	A	i	PE
4502	TGV 380003	TGV 380004	A	i	PE
4503	TGV 380005	TGV 380006	A	i	PE
4504	TGV 380007	TGV 380008	A	i	PE
4505	TGV 380009	TGV 380010	A	i	PE
4506	TGV 380011	TGV 380013	A	i	PE
4507	TGV 380013	TGV 380014	A		LY
4508	TGV 380015	TGV 380016	A		LY
4509	TGV 380017	TGV 380018	A		LY
4510	TGV 380019	TGV 380020	A		LY
4511	TGV 380021	TGV 380022	A		LY	VILLENEUVE D'ASCQ
4512	TGV 380022	TGV 380023	A		LY
4513	TGV 380024	TGV 380025	A		LY
4514	TGV 380027	TGV 380028	A		LY
4515	TGV 380029	TGV 380030	A		LY
4516	TGV 380031	TGV 380032	A		LY
4517	TGV 380033	TGV 380034	A		LY
4518	TGV 380035	TGV 380036	A		LY
4519	TGV 380037	TGV 380038	A		LY
4520	TGV 380039	TGV 380040	A		LY
4521	TGV 380041	TGV 380042	A		LY
4522	TGV 380043	TGV 380044	A		LY
4523	TGV 380045	TGV 380046	A		LY
4524	TGV 380047	TGV 380048	A		LY
4525	TGV 380049	TGV 380050	A		LY
4526	TGV 380051	TGV 380052	A		LY
4527	TGV 380053	TGV 380054	A		LY
4528	TGV 380055	TGV 380056	A		LY
4529	TGV 380057	TGV 380058	A		LY
4530	TGV 380059	TGV 380060	A		LY
4531	TGV 380061	TGV 380062	N		LY
4532	TGV 380063	TGV 380064	N		LY
4533	TGV 380065	TGV 380066	N		LY
4534	TGV 380067	TGV 380068	N		LY
4535	TGV 380069	TGV 380070	N		LY
4536	TGV 380071	TGV 380072	N		LY
4537	TGV 380073	TGV 380074	N		LY
4538	TGV 380075	TGV 380076	N		LY
4539	TGV 380077	TGV 380078	N		LY
4540	TGV 380079	TGV 380080	N		LY
Spare		TGV 380081	A		LY

▲ X 2206 in "Regional" blue livery at Paris Sud Ouest depot on 16th March 1996. **T.M. Wallis**

▼ X 2877 in "Massif Central" livery at St Germain des Fossés on 29th October 1993. **T.M. Wallis**

▲ X 4543 in standard 1980s DMU livery forms the 09.52 Évreux–Mantes-la-Jolie service at Bréval on 12th June 1994. **George Allsop**

▼ Refurbished 2-car set X 4402/8502 waits for its next duty at Chartres on 31st August 1993. **Les Nixon**

▲ New 2-car DMU X 72503/4 in "TER" livery at Châteaudun on 26th September 1997. **David Haydock**

▼ Y 7242 in the now-standard orange shunter livery at Sète on 20th October 1996. **Peter Fox**

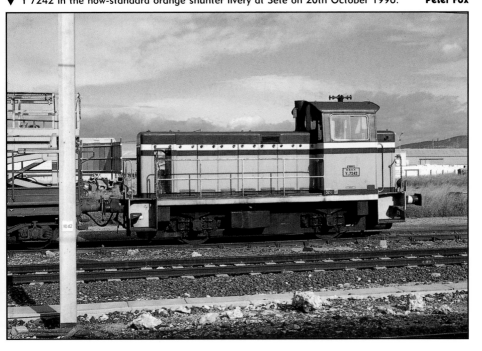

116

▲ Y 7591 shunts a trip freight from Grenoble at Monestier de Clermont on 20th May 1996.

Les Nixon

▼ Y 8126 stabled at Abbeville on 29th August 1993.   **Les Nixon**

▲ Y 8420 at Lens depot on 18th May 1992. The panel above the cab window, marked TELE, illuminates when the locomotive is operating under remote control. **David Haydock**

▼ LOCMA 0038 (formerly Y 2502) at St Pierre des Corps on 25th March 1995. **T.M. Wallis**

▲ Paris suburban EMU Z 5323 waits at Thiverval-Grigon with a service for Paris Montparnasse on 13th June 1994. **George Allsop**

▼ SNCF Class Z 5600 (RER) unit no. 43C, with car 5685 leading, at St Pierre des Corps on 6th July 1993. **Dr A.T. Sumner**

▲ Two Class Z 6400 stabled at Pont-Cardinet station, near to their home depot of Paris Saint Lazare, in August 1995. **David Haydock**

▼ Z 7116 forming an evening Dijon-Ville–Chalon-sur-Saône 'all stations' service works along the PLM main line near Gevrey-Chambertin on 29th August 1994. **Michael J. Collins**

▲ Z 11507 in "Lorraine" yellow livery at Thionville on 24th March 1993. **T.N. Hall**

▼ Class Z 20500 unit No. 20518/17 leaves Orry-la-Ville-Coye with a RER line D service. **David Haydock**

▲ Z 23502 stands at Hellemmes on 19th September 1998, whilst forming a special shuttle service in connection with the SNCF works open day. **David Haydock**

▼ Class Z 92050 is a small class of regional EMUs, adapted from Class Z 20500, for use in the Lille area. Here, 92055/56 approaches Douai with an evening service from Lens to Valenciennes. **David Haydock**

▲ TGV Sud-Est set 06 in the obsolescent orange livery near Marseillan Plage in the south of France, forming the 07.54 Béziers–Paris Gare de Lyon on 2nd June 1995. **Chris Wilson**

▼ TGV-R set 515 near Roeux on the classic line with the 08.22 Paris Nord–Valenciennes on 12th March 1994. **Chris Wilson**

TGV Duplex sets 208 and 219 form the 17.16 Lyon Part Dieu–Paris Gare de Lyon service near Tonnerre on 7th August 1998. **David Haydock**

▲ Thalys PBKA set 4301 was tested on 15 kV a.c. in Germany during July 1996. The set is seen here at Rohrbach, north of Würzburg. **David Haydock**

▼ Eurostar sets 3208/7 pass along the LGV Nord Europe near Beaumont on 11th July 1996, whilst forming the 15.23 London Waterloo–Paris Nord. **Chris Wilson**

▲ **"La Petit Train Jaune" (The little yellow train), alias SNCF Ligne de Cerdagne.** The 14.12 Villefranche-de-Conflent–La Tour de Carol is seen at Thuès-Carança on 6th July 1997 formed of power car Z 108, open trailer 20031, balcony trailer 20039 and power car Z 118. **Peter Fox**

▼ **SNCF Ligne de Savoie.** A Z 600 unit is seen at Chamonix on a Vallorcine–St Gervais train.
David Cable

▲ **Chemins de Fer Corses**. Soulé railcar X 9701 with trailer 97051 at Casamozza on 25th September 1991 with an Ajaccio–Bastia service.   **Pete Moody**

▼ **RATP**. An original RER line A Type MS61 set (15070/18013/15071) at Rueil-Malmaison.
David Haydock

▲ **CFD.** Class 20 No. 2003 (ex-BR 20139) at the head of four sand wagons at Autun on 30th August 1994. **Michael J. Collins**

▼ **CFTA.** Railcar X 2416 at Paimpol with the 13.05 to Guingamp on 5th July 1993. **Chris Wilson**

▲ **Chemins de Fer de la Provence.** Unreliable Soulé/Garnero two-car unit XR 351/X 351 receives attention at Nice CP station on 11th June 1991. **Peter Fox**

◄ Railcar X 302 sports the new CP livery on 14th June 1999. **Peter Fox**

▼ **Train à Vapeur de Touraine (TVT).** 2–8–2 No. 141C100 is seen near Chinon with a train from Richelieu. **Les Nixon**

1.8. SNCF NARROW GAUGE LINES

There are three metre gauge lines in France operated by the SNCF, plus the Chemins de Fer de la Corse (Corsica) which is now owned by the SNCF.

1.8.1. SNCF LIGNE DE CERDAGNE (LE PETIT TRAIN JAUNE)

This line opened 1910–29 was electrified from opening at 850 V d.c. third rail. Running from Villefranche-de-Conflent to La Tour-de-Carol, a distance of 62 km, it traverses mountain scenery with extremely sharp curves and steep gradients and several spectacular bridges. The line was under threat of closure for several years and freight traffic ceased in 1974. However efforts to promote the tourist potential of the line seem to have been successful. All the stock was refurbished in 1962–8 and painted in the then current red and yellow railcar livery. Commencing in 1983 the stock underwent further refurbishment and painting in a mainly yellow livery. The depot is at Villefranche-de-Conflent, although stock is nominally allocated to Béziers where major overhauls are carried out. The Languedoc-Roussillon region is to buy some new panoramic EMUs for the line.

POWER CARS   ZBD

Formerly Midi EABDe 2-9/11/3/5–8. Cars marked * were built as trailers but were converted to motor cars in 1912/21. They were originally Midi ABDe 14/11/3/5–8 respectively. EABDe 5 replaced an accident victim.

Built: 1908–09.
Builder-Mech. Parts: Carde & Cie.   **Builder-Elec. Parts:** Sprague-Thomson.
Traction Motors: Four 66 kW.   **Accommodation:** –/40.
Weight: 30 tonnes.   **Length:** 14.904 (14.384*) m.
Wheel Arrangement: Bo-Bo.   **Max. Speed:** 55 km/h.

Note: Car 103 has not been refurbished and is used for storage at Villefranche-de-Conflent depot.

Z 102	Z 105 *	Z 108	Z 111 *	Z 115 *	Z 117 *
Z 103 (U)	Z 106	Z 109	Z 113 *	Z 116 *	Z 118 *
Z 104	Z 107				

TRAILERS   ZRB

Built: 1908–09. These are the surviving original cars not converted to motors (ex Midi ABDe 1–4).
Builders: Carde & Cie.
Accommodation: –/44 1T   **Weight:** 16 tonnes.
Length: 14.384 m.   **Max. Speed:** 55 km/h.

ZR 20001	ZR 20002	ZR 20003	ZR 20004

OPEN-TOP TRAILERS   ZRB

Built: 1912. These cars were originally roofed (ex Midi Be 30–4).
Builders: Carde & Cie.
Accommodation: –/72.   **Weight:** 11 tonnes.
Length: 10.50 m.   **Max. Speed:** 55 km/h.

ZR 20030	ZR 20031	ZR 20032	ZR 20033	ZR 20034

BALCONY TRAILERS   ZRB (*ZRBD)

Built: 1910–12. Cars obtained second-hand from the CF Economiques du Nord in 1936.
Builders: Decauville.
Accommodation: –/46 1T.   **Weight:** 15 tonnes.
Length: 13.37 m.   **Max. Speed:** 55 km/h.

ZR 20023*	ZR 20036	ZR 20037	ZR 20038	ZR 20039

1.8.2. SNCF LIGNE DE SAVOIE

This line, opened in 1901, is one of the steepest adhesion railways in the world. Electrified from opening at 750 V d.c. third rail, it extends from St. Gervais les Bains to Vallorcine, a distance of 33 km, where a connection is made with the Swiss Martigny-Châtelard Railway.

The original stock was unusual since all vehicles were powered and multiple working fitted (including wagons!). However freight operations ceased in 1970, the remaining wagons being in departmental use until withdrawn in 1986. Modern stock introduced in 1958 included trailer cars. The depot is at St. Gervais-les-Bains.

CLASS Z 600   ZABD

Built: 1958.
Builder-Mech. Parts: Decauville.   **Builder-Elec. Parts:** Oerlikon.
Continuous Rating: 802 kW.   **Accommodation:** 8/34.
Weight: 40.9 tonnes.   **Length:** 18.20 m.
Wheel Arrangement: Bo-Bo.   **Max. Speed:** 70 km/h.
Livery: Orange with grey band and grey roof.

| Z 601 | Z 603 | Z 605 | Z 606 | Z 607 | Z 608 |
| Z 602 | Z 604 | | | | |

Name: Z 601 CHAMONIX-MT BLANC

Z 691   ROTARY SNOWPLOUGH

Built: 1958.
Builder-Mech. Parts: SNCF.   **Builder-Elec. Parts:** Oerlikon.
Weight: 33.5 tonnes.   **Length:** 9.015 m.
Wheel Arrangement: 1-Bo.   **Max. Speed:** 40 km/h.
Livery: Orange with grey band and grey roof.

Z 691

CLASS Z 800   2-CAR UNITS (ZB+ZB)

These units were developed in order to allow through operation between the SNCF St. Gervais–Vallorcine line and Martigny in Switzerland via the Martigny Châtelard (MC) railway. This task is very complicated as there are sections electrified by third rail and others with overhead catenary plus rack-worked sections on the MC. The units have asynchronous-motored power bogies at each end. All are rack-fitted. There are five types of brakes – electro-pneumatic tread brakes, rheostatic and regenerative brakes, rack brakes and emergency electro-magnetic brakes. Features for the passenger are air-conditioning and panoramic windows. MC units are numbered Z 821/22 and Z 823/24 and classified BDeh 4/8. All five EMUs are maintained by SNCF at St. Gervais. The Rhone-Alpes region intends to order two more units without equipment for the MC line to replace the remaining Z 600 units.

Built: 1996/97.   **Systems:** 850 V d.c. third rail/overhead.
Builder-Mech. Parts: Vevey Technologies/SLM.   **Builder-Elec. Parts:** Adtranz.
Continuous Rating: 1000 kW.   **Accommodation:** –/48 + –/48.
Weight: 36 + 36 tonnes.   **Length:** 18.90 m + 18.90 m.
Rack system: Strub.   **Max. speed:** 70 km/h (16 km/h on rack).
Livery: Red and white with white stars.

| Z 801 Z 802 | Z 803 Z 804 | Z 805 Z 806 |

CLASS Z 20600   TRAILERS (ZRAB)

Intermediate trailers for Z 601–8.

Built: 1958.   **Builder:** Decauville.
Accommodation: 24/35.   **Weight:** 19.7 tonnes.
Length: 18.20 m.   **Max. Speed:** 70 km/h.
Livery: Orange with grey band and grey roof.

| ZR 20601 | ZR 20602 | ZR 20603 | ZR 20604 |

1.8.3. CHEMIN DE FER DU BLANC-ARGENT

This line, owned by the SNCF is operated by the above company. Formerly running between the towns in its title, it now operates a passenger service only between Salbris and Luçay le Mâle. The passenger stock has been modernised, but freight traffic ceased in 1989. The depot and workshops are located in Romorantin.

DIESEL LOCOS   C

Formerly steam locos 25/28, built by Blanc Misseron in 1901. Owned by BA.

Rebuilt: 1953.
Engine: Willème 517F8 (132 kW).
Weight: 17 tonnes.
Wheel Dia.: 1050 mm.

Builder: SNCF Périgueux Works.
Transmission: Mechanical.
Length: 8.45 m.
Max. Speed: 30 km/h.

BA 13 | BA 14

RAILCARS

CLASS X 200   XBD

The last survivor of 6 cars (X 201–206) transferred from the Réseau Breton in 1967. Reserve car.

Built: 1948.
Engine: Willème 517F8 (132 kW).
Accommodation: –/51 1T.
Length: 19.12 m.
Wheel Arrangement: 1A-A1.

Builder: De Dion Bouton.
Transmission: Mechanical.
Weight: 18 tonnes.
Max. Speed: 70 km/h.
Livery: Cream & red.

X 205

CLASS X 210   XBD

X 211/2 came from the PO Corrèze in 1967. All four cars were refurbished in 1983–4 and fitted with new engines,when X 213/4 were renumbered from X 223/1 respectively.

Built: 1950–51.
Engine: Poyaud 6L520S1 (185 kW).
Transmission: Hydro-mechanical. Voith DiWA D501.
Accommodation: –/54 1T.
Length: 18.535 m.
Wheel Arrangement: B-2.

Builder: Verney.

Weight: 21 tonnes.
Max. Speed: 85 km/h.
Livery: Blue.

X 211 | X 212 | X 213 | X 214

CLASS X 220   XBD

The last survivor in original condition of 4 cars (X 221–4) purchased new in 1950–1. Two others have been refurbished (see X 211–4). In reserve.

Built: 1951.
Engine: Willème 517F6 (103 kW).
Accommodation: –/53 1T.
Length: 18.535 m.
Wheel Arrangement: B-2.

Builder: Verney.
Transmission: Mechanical.
Weight: 18 tonnes.
Max. Speed: 80 km/h.
Livery: Blue.

X 224

CLASS X240   XBD

Delivered as part of the modernisation programme for passenger stock.

Built: 1983.
Engine: Poyaud 6LC 520S2 (175 kW).
Accommodation: –/52 1T.
Length: 18.28 m.
Wheel Arrangement: B-2.

Builder: CFD Montmirail/Socofer, Tours.
Transmission: Hydraulic. Voith T211r.
Weight: 25 tonnes.
Max. Speed: 85 km/h.
Livery: Cream & brown (X 241), blue (X 242).

X 241 ROMORANTIN-LANTHENAY | X 242 VALENÇAY

CLASS XR 700

Built: 1951.
Accommodation: –/57 1T.
Length: 12.975 m.
Livery: Blue.

TRAILERS (XRBD)

Builder: Verney.
Weight: 9.5 tonnes.
Max. Speed: 85 km/h.

All refurbished 1983–4. XR 701 is ex PO Corrèze 1967.

XR 701 | XR 702 | XR 703

CLASS X 74500   SIX-AXLE ARTICULATED UNITS

New Units on order. They feature an off-centre bogie so that the body sections will be of different lengths.Air conditioned. Panoramic windows.

Built: 2001.
Engine: MAN of 265 kW.
Accommodation: –/66 1T.
Weight: 45 t.
Wheel Arrangement: B-2-B.

Builder: CFD.
Transmission: Hydraulic. Voith T211.

Length:
Max. Speed:

Multiple working within class and with X 240.

X 74501 | X 74502 | X 74503 | X 74504 | X 74505

▲ **Chemin de Fer du Blanc-Argent.** Railcars X 213 and X 211 stand side-by-side at Romorantin.
David Haydock

1.8.4. CHEMINS DE FER CORSES (CORSICA)

The SNCF took over operation of this system on 01/01/83 after the last of a series of concessionary companies gave up. The main line runs from Bastia to Ajaccio (157 km) with a branch from Ponte Leccia to Calvi (73 km). The central section of the main line is particularly scenic. There is a depot and workshop at Casamozza, and a depot at Bastia.

DIESEL LOCOMOTIVES

001   B-B
Built: 1995.
Engine: Two Poyaud (310 kW).
Builder: CFD Industrie Type BB650.
Transmission: Hydraulic.

001

114   B-2
Nicknamed the "Submarine". Now stored at Cassamozza.
Built: 1958 using bogies from Billard A150D No. 114 (built 1938).
Builder: Bastia depot.
Engine: 75 kW.
Transmission: Mechanical.

114 (U)

CLASS BB 400   B-B
Built: 1963/6.
Engine: Two Poyaud (310 kW).
Builder: CFD.
Transmission: Hydromechanical.

404 was formerly Chemins de Fer de la Provence 403, and carries no number. It was bought in 1974.

404 | 405

DIESEL RAILCARS & TRAILERS

TRAILERS   XRBD
Rebuilt: 1977 by Garnero. Ex Billard A210D built 1935 (formerly X 104/5).
Wheel Arrangement: 2-2.
Weight: 13 t.
Accommodation: –/44 1T.
Length: 19.80 m.

R 104 | R 105

113   DRIVING TRAILER (Xrbdx)
The only survivor of a batch of six (111–6), this car was rebodied by Carde & Cie. in 1966, and converted to a driving trailer to run with 204 in 1987. Works between Calvi and Île Rousse.

Rebuilt: 1987. Ex Billard A150D built 1938.
Accommodation: -/37 1T.
Wheel Arrangement: 2-2.
Length: 14.50 m.
Max. Speed: 75 km/h.

113

CLASS 200   XBD
Originally a batch of eight. Seating is 2+1 except refurbished vehicles which are 2+2 and 202 which is 3+0!

Built: 1949–50.
Engine: Renault (195 kW).
Accommodation: –/28 1T, (–/40 1T r, –/24 1T *).
Wheel Arrangement: B-2.
Builder: Renault. Type ABH8.
Transmission: Mechanical.
Length: 19.50 m.
Max. Speed: 60 km/h.

m Fitted for working with driving trailer.
r Refurbished.

201 r | 202 *m | 204 m | 206 r | 207 r (U)

VARIOUS   TRAILERS (XRBD)

Built: 1938/49. Converted from power cars.   **Builder:** Billard type A80D.
Accommodation: –/28 1T (–/27 1T§, –/30 1T*). **Length:** 11.50 m.

Ex CFD Tarn 1966 (CFE Tramways de Seine et Marne 1966*). Rebodied except 212.

| 7 | | 210 | | 211 § | | 212 * |

CLASS X 240   VANS (XRD)

Built: 1938/49. Converted 1970 from power cars.
Builder: Billard type A80D.   **Length:** 11.50 m.

Ex PO Corrèze 1970.

| 242 | | 243 |

CLASS X 500

Departmental units for the Civil and Mechanical Engineering Depts respectively.

Built: 1938/38.   **Builder:** Billard. Type A150D6.
Engine: Deutz (75 kW).   **Length:** 13.35 m.
Wheel Arrangement: B-2.

503 was ex CFE Tramways de Seine et Marne 1966. 513 was ex CFD Tarn 1966.

| 503 (D) | | 513 (D) |

526   DRIVING TRAILER (XRBDx)

Converted from Billard type A150D6. Works between Calvi and Île Rousse.

Built: 1947.   **Builder:** Billard. Type A150D6.
Length: 13.35 m.

Ex tramways d'Ille et Villaine (until 1952) and Réseau Breton (until 1966).

526

CLASS X 2000   XB

Built: 1975–76.   **Builder:** CFD.
Engine: Two Poyaud (123 kW).   **Transmission:** Hydraulic.
Wheel Arrangement: B-B.   **Accommodation:** –/48 1T.
Length: 15.90 m.   **Max. Speed:** 85 km/h.

Originally numbered X 1201–5.

| X 2001 | | X 2002 | | X 2003 | | X 2004 | | X 2005 |

CLASS X 5000   XB

A longer and more powerful version of X 2000.

Built: 1981.   **Builder:** CFD.
Engines: Two Poyaud (179 kW).   **Transmission:** Hydraulic.
Accommodation: –/48 1T.
Weight: tonnes.   **Length:** 16.50 m.
Wheel Arrangement: B-B.   **Max. Speed:** 85 km/h.

| X 5001 | | X 5002 |

CLASS X 97050   XBD

Recently-built railcars for the Bastia–Ajaccio service. Multiple working fitted.

Built: 1989–90/2/7.   **Builder:** Soulé.
Engine: Two 6 cylinder SACM UD18H6R3 (177 kW) at 2250 r.p.m.
Transmission: Hydraulic. Voith T211r   **Accommodation:** –/44 1T.
Weight: 35.6 tonnes.   **Length:** 18.28 m.
Wheel Arrangement: B–B.   **Max. Speed:** 90 km/h.

| X 97051 | X 97053 | X 97054 | X 97055 | X 97056 | X 97057 |
| X 97052 | | | | | |

CLASS XR 9700   XRBDx

Driving trailers to work with Class X 97050.

Built: 1989–90/2/7.   **Builder:** Soulé.
Accommodation: –/54 1T.   **Weight:** 22.4 tonnes.
Length: 18.28 m.   **Max. Speed:** 90 km/h.

| XR 9701 | XR 9703 | XR 9704 | XR 9705 | XR 9706 | XR 9707 |
| XR 9702 | | | | | |

▲ **Chemins de Fer Corses.** CFD railcar X 5002 and rebodied trailer X 104 at Ponte Lecchia forming the 14.40 Bastia–Ajaccio on 23rd September 1991.   **Pete Moody**

2. RÉSEAU EXPRESS RÉGIONAL – LINES OPERATED BY RÉGIE AUTONOME DES TRANSPORTS PARISIENS (RATP)

RATP is the Paris transport operator which is in charge of running buses, two tramway routes, 14 metro lines and the Réseau Express Régional (RER) regional express network of suburban trains. The RER network now totals five lines – A to E. Operation of the RER is complicated by the involvement of both RATP and SNCF. SNCF is entirely responsible for operating lines C, D and E while the two operators share operation of lines A and B. When opened in 1969 and after, line A originally ran from Boissy St. Leger to St. Germain-en-Laye and was entirely operated by RATP with Type MS61 EMUs. These still operate, having all received a mid-life overhaul. Line B originally ran from Châtelet to St. Rémy-les-Chevreuse and was operated by RATP Class Z 23000 EMUs which have now disappeared. Both of these lines are electrified at 1500 V d.c. overhead. Line B was then joined to SNCF lines from Gare du Nord and, later, line A gained a branch to Poissy and Cergy over SNCF lines. Both service extensions required dual-voltage EMUs for operation under 25 kV a.c. 50 Hz. These were MI79 (MI = Matériel Interconnexion or intercon-nection stock) and MI84 stock which is included in the SNCF section as Class Z 8100. Renewal of Line A stock has now become necessary, the answer being MI2N double-deck stock. We include RATP EMUs for RER services here as they are not documented in any other publication. We also include RATP's small fleet of diesels for maintenance. We do not include Metro stock as it is fully documented in the excellent Paris Metro Handbook by Brian Hardy and published by Capital Transport.

ELECTRIC LOCOMOTIVES
TYPE 4900   Bo-Bo
The last of seven electric locos originally numbered 4901–4907. These locos are very similar looking to the Class Z 23000 EMUs used on the Sceaux line until the 1980s. 4901 has been withdrawn. Units 4902/3/6/7, which have been modernised, are used to haul trains of compo-nents between Rueil depot on line A and Massy depot on line B. 4904 shunts at Rueil and 4905 at Massy.

Built: 1935/36.
Builder: CGC.
Weight: 54 tonnes.
Wheel dia.: 1100 mm.
Livery: Yellow/black.

System: 1500 V d.c.
Power rating: 736 kW.
Length: 12.60 metres.
Max. Speed: 80 km/h light, 60 km/h with train.

4902	4903	4904	4905	4906	4907

DIESEL LOCOMOTIVES
TYPE C 61000   C
These shunters are the same as SNCF Class C 61000 of which 48 were once used in the Lille, Paris and Le Havre/Rouen areas, some of them with "calf" units doubling power. T 101 was bought direct by RATP, and the company bought another 9 from SNCF in 1973/78, numbered T 104–109 and T 130–133. Only three are now left. The locos tend to be used on maintenance trains in tunnels as they smoke less than Type BB 63500.

Built: 1946–48 (T 101 1950).
Engine: Sulzer (375 kW).
Weight: 51 tonnes.
Wheel dia.: 1400 mm.
Livery: Dark green/yellow.

Builder: CEM.
Transmission: Electric.
Length: 9.50 m.
Max. Speed: 60 km/h.

T 101 RU	T 105 (C 61025) BY	T 132 (C 61033) MY

TYPE Y 7400   B

These shunters are the basically the same as SNCF Class Y 7400 of which almost 500 are in service. They are used for shunting at their respective depots and to form works trains.

Built: 1969.
Engine: Poyaud 6PYT of 147 kW.
Weight: 32 tonnes.
Wheel Dia.: 1050 mm.
Livery: Orange/brown.

Builder: Moyse.
Transmission: Mechanical.
Length: 8.94 m.
Max. Speed: 60 km/h.

T 102 BY |T 103 RU

TYPE BB 63500   Bo-Bo

These locos are similar to SNCF Class BB 63500 but were bought second-hand in 1992 from the northern French coal mines (HBNPC), which also supplied the locos used by CFTA. The locos were refurbished by Fauvet-Girel in Lille but work carried out on three batches differed. T 160–163 only received a minimal overhaul and a repaint. T 165–167 were refurbished more extensively and a received a modified cab unit. Finally, T 168–170 were modernised like the previous batch but also received a turbocharger which increased their power output. RATP is considering upgrading all locos to the same standard. All can work in multiple with one another. The locos are used for works trains on the exterior sections of RER lines A and B.

Built: 1959–63.
Engine: SACM MGO V12A (442 kW) or MGO V12ASH (602 kW) (T 168–170).
Transmission: Electric.
Weight: 72–80 tonnes.
Wheel Dia.: 1050 mm.
Livery: Orange/brown.

Builder: Brissonneau & Lotz.
Length: 14.48 m.
Max. Speed: 80 km/h.

T 160 MY |T 162 BY |T 165 MY |T 167 MY |T 169 BY |T 170 BY
T 161 BY |T 163 MY |T 166 RU |T 168 RU

ELECTRIC MULTIPLE UNITS
TYPE MS61   3-CAR UNITS

These units are owned by RATP and operate only on Line A from Boissy-St.-Leger to St. Germain-en-Laye in trains of up to three units. Each unit is composed of an even and odd numbered Type M15000 power car and a Type AB18000 central composite trailer. Formations are relatively stable, but unlike MI79 and MI84 stock, can change from time to time. The units were built in five batches, with minor differences, coded A to E. Sets in the A and B batches, 15001–15124, have a different front end design to batches C to E. All of the A/B batch are allocated to Boissy-St-Leger (BY), the depot at the eastern end of Line A whilst the later units are allocated to Rueil Malmaison (RU) on the branch from Nanterre to St.-Germain-en-Laye. The exceptions are 15074 at RU and 15240 at BY. The original livery was two-tone blue but sets have had a mid-life overhaul and have been repainted in Paris red, white and blue (SNCF livery I). All units are equipped with the SACEM in-cab signalling system.

Built: 1966–80.
Builder-Mech. Parts: B&L/CIMT/ANF.
Traction Motors: Four TCO (200 kW) per power car.
Formation: Bo-Bo + 2-2 + Bo-Bo.
Accommodation: –/64 + 32/40 + –/64 & 16/76 fold down.
Weight: 40 + 32 + 40 tonnes.
Maximum Speed: 100 km/h.

Systems: 1500 V d.c. overhead.
Builder-Elec. Parts : TCO/MTE.

Length: 24.555 m + 24.110 m + 24.555 m.

15001 18044 15026 BY	15009 18002 15010 BY	15017 18019 15018 BY
15002 18001 15007 BY	15011 18004 15130 BY	15019 18038 15068 BY
15003 18041 15004 BY	15012 18018 15075 BY	15020 18034 15089 BY
15005 18020 15112 BY	15013 18026 15086 BY	15021 18057 15046 BY
15006 18045 15035 BY	15014 18009 15039 BY	15022 18022 15023 BY
15008 18053 15099 BY	15015 18024 15016 BY	15024 18023 15087 BY

15027	18054	15098	BY	15100	18025	15101	BY	15176	18100	15193	RU
15025	18033	15028	BY	15095	18063	15096	BY	15175	18086	15216	RU
15027	18054	15098	BY	15100	18025	15101	BY	15176	18100	15193	RU
15029	18012	15030	BY	15102	18015	15105	BY	15177	18101	15178	RU
15031	18061	15124	BY	15104	18011	15123	BY	15179	18102	15180	RU
15032	18035	15045	BY	15106	18059	15107	BY	15181	18103	15182	RU
15033	18006	15078	BY	15109	18052	15240	BY	15183	18104	15184	RU
15034	18056	15055	BY	15110	18032	15111	BY	15185	18105	15186	RU
15036	18060	15113	BY	15114	18062	15115	BY	15187	18081	15188	RU
15037	18016	15038	BY	15116	18058	15117	BY	15189	18106	15190	RU
15040	18007	15079	BY	15118	18042	15119	BY	15191	18083	15192	RU
15041	18047	15042	BY	15126	18108	15131	RU	15194	18073	15195	RU
15043	18036	15044	BY	15127	18066	15148	RU	15196	18074	15197	RU
15047	18013	15048	BY	15128	18071	15129	RU	15198	18085	15199	RU
15049	18021	15050	BY	15132	18068	15133	RU	15200	18076	15201	RU
15051	18050	15052	BY	15134	18128	15135	RU	15202	18077	15203	RU
15053	18046	15054	BY	15136	18099	15173	RU	15204	18078	15205	RU
15056	18029	15057	BY	15137	18069	15138	RU	15206	18079	15207	RU
15058	18049	15081	BY	15139	18067	15140	RU	15208	18080	15209	RU
15059	18003	15130	BY	15141	18110	15142	RU	15210	18082	15211	RU
15060	18040	15061	BY	15143	18065	15144	RU	15212	18088	15213	RU
15062	18043	15063	BY	15145	18072	15146	RU	15214	18107	15215	RU
15064	18008	15103	BY	15147	18084	15254	RU	15217	18118	15218	RU
15065	18005	15076	BY	15149	18087	15150	RU	15219	18127	15220	RU
15066	18048	15067	BY	15151	18116	15250	RU	15222	18075	15227	RU
15069	18031	15122	BY	15152	18109	15245	RU	15223	18123	15224	RU
15070	18017	15071	BY	15153	18089	15154	RU	15225	18111	15226	RU
15072	18010	15229	BY	15155	18090	15156	RU	15228	18112	15239	RU
15073	18051	15108	BY	15157	18091	15158	RU	15230	18125	15253	RU
15074	18092	15125	RU	15159	18124	15160	RU	15233	18117	15234	RU
15077	18055	15082	BY	15161	18093	15162	RU	15235	18115	15236	RU
15080	18119	15083	BY	15163	18094	15164	RU	15237	18120	15238	RU
15084	18027	15085	BY	15165	18095	15166	RU	15241	18121	15242	RU
15088	18030	15121	BY	15167	18096	15168	RU	15243	18064	15244	RU
15090	18039	15091	BY	15169	18097	15170	RU	15246	18126	15249	RU
15092	18028	15093	BY	15171	18098	15172	RU	15247	18122	15248	RU
15094	18014	15097	BY	15174	18070	15221	RU	15251	18113	15252	RU

TYPE MI2N   5-CAR DOUBLE-DECK UNITS

These units were designed as a common project for RATP and SNCF whose units are Class Z 22500 (see SNCF section of book). The only significant differences are that RATP units have three power cars instead of two, in order to give better acceleration on RER line A where a two-minute frequency operates in the rush-hour, and that there is stair access to the upper level from all doors in the RATP sets. 17 units have been delivered. RATP has an option for a further 23. RATP are now nicknaming these units "Alteo".

For details see SNCF Class Z 22500 except:

Total power: 3500 kW.
Accommodation: 48/480 seats total.

Formation: ZRB + ZB + ZB + ZAB + ZRB.
Weight: 288 tonnes total.

All trains equipped with SACEM computer aided driving system.

1501	2501	3501	2502	1502	BY	1519	2519	3510	2520	1520	BY
1503	2503	3502	2504	1504	BY	1521	2521	3511	2522	1522	BY
1505	2505	3503	2506	1506	BY	1523	2521	3512	2524	1524	BY
1507	2507	3504	2508	1508	BY	1525	2523	3513	2526	1526	BY
1509	2509	3505	2510	1510	BY	1527	2525	3514	2528	1528	BY
1511	2511	3506	2512	1512	BY	1529	2527	3515	2530	1530	BY
1513	2513	3507	2514	1514	BY	1531	2529	3516	2532	1532	BY
1515	2515	3508	2516	1516	BY	1533	2531	3517	2534	1534	BY
1517	2517	3509	2518	1518	BY						

3. PRIVATE RAILWAYS

The following gives details of French private railways (other than preserved lines).

3.1. CHEMINS DE FER DE LA PROVENCE   CP

This is the only non-SNCF adhesion non-preserved passenger railway left in France. It runs from Nice Gare du Sud to Digne, a distance of 151 km, and is the last remnant of the Chemins de Fer du Sud whose network included lines from Nice to Vence, Grasse, Draguignan & Meyrargues and from Saint Raphael to Toulon via St. Tropez. Depots are at Nice and Digne, with steam locos based at Puget-Théniers. There is a works at Lingostière.

Gauge: 1000 mm.
Liveries: The standard livery is white with a blue window band. Other liveries are as follows:
N   New livery of white with a blue window band and a yellow stripe below the window.
R   Old livery of white with a red window band.

DIESEL LOCOMOTIVES

T62   Bo-Bo
Built: 1951.   **Builder:** Brissonneau & Lotz.
Engine: Two Renault (220 kW).   **Transmission:** Electric.
Weight: 48.5 tonnes.

T 62

CLASS BB 400   B-B
Ex PO Corrèze in 1971. Dumped at Lingostière. The remains of BB 402 are also there.

Built: 1962.   **Builder:** CFD.
Engine: Two Poyaud (152 kW).   **Transmission:** Mechanical.
Weight: 44 tonnes.

BB 401 (U)

CLASS BB 1200   B-B
Ex FEVE 1404 in 1992. A metre gauge version of the DB V 160 design.

Built: 1966.   **Builder:** Henschel.
Engine: SACM BZSHR (900 kW).   **Transmission:** Hydraulic.
Weight: 56 tonnes.   **Max. Speed:** 25 km/h.

BB 1200

RAILCARS

CLASS X 200   XD
Ex-Vivarais. 213 & 214 still exist on the Vivarais.

Built: 1937.   **Builder:** Billard. Type A 150 D.
Engine: Berliet (172 kW).   **Transmission:** Mechanical.
Wheel Arrangement: B-2.   **Weight:** 14.5 tonnes.

212 (U)

CLASS X 300 SERIES 1   XB
Built: 1972.   **Builder:** CFD.
Engine: Two MAN of 123 kW.   **Transmission:** Hydromechanical.
Accommodation: –/48 1T (*–/46 1T & coffee machine).
Weight: 22 tonnes.
Wheel Arrangement: 1A-A1.   **Max. Speed:** 75 km/h.

These units have flat ends.

X 301 (SY 01) **R** | X 302 (SY 02) * | X 303 (SY 03) | X 304 (SY 04)

CLASS X 300 SERIES 2 XB

Built: 1977.
Engine: Two MAN (123 kW).
Accommodation: –/50 1T.
Wheel Arrangement: 1A-A1.

Builder: CFD.
Transmission: Hydromechanical.
Weight: 23 tonnes.
Max. Speed: 75 km/h.

These units have angled ends.

X 305   (SY 05) **N** | X 306   (SY 06)

CLASS ZZ XB

The survivors of twelve cars (ZZ 1-12) built 1935-45. ZZ 21/2 were formerly ZZ 1/2. The cars were allocated new numbers in the X 320 series, but were never renumbered.

Built: 1935–42.
Engine: Poyaud (243 kW).
Accommodation: –/44 1T (§–/56 1T).
Wheel Arrangement: B-2.

Builder: Renault. Type ABH 1 (ABH 5*).
Transmission: Mechanical.
Weight: 32 (*31) tonnes.
Max. Speed: 60 km/h.

ZZ 6   § | ZZ 8   * (U) | ZZ 10   **R** * | ZZ 22

The remains of ZZ 3 and ZZ 21 are dumped at Lingostière.

CLASS X 350 XBD+Bx

This two-car unit was built for the "Alpazur" service, but is now in general use. It is unreliable and cannot keep time on the Nice–Digne run because of its low power/weight ratio.

Built: 1984.
Engine: One Poyaud (365 kW).
Accommodation: –/56 1T + –/65 1T.
Wheel Arrangement: BoBo + 2-2.

Builder: Soulé/Garnéro.
Transmission: Hydraulic. Voith.
Weight: 40 + 31.7 tonnes.
Max. Speed: 75 km/h.

X 351 + XR 1351

CLASS XR 1330 TRAILERS

Built: 1937–58.
Accommodation: –/32 1T.

Builder: Billard. Type R 210.
Weight: 15 tonnes (9.1 tonnes p).

p Used as a parcels van.
r Rebodied by CP Lingostière Works.
v ex Vivarais 1969.

XR 1331 (RL 1) **N** r | XR 1333 (RL 3) **W** p | XR 1337 (RL 7) **N** rv

The remains of trailer XR 1336 which was rebodied by Garnéro and four-wheeled ex-CF du Tarn trailer RL 4 are dumped at Lingostoère.

CLASS XR 1340 HAULED STOCK

Built: 1951–53.
Accommodation: –/52 1T.
Wheel Arrangement: 2-2.

Builder: CP Lingostière Works.
Weight: 18 tonnes.

XR 1341 (AT 1) **B** | XR 1342 (AT 2) **B** | XR 1343 (AT 3) **B** | XR 1344 (AT 4) **B**

PRESERVED STEAM LOCOMOTIVES

No.	Type	Builder	Built	Notes
E 211§	2-4-6-0T (1BCh4vt)	Henschel	1923	ex CP (Portugal) (U)
E 327*	4-6-0T (2Cn4t)	Fives-Lille	1909	ex Réseau Breton

* Preserved by FACS (Fédération des Amis des Chemins de Fer Secondaires).
§ Preserved by Groupe d'Étude des Chemins de Fer de la Provence.

Chemins de Fer de la Provence.

▲ Renault type ABH1 railcar No.
ZZ 22 stands outside Nice Gare CP
on 11th June 1999.   **Peter Fox**

▶ Henschel loco BB 1200 (ex-
FEVE) on a permanent way train at
Mézel-Chateauredon on 14th June
1999.   **Peter Fox**

3.2. CHEMIN DE FER DE LA RHUNE

This rack line is the last remnant of the once extensive Voies Ferrées Départementales du Midi
metre gauge system. Running from St. Ignace to La Rhune, it has been isolated from other
railways since the closure of the line to St. Ignace in 1936. The line climbs into the Pyrénées
giving views of the Basque coast. Electrified since opening in 1924 at 3000 V 50 Hz three-phase,
the original locos are still in use together with others from the similar closed line at Luchon. The
line can be reached by bus from St. Jean de Luz. Now managed by CFTA (see below).

Gauge: 1000 mm.

4 WHEEL RACK LOCOS

Built: 1912–15.
Builder-Mech. Parts: SLM.
Power: 240 kW.
Length: 5050 mm.

Builder-Elec. Parts: Brown Boveri.
Weight: 12 tonnes.
Max. Speed: 8.5 km/h.

* ex Luchon–Superbagnères 1966.

1 |2 |3 * |4 * (U) |5 * |6

3.3. CHEMIN DE FER DE CHAMONIX AU MONTENVERS

This rack line, opened 1908-09 climbs into amazing mountain and glacier scenery. The 5 km line was electrified in 1954 at 11 kV ac 50 Hz. However diesel traction is used for works trains and in emergency and also for extra trains at peak periods.

Gauge: 1000 mm.

DIESEL LOCOS   1-B

These locos work with articulated coaches 61–63.

Built: 1967/72*.   **Builder:** SLM.
Engine: Poyaud A12-150 Se (485 kW or 520 kW*).
Transmission: Hydraulic.
Weight: 23.3 tonnes.   **Length:** 7.50 m.
Driving Wheel Dia: 790 mm.   **Max. Speed:** 21 km/h.

31 |32 * |33 *

ELECTRIC RAILCARS

These railcars have driving cabs at the lower end only. They normally work coupled to trailers 51–56. Classified by the Swiss system as Bhe 4/4.

Built: 1954/60*/79§.
Builder-Mech. Parts: SLM.   **Builder-Elec. Parts:** TCO.
Power: 475 kW.   **Accommodation:** –/84 (–/80*§).
Weight: 29.5 tonnes.   **Length:** 15.37 (15.94*§) m.
Wheel Arrangement: Bo-Bo.   **Max. Speed:** 20 km/h.

41 |42 |43 |44 |45 * |46 §

PRESERVED STEAM LOCOMOTIVES

Three of the eight steam locomotives used on the line before electrification still survive at Chamonix:

No.	Type	Builder	Built	Notes
6	0-4-2T (B1zzh2t)	SLM	1923	
7	0-4-2T (B1zzh2t)	SLM	1926	stored
8	0-4-2T (B1zzh2t)	SLM	1927	for spares

◀ **Chemins de Fer de Chamonix au Montenvers.** Railcar 45 plus trailer 55 at Chamonix on 11th August 1995. **Pete Moody**

3.4. TRAMWAY DU MONT BLANC

This rack line in the Savoy Alps was opened in 1909–14 between St. Gervais les Bains and Glacier Bionnassay, but never achieved its intended terminus closer to Mont Blanc. The 12 km line was electrified in 1957 at 11 kV a.c. 50 Hz. The depot is located at St. Gervais.

Gauge: 1000 mm.

RACK RAILCARS

These cars have driving cabs at the lower end only. They normally work with a trailer coupled at the upper end. the cars do not carry any numbers, but are identifiable by their different liveries.

Built: 1956.
Builder-Mech. Parts: SLM/Decauville.   **Builder-Elec. Parts:** TCO.
One hour Rating: 475 kW.   **Accommodation:** –/84.
Weight: 12 tonnes.   **Length:** 15.37 m.
Wheel Arrangement: Bo-Bo.   **Max. Speed:** 20 km/h.

blue/yellow
yellow/blue
orange/cream

PRESERVED STEAM LOCOMOTIVES

Three of the six steam locomotives used on the line before electrification still survive:

No.	Type	Builder	Built	Notes
2	0-4-0T (Bzn2t)	SLM	1906	Evires
3	0-4-0T (Bzn2t)	SLM	1909	St. Gervais (stored in depot)
4	0-4-0T (Bzn2t)	SLM	1909	St. Gervais (stored in depot)

▲ **Tramway du Mont Blanc.** The orange and cream set at St. Gervais-les-Bains on 11th August 1995.
Pete Moody

3.5. RÉGIE DÉPARTMENTALE DES TRANS-PORTS DES BOUCHES-DU-RHÔNE

This railway operates a number of freight-only lines between Marseille and Avignon. Locos are yellow with red stripes and labelled "RDT 13" – 13 is the number of the Bouches-du-Rhône département.

Pas-des-Lanciers–Bel Air-La Mède (14 km).
Arles–Fontvieille (8 km).
Tarascon–St Rémy-de-Provence (13 km).
Barbantane-Rognognas–Plan d'Orgon (23 km).

Gauge: 1435 mm.
Depots: Arles, Marignane.

CLASS 50   Bo

Shunters which can operate in multiple on heavy trains.

Built: 1957–62.   **Builder:** CEM/Fauvet Girel.
Engine: **Transmission:** Electric.
Weight: 33–38 tonnes.   **Length:**

| 51 | |53 | |54 | |55 | |56 | |57 |
| 52 | | | | | | | | | | |

CLASS 300   Bo

Built: 1958–60.   **Builder:** CEM/Fauvet Girel.
Engine: **Transmission:** Electric.
Weight: 35 tonnes.   **Length:**

301 |302

CLASS 1200   Bo-Bo

These locos are similar to the SNCF Class BB 63500 but with more powerful engines. Despite this, two or three locos in multiple are used on heavy tank trains from La Mède refinery to Pas-des-Lanciers SNCF station.

Built: 1964 (1201–03), 1969 (1204).   **Builder:** Brissonneau & Lotz.
Engine: MGO ASHR or BSHR 16-cylinder (1200 h.p.).
Transmission: Electric.
Weight: 64 tonnes.   **Length:** 14.68 m.
Wheel Dia.: 1050 mm.   **Max. Speed:** 80 km/h.

Equipped for multiple operation.

1201 |1202 |1203 |1204

CLASS 1400   Bo-Bo

Built: 1978.   **Builder:** Moyse.
Engine: SACM AGO (1030 kW).   **Transmission:** Electric.
Weight: **Length:**

1401

3.6. VOIES FERRÉES DES LANDES   VFL

This railway, now taken over by SNCF but with special status, operates freight-only branches off the SNCF Bordeaux-Dax line. Several have been closed and VFL has taken over wagonload services from Mont-de-Marsan to Roquefort and Hagetmau as well as on the main line to Labouheyre.

Ychoux–Lipostey Zone Industrielle (2 km).
Laluque–Tartas (14 km).

Gauge: 1435 mm.
Depot: Morcenx.
Livery: Red and grey.

CLASS BB 01   BB

Built: 1957.   **Builder:** CFD.
Engine: **Transmission:** Mechanical.

BB 01

CLASS Y 01   B

Usually found at Dax. Purchased 1974 from CFD.

Details as SNCF Class Y 7400, except:

Built: 1967.   **Builder:** De Dietrich.

Y 01 | Y 02

CLASS BB 63500   Bo-Bo

Purchased from SNCF in 1999 (1996*). Still carry these numbers.

For details see SNCF Class BB 63500.

BB 63540 | BB 63622* | BB 63795

CLASS BB 71000   BB

Purchased from SNCF in 1988/9. These plus the BB 63500 are used on daily trip freights from Mont-de-Marsan.

Built: 1965–6.   **Builder:** Fives/Lille/CFD.
Engine: Poyaud V12 (615 kW).   **Transmission:** Mechanical.
Weight: 55 tonnes.   **Length:** 11.85 m.
Wheel Dia.: 860 mm.   **Max. Speed:** 80 km/h.

BB 71003 | BB 71011

3.7. SOCIÉTÉ GÉNÉRALE DE CHEMINS DE FER ET DE TRANSPORTS AUTOMOBILES   CFTA

This is a light railway organisation, part of the Vivendi group (formerly CGEA) which owns or leases the following lines on behalf of SNCF:

- Paimpol–Guingamp (36 km). Guingamp–Carhaix (53 km). These lines were formerly part of the metre-gauge Réseau Breton which was converted to standard gauge in 1967, although the section from Paimpol to Guingamp had been dual gauge since 1924.
- Gray–Is-sur-Tille (42 km). Gray–Fresne St. Mamès. (28 km).
- Troyes–Mussy-sur-Seine (45 km). Brion-sur-Ource–Châtillon-sur-Seine–Nuits-sous-Ravières. (45 km).
- Clamecy–Tamnay-Châtillon–Cercy la Tour (75 km). Clamecy–Nevers (70 km). Clamecy–Entrains-sur-Nohain (20 km). Tamnay-Châtillon–Château Chinon. (22 km).
- Longueville–Provins–Villiers St. Georges (25 km). Mézy-Montmirail (24 km).
- Sézanne–Anglure (19 km). Esternay–Sézanne–Connantre (29 km).

Gauge: 1435 mm.
Depots: Carhaix, Châtillon, Clamecy.   **Main works:** Gray.
CFTA has made do over the years with second hand locomotives. It took delivery of a batch of surplus diesels from the Houillères du Bassin du Nord et du Pas de Calais (HBNPC – northern France coal field) and for its lines in Brittany acquired its first newly built stock for many years in the shape of three four-wheeled diesel railcars. All locos are in blue livery with red lining. In the late 1990s CFTA was expanding into servicing industrial branches and has thus acquired a large fleet of shunters which we cannot document here. In addition, the company occasionally hires in diesel locos from preservation groups in order to fulfil occasional track maintenance contracts.

CLASS BB 4000   Bo-Bo
These locos were originally built for the US Army Transportation Corps (USATC). They went on to operate for the Chemins de Fer Économiques de la Gironde. Other members of the class are still in service – BB 4028 with the CF des Landes de Gascogne at Sabres and BB 4033 at Guîtres with Train Touristique Guîtres–Marcenais.

Built: 1946.   **Builder:** General Electric.
Engines: Two Baudouin (235 kW).   **Weight:** 67 tonnes.

BB 4032   Gray | BB 4036   Gray

CLASS BB 4500   BB
31 locos out of fleet of 109 were purchased from HBNPC at the beginning of the 1990s. Four were cannibalised and scrapped and four more retained for spares. The other 23 were over-hauled and converted at Gray from 1990 to 1995. After initial light overhauls producing Class 4500, CFTA decided to add turbochargers, increasing power, as well as equipping locos for multiple operation. BB 4500 locos have neither. In 1999 4501/3/4 were on hire at the ore loading terminal in Dunkerque docks. Details are generally as SNCF Class BB 63500 except:

Built: 1959–63.   **Builder:**
Engine: SACM MGO A (442 kW).

BB 4501 Gray	BB 4503 Gray	BB 4510 Gray
BB 4502 Gray	BB 4504 Gray	

CLASS BB 4800   Bo-Bo
As Class BB 4500 but with turbochargers, pushing up power to 825 h.p. Equipped for multiple operation. Purchased from HBNPC. For details see SNCF BB 63500.

Built: 1960–63.   **Builder:** Brissonneau & Lotz.

BB 4801	Sézanne	BB 4807	Clamecy	BB 4813	Is-sur-Tille
BB 4802	Sézanne	BB 4808	Clamecy	BB 4814	Provins
BB 4803	Châtillon	BB 4809	Clamecy	BB 4815	Châtillon
BB 4804	Châtillon	BB 4810	Clamecy	BB 4816	Châtillon
BB 4805	Clamecy	BB 4811	Clamecy	BB 4817	Carhaix
BB 4806	Clamecy	BB 4812	Clamecy	BB 4818	Clamecy

OTHER LOCOMOTIVES

BB 551   Built CFD 1962. Two Baudouin engines of 315 h.p. each.
Now shunting Lavera refinery near Marseille.

Y 6232   As LOCMAs ex SNCF X 6200. Gray.

DIESEL MULTIPLE UNITS
CLASS X 97150   XBD

France's first one-person operated railcars for Guingamp–Carhaix and Guingamp–Paimpol. Known as type 'A2E' (Autorail à 2 essieux).

Built: 1990.
Engine: Cummins (210 kW).
Accommodation: –/38 1T.
Weight: 26.5 tonnes.
Wheel Arrangement: A-A.
Livery: White and green ("Région Bretagne").

Builder: Soulé.
Transmission: Hydraulic.

Length: 15.57 m.
Max. Speed.: 90 km/h.

X 97151	X 97152	X 97153

OTHER Dmus

Used on same service as X 97150 at peak times.

X 2416   ex SNCF. For details, see SNCF Class X 2400.
X 2423   ex SNCF. For details, see SNCF Class X 2400.
X 2429   ex SNCF. Kept at Carhaix for spares.
X 2882   ex SNCF. For details, see SNCF Class X 2800
X 4051   ex SNCF. "Picasso" railcar. See Preserved DMUs for details.
XR 8264   ex SNCF. DMU trailer.
XR 8292   ex SNCF. DMU trailer.

3.8. CHEMINS DE FER DÉPARTEMENTAUX   CFD

CFD is what remains of a much larger operator of regional light railways. The company now only operates the Avallon–Autun line (87 km) on behalf of SNCF. The line is of great interest to British readers as the company acquired four British Rail Class 20 diesels in 1993 for freight services. One multiple pair is used on the Monday–Friday Cravant-Bazarnes–La Roche-en-Brénil return freight which extends to Saulieu on Mondays and Thursdays. The depot is at Autun.

CLASS 20   Bo-Bo

Built: 1957–68.
Builder: English Electric/Robert Stephenson & Hawthorn.
Engine: EE 8SVT Mk. II (746 kW).
Weight: 73.5 tonnes.
Max. T.E.: 187 kN.
Wheel Dia.: 1092 mm.

Transmission: Electric.

Length: 14.25 m.
Max. Speed: 100 km/h.

2001 (20035)	2002 (20063)	2003 (20139)	2004 (20228)

3.9. CHEMIN DE FER DE LA MURE

This line, electrified at 2400 V d.c. overhead, originally extended from St Georges de Commiers to Corps with several short branches. Most of the system was electrified from 1903, but closures commenced in 1936, and all passenger services ceased in 1950. The section to La Mure survived as a coal carrier. During recent years tourist trains have commenced, and this is now the sole traffic with the closure of the colliery. The second generation of electric locomotives are the principle motive power, but there is an assortment of other stock from various sources.

Gauge: 1000 mm.
Livery: Red (except T9 which is green).

SÉCHERON LOCOS   Bo-Bo

These locos can haul 360 tonne-trains downhill and 175 ton-trains uphill. When delivered, these locomotives could operate under two d.c.-voltage systems: +1200 V/0 V/ −1200 V d.c. (two wires), and second, 0 V/2400 V d.c. (one wire). On the roof four twin-arm pantographs were installed (two at each end). They were "high tech" for their time having suspended traction motors and flexible drive.

Built: 1932.
Builder-Mech. Parts: ANF.   **Builder-Elec. Parts:** Secheron.
Weight: 60 tonnes.   **Length:** 12 m.
Power: 690 kW (920 h.p.).   **Max. Speed:** 40 km/h.
Braking Systems: vacuum, rheostatic, and magnetic track.

T6	ST. GEORGES DE COMMIERS
T7	LA MURE D'ISÈRE
T8	
T9	
T10	

THOMSON-BUIRE ELECTRIC RAILCARS

These electric railcars were built for the La Mure–Gap section. These were designed for passenger trains and sundries traffic. They could haul 300 tonne trains at a minimum speed of 14 km/h on a 6.5% gradient.

Built: 1913–1927
Builder-Mech. Parts: Chantiers de La Buire.
Builder-Elec. Parts: Compagnie Française Thomson-Houston (later Alsthom).
Traction Motors: Four 75 kW (100 h.p.).   **Wheel Arrangement:** Bo-Bo.
Weight: 42 tonnes.   **Length:** 16 m.

A1 (U)	A3 (U)	A5 (U)

SWS ELECTRIC RAILCARS

These railcars were built for the the Nyon–St. Cergue–Morez Railway in Switzerland as Class ABDe4/4 where they worked until 1984. They were transferred to the SG La Mure between 1985 and 1993. Designed for operation under 2200 V d.c. they were modified with new pantographs and additional resistors on the roof.

Built: 1914–18.
Builder-Mech. Parts: Brown-Boveri.   **Builder-Elec. Parts:** SWS.
Tracton Motors: Four 75 kW (100 h.p.).   **Accommodation:** −/50.
Weight: 32 tonnes.   **Length:** 16.4 m.
Wheel Arrangement: Bo-Bo.   **Braking Systems:** air and electric.

1 (S)	5	T10 (U)	11 (U)

BRISSONNEAU & LOTZ LOCOMOTIVES   B-B

In 1984, the Isère Department gave two diesel locos to the line which had worked on the Voies Ferrées du Dauphiné (VFD) until 1964. They had been out of use for 20 years, and were transfered to St Georges de Commiers to serve as assisting engines (in case of major electrical problems). They can haul 300 tonne trains on the level, or 120 tonne trains on a 1 in 80 gradient. They belong to a series of ten machines built after the Second World War. Two other locos of the same type are still in service on the CP (see section 3.1.) and on the Chemin de Fer du Jura in Switzerland (Gm 4/4 508).

Built: 1951.   **Builder:** Brissonneau & Lotz.
Engines: Two Renault 12-cylinder of 224 kW (300 h.p.) at 1500 r.p.m.
Weight: 50 tonnes.   **Max. Speed:** 60 km/h.

Multiple working within class.

T2 (U) |T4 (S)

DECAUVILLE RAILCAR

This vehicle can haul 240 tonnes on the level or 30 tonnes on a gradient of 2.7% at a maximum speed of 8 km/h. It is used by the permanent way department.

Built: 1966.   **Builder:** Decauville.
Engine: 4 cylinders.   **Accommodation:** –/18.
Transmission: Mechanical. Chain drive to each axle.
Weight: 7 tonnes.   **Length:** 7.1 m.
Wheel Arrangement: A-A.   **Max. Speed:** 50 km/h.

Unnumbered

▲ **Chemins de La Mure.** Sécheron loco T7 "LA MURE D'ISÈRE"at Viaduc de Vaulx on 23rd May1998 during the Today's Railways/TBR "Taste of France" tour.   **Peter Fox**

3.10. HOUILLÈRES DU BASSIN DE LORRAINE   HBL

Houilleres du Bassin de Lorraine (HBL) is the network of railways serving the coal mines in the Lorraine area of north-east France. The present 210 km network consists of a 50 km double track main line parallelling the electrified SNCF line from Creutzwald to Béning and Béning to Forbach, with branches serving mines and factories. The network hauled 9 million tonnes in 1995, employs 450 staff and operates 24 hours a day although operations are reduced on Saturdays and almost non-existant on Sundays. Trains are often hauled by two locos in multiple and can be banked by a third machine. Until September 1977, HBL operated passenger trains between sites but these have been replaced by buses except one, between Reumaux and Merlebach Nord which is in Germany. This was operated by a Picasso railcar until 1992 when it was replaced by a single coach powered by a shunter. Although there are three different loco types, all have the same power unit and can be used in multiple with each other. Livery for all locos is dark green.

Depots: La Houve, Carling, Merlebach, Petite Rosselle.
Works: Petite Rosselle.

BB 01–16   Bo-Bo

These locos are basically the same as ex NS Class 2400 which became SNCF Class 62400. BB 14–16 are equipped with remote-control equipment for use at the washing plant at Freyming, signalled by the suffix T.

Built: 1955–63.
Engine: SACM MGO V 12 A (441 kW).
Weight: 70 tonnes.
Wheel dia.: 1000 mm.

Builder: Alsthom.
Transmission: Electric.
Length: 12.518 m.
Max. Speed: 50 km/h.

01	04	07	10	13	15 T
02	05	08	11	14 T	16 T
03	06	09	12		

BB 20–35   B-B

These locos have monomotor bogies with chain drive to the axles giving them a characteristic noise. The first two locos have a different gear ratio giving them a lowere maximum speed.

Built: 1965–66.
Engine: SACM MGO V 12 A (441 kW).
Weight: 83 tonnes.
Wheel dia.: 1000 mm.

Builder: CEM-Fauvet Girel.
Transmission: Electric.
Length: 12.44 m.
Max. Speed: 42 km/h (* 35 km/h).

20	23	26	29	32	34
21	24	27	30	33	35
22	25	28	31		

BB 40–51   Bo-Bo

These locos are almost identical to SNCF Class BB 63500 and only arrived on the HBL network in 1969/70 after becoming surplus in the Nord-Pas-de-Calais area.

Built: 1958–60.
Engine: SACM MGO V 12 A (441 kW).
Weight: 72 tonnes (* 82 tonnes).
Wheel dia.: 1050 mm.

Builder: Brissonneau & Lotz.
Transmission: Electric.
Length: 14.68 m.
Max. Speed: 50 km/h.

m equipped for multiple working operation.

40	42	44 m	46	48	50
41 *	43 m	45 m	47	49	51

M 70–76   Bo

These shunters consist of two batches with different engines – 70–72 were originally numbered 3–5 whilst 73-76 were originally 1009–1013. 73 is normally based at Merlebach shunting the wagon works and in reserve for the passenger train to Merlebach Nord. Others are based at Carling Poste 12.

Built: 1958–62.
Engine: Moyse V8B (210 kW) or Daimler-Benz OM 442LA (210 kW).
Transmission: Electric.
Weight: 35 tonnes.

Builder: Moyse.
Max. Speed: 32 km/h.
Length: 7.28 m.

70	72	73	74	75	76
71					

81/82   Bo+Bo

These are double units consisting of a shunter plus cabless "mule". The locos were originally numbered Y 50 + Y 50T and Y 51 + Y 51T. Unlike the rest of the fleet, the locos are in yellow livery. They are used at the VAC and at Carling coking plant.

Built: 19 .
Engine: Berliet.

Builder: Moyse.
Transmission: Electric.

BNY 81 + BNT 81 |BNY 82 + BNT 82

4. EX-SNCF LOCOMOTIVES IN INDUSTRIAL USE

Many SNCF locomotives have been sold to industrial concerns for further use. In some cases they still carry their SNCF numbers. The following covers all known locomotives except for those covered in other sections. The number in brackets is the French "département". The author thanks Eric Dunkling and Keith Clingan of the Industrial Railway Society for much of the information on shunters here. Further news and observations are welcome.

Number	Location	Notes
BB 13044	Eurotunnel, Coquelles.	Stationary transformer
C 61037	Béghin-Say, Sermaize les Bains (51).	
BB 63195	Potasses d'Alsace, Richwiller.	
BB 63213	ZI de la Martinerie, Déols.	
BB 63218	Ciments Lafarge, Le Teil.	Green/white
BB 63220	Ciments Lafarge, La Couronne.	Green
BB 63230	ASUEPA, Artix.	Green
BB 63242	Bocahut quarry, Fourmies.	Blue
BB 63245	Decoexa, Irún (Spain).	Blue
BB 63246	Aciéries de l'Atlantique, Tarnos.	Blue
BB71001	Enterprises Méditerranée (Semer), Rivesaltes.	White/blue
BB71006	CDRA, St Gaudens (31).	Blue/white/yellow
BB71008	Cipha, Le Havre (Terminal Pondereux).	
BB71014	Halavau, Neuilly ?	
BB71015	Cellulose du Pin, Tartras (40).	
BB71018	Soc Métallurgique d'Epernay (51).	
BB71019	Kronenbourg, Corbas (69).	or Strasbourg, Port du Rhin?
BB71020	Transports Bridier, La Chapelle St Ursin (18).	
BB71022	Kronenbourg, Strasbourg, Port du Rhin.	
BB71028	Metalinor, Dunkerque.	
Y2101	Sablières de Bourron-Marlotte (77).	
Y2104	SERAGRI, Chatel Censoir (89).	
Y2105	Soufflet, Polisot (10).	
Y2106	Coop Agricole de la Charente, Angoulême.	
Y2108	Potain, Moulins (03).	
Y2109	SA Patry (dealer), Persan-Beaumont (95).	
Y2110	Graines Selectif Tezier, Portes-les-Valence.	
Y2111	Coop Agricole du Dunois, Bailleau-le-Pin (28).	
Y2116	Franciade, Lamotte-Beuvron (41).	Green
Y2121	MAGEFI, Nouveaux Ports de Metz (37).	
Y2122	Soufflet Agriculture, Anglure (51).	
Y2126	CAPROGA La Meunière, Ladon (45).	Blue
Y2127	Coop Agricole de Gien (45).	
Y2128	Coop Agricole La Dauphinoise, Port de Lyon.	
Y2134	SICA SERROGRAIN, Sens (89).	
Y2135	Coop Agricole du Dunois, Châteaudun (28).	
Y2139	Franciade, Mondoubleau (41).	AT2 PM 029
Y2140	Coop Agricole du Dunois, Allonnes-Boisville.	
Y2141	Charpente, Carcassone (11).	
Y2146	Coop Agricole, Corbeille-en-Gatinais (45).	
Y2205	Enterprise Monin, Ste. Foy l'Argentière (69).	
Y2206	CEGELEC, Paris.	
Y2210	Papeteries du Limousin, Saillat (87).	
Y2212	Coop Agricole du Dunois, Gommiers (28).	
Y2217	Coop Agricole du Dunois, Janville (28).	
Y2223	Cornet et Fils, Lignerolles (28).	
Y2227	France Appro, Pleine Fougères (35).	
Y2229	Sopalin, Sotteville (76).	AT1 RO 239
Y2230	Sablières de Bourron-Marlotte (77).	

Y2235	Coop des Pyrénées Orientales, Perpignan.	
Y2244	Coop Agricole du Dunois, Vieuvicq (28).	
Y2245	Cooperative de Verneuil, Breteuil sur Iton (27).	
Y2253	Cie. Bases de Lubrifiants, Port Jerome (76).	
Y2256	SCAEL, Bonneval (28).	
Y2261	Potain, St. Nizier sous Charlieu (42).	
Y2265	Usine Metal de Massily, Massily (71).	
Y2268	Bourgeois, Besançon (25).	
Y2272	Coop Agricole, Brienon (89).	Orange
Y2286	Van Leer, Grand Quevilly (76).	AT1 RO 249
Y2290	Agralco, Coutances (50).	AT1 RO 258
Y2302	SA Patry (dealer), Persan-Beaumont (95).	
Y2309	SA Patry, Persan-Beaumont (95).	
Y2314	André Recerdier, Pernes-le-Fontaines (84).	
Y2323	Map Metal, ?	
Y2325	Cornet et Fils, Orgeres en Beauce (28).	
Y2327	Coop Agricole du Dunois, Auneau (28).	
Y2329	Ets. Desbrugeres (dealer), Noyon (60).	
Y2333	Epis Centre, Jean Varenne, near Issoudun (36).	
Y2335	Scrapyard, St Avre le Chambre (73).	
Y2338	Ateliers d'Occitanie, Narbonne (11).	
Y2408	Factory, St. Etienne (42).	
Y2421	B. M. Traction (dealer), Lyon (69).	
Y2422	SAM, Follingy.	ATIRO 256
Y2426	Factory, St. Julien-Montrichier (73).	
Y2430	Ets. Fonlupt, Bourg-en-Bresse.	AT2 DJ 033
Y2437	Carrières de Pagnac, Pagnac (87).	
Y2442	Carrières de Pagnac, Pagnac (87).	
Y2454	Scrapyard, Cluses (74).	
Y2466	Ets. Lambiotte, Prémery (58).	
Y2472	Soc. Kaolins du Finistere, Pleyber-Christ (29).	
Y2473	Rhône Poulenc Films, Miribel (01).	
Y2503	Soc. Nouvelle de Transports, Chambéry (73).	
Y2512	C. Alpine de Recyclage, Aiton-Bourgneuf (73).	
Y2513	SA Gaston Arnould, Vittel (88).	
Y2516	Moullins de Savoie, Chambéry (73).	
Y2517	Carbone Savoie, N. Dame de Briançon (73).	
Y5113	Allevard Ressorts, Douai (59).	
Y5120	Chartenay, St. Imbert (58).	
Y5128	Coop Agricole du Dunois, Châteaudun (28).	
Y5149	Leclerc, Bordeaux (33).	
Y5154	Butagaz, Corbehem (62).	
Y6023	Imes France, Culoz (01).	
Y6032	Sapprime, ?	
Y6036	Rhône-Progil, ?	
Y6208	Metaux Spéciaux, Pomblières-St. Marcel (73).	
Y6211	SCAEL, Courville sur Eure (28).	
Y6213	Factory, Dannemarie-Velesmes (25).	
Y6218	SCAB, Bonneval (28).	AT2 PSO 066
Y6223	Champagne Céréales, Coucy-les-Eppes (02).	
Y6226	Générale Sucrerie (SOL, St Louis), Laon (02).	
Y6228	CFRT, Flixecourt (80).	AT1 AM 53
Y6235	Grande Minoterie Dijonnaise, Dijon (21).	
Y6236	Sogeloc, Gargenville (78).	
Y6237	Guyomar'ch, Questembert (56).	
Y6241	Total Gaz, St. Loubes (33).	White
Y6249	Cereal Coop, ?	
Y6250	Coop Agricole, Morigny, Etampes (91).	
Y6254	Norsk Hydro Azote, Le Havre.	AT2 RO 244
Y6259	DOMAGRI, Gerzat (63).	
Y6262	SPAD, Canals near Grisolles (31).	Grey
Y6277	Sucrerie de Pithiviers (45).	

Y6278	Coop Agricole La Brie, Coulommiers (77).	
Y6279	Factory, Montaudran, Toulouse (31).	
Y6292	Sonegra, Darcey (21).	
Y6303	Total Gaz, Frontenex (73).	
Y6308	Champagne Céréal., Fere Champenoise (51).	
Y6315	Providence Agricole, Gondrecourt-le-Château.	
Y6316	Siciété CA, Thouars (79).	
Y6318	Coop Agricole, Longuejumelles.	
Y6321	Champagne Céréales, ZI de Pompelle, Reims.	
Y6322	La Providence Agricole, Matougues (51).	
Y6324	Sogemi-Fillod, St. Amour (39).	AT2 DJ 046
Y6325	Soufflet, Polisot (10).	AT2 RS 128
Y6330	UCOP Silo, Breteuil Ville (60).	
Y6403	Calcia, Port de Rouen (76).	AT2 RO 226
Y6405	???, Reims (51).	
Y6407	Silo, Châtel-Censoir (89).	
Y6411	Transagra, Tracy-sur-Loire (58).	
Y6418	UNCAC, St Jean de Losne (21).	
Y6421	SOCOMAC, La Rochelle (17).	
Y6422	SPAD 69, Vénissieux (69).	
Y6425	Heineken/Pelforth, Schiltigheim (67).	
Y6427	Silo Vicois, Eauze (32).	
Y6431	Silo, Monthois (08).	
Y6439	Coop Agricole de la Champage, Coligny (51).	
Y6452	Distrilux, Gonfreville l'Orcher.	AT2 RO 201
Y6454	FRET SNCF, Rouen (76).	
Y6455	Sucrerie de Colville (76).	AT2 RO 247
Y6466	Iton-Seine, Bonnières-sur-Seine (78)	
Y6473	Sablières, Les Andelys (27).	AT2 RO 225
Y6475	VAHOMILLS, Sète (34).	
Y6479	SICA, Port-la-Nouvelle (11).	
Y6480	Factory, Montluçon (03).	
Y6481	Cie. Nord du Rhône, Port de Lyon (69).	
Y6484	UCASPORT, Rouen (76).	AT2 RO 219
Y6485	Coop de Chemin, Chemin (39).	
Y6496	Kaisersberg, Hondouville (27).	AT2 RO 206
Y6498	TRANSAGRA, Chateauneuf-sur-Cher (18).	
Y6499	Lesaffre, Sucrerie de Nangis, Nangis (77).	
Y6503	SONOGRA, Nuits sous Ravières (89).	
Y6504	Sollac, Desvres (62).	
Y6508	Tioxide, Calais (62).	
Y6511	Comurex, Malvesi, near Narbonne (11).	
Y6523	Générale Sucrerie, Etrepagny.	AT2 RO 232
Y6524	Garon Lepuix, Giromagny (90).	
Y6526	Silos du Port de Rouen (76).	AT2 RO 210
Y6528	Général Sucrerie, Roye (80).	
Y6530	Decoexa, Hendaye/Irún.	Blue
Y6536	Société des Talcs de Luzenac, Luzenac (09).	
Y6542	Champagne Cereales, Coolus (51).	
Y6543	Factory, Cosne-sur-Loire (58).	
Y6545	Transagra, Poilly-les-Gien (45).	
Y6546	C.F. des Pyrénées Orientales, Perpignan.	
Y6548	Distrilux, Marly-la-Ville (93).	
Y6550	FRET SNCF, Rouen, "FRET 2".	AT2 RO 253
Y6552	Factory, Breteuil (27).	
Y6554	Factory, Bergerac (24).	
Y6556	BSN, Wingles (62).	
Y6572	Union Sud Alim., Villefranche-de-Rouergue.	
Y6579	UCACEL, Rouen (76).	AT2 RO 213
Y6580	B. Secula, ZI Beaune Vignolles, Beaune (21).	
Y6581	BSN, Wingles (62).	
Y6582	Champagne Céréales, Dontrien (51).	
Y6583	Ciments Lafarge, Boussens (31).	

Y6588	FRET SNCF, Rouen.	AT2 RO 203. Green
Y6593	SCAN, Guérigny (58).	
Y6597	Rouen area.	Yellow
Y6598	Silo Coop Bretagne, Chatelaudren Plouaget.	
Y6602	St. Gobain, Chalons-sur-Saone (71).	
Y6603	Soufflet, Rouen (76).	
Y6610	Soufflet, Sotteville (76).	
Y6620	SOGEMA, Grand Couronne (76).	
Y6624	Soferti, Caen (14).	AT2 RO 243. Blue/white
Y7026	Lacombe, Boutrassol-Justarette, near Pinsaguel.	
Y7030	Ph Rey Transit Groupages, Perpignan (66).	
Y7038	SCAEL, Marchezais-Broué (28).	
Y7118	Cie. Normande de Manutention, Rouen docks.	
Y7128	SCAC, Rouen docks.	
Y50101	Magasins Généraux, Toulouse (31).	
Y50102	Patry (dealer), Persan-Beaumont (95).	
Y50103	Cooperative Scara, Mailly (10).	
Y50104	Compagnie Parisienne des Asphaltes, ?	
Y50107	Patry (dealer), Persan-Beaumont (95).	
Y50108	Quarry, Bellignies, near Bavay (59).	
Y50109	Gardi-Loire, near Montoir-de-Bretagne (44).	
Y50110	Leno/Limagrain, near Clermont-Ferrand (63).	
Y51122	CCI Vaucluse, ZI Avignon Courtine (84).	
Y51129	Magasins Généraux, Toulouse (31).	
Y51130	Coop du Mans, Le Mans (72).	
Y51139	Coop du Mans, Le Mans (72).	
Y51207	La Cellulose du Rhône, Tarascon.	Yellow/red
Y51219	Coop Agricole des Charente, Charmant (16).	

▲ **Seco (private track maintenance company)** SECO loco No. 138 01 (formerly SNCF 65507) at Achères on 6th March 1993. **Brian Leighton**

5. PRIVATE TRACK MAINTENANCE COMPANIES

In France, four major and two minor private companies share contracts for track laying and renewal. Each has its own fleet of second-hand locos to haul trains. Although independent, the companies work together on large contracts and the smaller of the four "majors" now largely work together. The two "minors" share the same depot facilities. Between them, the companies have almost 60 ex DB Class 211 locos! The locos can be found anywhere track work is taking place in France and even in other countries where the companies win contracts.

The Class 211 locos operated by Drouard and COGIFER/ETF were imported by Sifel at Mitry-Mory north of Paris and re-engined with Caterpillar 3512 V12 DT engines, which develop 940 kW at 1500 r.p.m., before entering service. Sifel is now owned by Travaux du Sud Ouest. During a visit in 1998, 211 269 was present in red livery numbered V142-41 after a long period in Guinea in Africa. Sifel also had 211 105 and 211 275 stored for spare parts in an industrial estate, some 2 km north of the depot. ÖBB shunter 2060 067 was with them.

The SNCF system of classification for private locomotives approved to operate over their tracks consists of a number such as AT3 RO 156. AT means "Agréement Technique" (technical approval); AT1 is a small tractor, AT2 a large tractor whilst AT3 is a main line locomotive. The following two letters represent the SNCF region which granted the approval – for example, RO for Rouen. Finally, the following three figures are a serial number which increases with time.

5.1. COGIFER TF

COGIFER TF is part of a large public works group owned by De Dietrich. The origins of COGIFER are with the companies Dehé and Montcocol. The Montcocol name disappeared and Dehé became associated with the COGIFER group around 1992. The name Dehé was dropped at the beginning of 1998. In 1996, Dehé started to work more closely with Drouard and created a common subsidiary – "Européene de Travaux Ferroviaires" or ETF – in order to bid for contracts against SECO DG and TSO which have greater resources. ETF is 50% owned by COGIFER and Drouard and incorporates both loco fleets. The major part of both fleets has now been transferred to ETF. COGIFER's livery is now yellow with a blue stripe. Dehé's livery was orange with a blue stripe. Some repainting of ETF locos in a new yellow livery with a green stripe has taken place since this merger. COGIFER and ETF locomotives are numbered in the 52000 series to a system which includes road and building construction equipment such as cranes and bulldozers! Numbers are carried on car-style number plates. Sadly, Dehé scrapped all of its ex DB Class 220 locos in early 1998.

Workshops: Montigny-Beauchamp.

SNCF Approval No.	ETF No.	Previous No.	Built	Type of Loco/Notes
COGIFER TF Fleet				
AT3 NT 129	52002 (272)	HBNPC 11	1960	600 h.p. B&L BB 63000
AT3 LL 047	52005 (273)	Works no. 1611	1973	1600 h.p. Fauvet Girel Bo-Bo. Stored at Montigny
AT3 DJ 032	52006	BB 4007	1975	660 h.p. Moyse type BB 40 EPA 680P. Shunts at Montigny
AT3 PN 133	52010	DB 211.115	1961	Re-engined with Caterpillar 3512
AT3 PN 181	52035	DB 211.???	1963	Layritz 142-5x
ETF Fleet				
AT3 CF 022	52003 (269)	SNCF BB 66691	1962	1800 h.p.
AT3 CF 023	52004 (270)	SNCF BB 66692	1962	1800 h.p.
AT3 PN 130	52007	DB 211.127	1962	
AT3 PN 131	52008	DB 211.285	1962	
AT3 PN 132	52009	DB 211.157	1962	
AT3 PN 150	52019	DB 211.???		
AT3 PN 170	52021	DB 211.???		Layritz 142-43
AT3 PN 171	52022	DB 211.???		Layritz 142-45
AT3 PN 134	52023	DB 211.167	1962	Ex Drouard
AT3 PN 135	52024	DB 211.139	1962	Ex Drouard

AT3 PN 136	52025	DB 211.187	1962	Ex Drouard
AT3 PN 137	52026	DB 211.248	1962	Ex Drouard
AT3 LY 243	52027	HBNPC ??	1963	Ex Drouard. BB 63000 de Bo-Bo B&L (2015)
AT3 LY 246	52028	HBNPC 71	1961	Ex Drouard. BB 63000 de Bo-Bo B&L (2016)
AT3 PSE 003	52029	SNCF CC 65510	1956	Ex Drouard. de Co-Co
AT3 PSE 006	52030	DB 211.081	1962	Ex Drouard
AT3 PSE 007	52031	DB 211.069	1962	Ex Drouard
AT3 PSE 002	52032	SNCF CC 65505	1955	ex Drouard. de 1470 kW
AT3 PN 182	52036	DB 211.???		
AT3 PN 183	52037	DB 211.???		

Notes: DB 211.305 stored at Creil (St. Lou d'Esseront) for spares. All Class 211 re-engined with Caterpillar 3512 DT. Locos 52016–18/20/33/34 are shunters and not included.

5.2. DROUARD

Drouard, previously Drouard Frères, is a subsidiary of the very large Spie-Batignolles public works and construction group. Livery is greenish blue and yellow. This is being replaced by yellow livery lined in black or with green for the locos in the ETF fleet.

Workshops: Juvisy. Drouard also use COGIFER's workshops.

SNCF Approval No.	Previous No.	Built	Type of Locomotive/Notes
AT3 PN 138	DB 211.136?	1962	Re-engined Caterpillar 3512 TA
AT3 PN 178	DB 211.???	1962	Re-engined Caterpillar 3512 DI TA. Layritz no. 142-48
	DB 211.???		Under conversion in September 1998. Layritz no. 142-53
AT3 LY 245	HBNPC 74	1961	BB 63500 de Bo-Bo (N° 2017)

5.3. SECO DG

Created after the merger of the companies SECO and Desquenne et Giral, SECO DG is a subsidiary of a holding company, Desquenne et Giral. SECO DG locos have an SNCF approval number as well as the company's own numbering system which covers all their equipment including wagons and track maintenance machines. Livery is orange with black and yellow warning markings. Again a new, mainly yellow livery is emerging at present. 136.01, which is known as "Le Teckel" or the dachshund is a low-slung design with two 500 h.p. Baudoin engines which is used to power tracklaying trains on new lines. The loco is cut down in order to allow gantry cranes picking up track to pass over it. It is limited to 40 km/h on the main line.

Workshops: Les Mureaux.

Types of locomotive: Class 131 are Decauville shunters, Class 132 are Brissoneau & Lotz 600 h.p. Bo-Bos (132.02 is 825 h.p.), Class 133 are ex DB Class 211 B-B, Class 135.01 are Fauvet Girel Bo-Bos, and Class 138 is ex SNCF Class CC 65500.

SNCF Approval No.	SECO DG No.	Previous No.	Built	SNCF Approval No.	SECO DG No.	Previous No.	Built
	131.01			AT3 PSL 199	133.08	DB 211.152	1962
	131.02			AT3 PSL 301	133.10	DB 211.185	1962
AT3 PSL 144	132.01	HBNPC ??	1962	AT3 PSL 302	133.11	DB 211.245	1962
AT3 PSL 012	132.02	HBNPC ??	1962	AT3 PSL 303	133.13	DB 211.113	1963
AT3 PSL 020	132.03	HBNPC ??	1960	AT3 PSL 304	133.14	DB 211.158	1962
AT3 PSL 132	132.04	HBNPC ??	1960	AT3 PSL 306	133.15	DB 211.137	1962
AT3 PSL 193	133.01	DB 211.238	1961	AT3 PSL 305	133.16	DB 211.131	1962
AT3 PSL 194	133.03	DB 211.111	1963		135.01		1970
AT3 PSL 192	133.04	DB 211.114	1961		135.02		1970
AT3 PSL 196	133.05	DB 211.234	1961	AT3 PSL 035	136.01		
AT3 PSL 197	133.06	DB 211.144	1962	AT3 PSL 171	138.01	SNCF CC 65507	1956
AT3 PSL 198	133.07	DB 211.156	1962				

Notes: 133.02, ex DB 211.154, was destroyed in a fire. Numbers 133.09 was reserved for 211.186 and 133.12 for 211.179 but were never used for spare parts then cut up. Number 134.01 was allocated to a CEM 0-6-0 shunter built to the same design as SNCF Class C 61000 but now cut up. Number 137.01 was allotted to Renault prototype CC 80001 (formerly 060 GA 1), nicknamed "Belphégor", now in the Renault museum.

5.4. TRAVAUX DU SUD OUEST (TSO)

This is a family company based east of Paris. Identifying the TSO locos has been very difficult as company records are incomplete and in some cases incorrect. In addition, most of the works plates, a sure way of telling the loco's origins, have now been removed from loco cabs.

AT3 PE 206/7 are both equipped with TVM 430 cab signalling so that they can operate on SNCF's high-speed lines anywhere in France. AT3 PE 700 has been numbered as such as it was recently equipped with a 700 h.p. Deutz engine. This is about half the power of the usual Class 211 engines. TSO wanted a loco which would act as a shunter on works sites but which could run at 100 km/h between jobs. TSO's other shunters always gave problems when moving between sites because of limitation to 40 km/h. As TSO's Class 211 have come for overhaul, it has been found necessary to re-equip them with Caterpillar 3512 DT engines. The majority are now thus equipped. TSO operated the German V 300 prototype for some time but scrapped it at Le Mans when the company pulled out of that site in 1995. Livery is yellow with red lining. At the end of 1998, TSO was about to test an ex DB Class 216 loco and may acquire more.

Workshops: Chelles.

SNCF App. No.	Previous or Works No.	Built	Type of locomotive
AT2 PE 006			B Tractor Moyse Type BN28 500 h.p.
AT1 PE 010			B Tractor U60
AT1 PE 011			B Tractor U60
AT2 PE 012			C Tractor Moyse BNC6
AT2 PE 021			B Tractor CFD
AT1 PE 033			B Tractor U60
AT2 PE 209			B Tractor U60
AT3 PE 024	1511	1979	B-B Type BB1500 CFD (80 t., 1540 h.p.)
AT3 PE 025	1512	1979	B-B Type BB1500 CFD (80 t., 1540 h.p.)
AT3 RO 006	SNCF CC 65512	1956	
AT3 RO 007	SNCF CC 65522	1957	
AT3 PE 137	DB 211.149	1962	MTU engine
AT3 PE 138	DB 211.180	1962	Caterpillar engine (02/97)
AT3 PE 139	DB 211.147	1962	MTU engine
AT3 PE 140	DB 211.151	1962	Caterpillar engine (02/97)
AT3 PE 169	DB 211.173	1961	MTU engine
AT3 PE 170	DB 211.087 (No. deduced)	1962	Caterpillar engine (1991)
AT3 PE 171	DB 211.090 (No. deduced)	1962	Caterpillar engine (1991)
AT3 PE 172	DB 211.322	1962	Mercedes engine
AT3 PE 173	DB 211.328	1962	Caterpillar engine (07/95)
AT3 PE 174	DB 211.329	1962	Caterpillar engine (02/97)
AT3 PE 200	DB 211.197 (No. deduced)	1962	Caterpillar engine (03/96)
AT3 PE 201	DB 211.280	1962	Caterpillar engine (06/96)
AT3 PE 202	DB 211.239	1961	Burnt out and scrapped
AT3 PE 203	DB 211.221	1962	Caterpillar engine (07/96)
AT3 PE 204	DB 211.310	1962	Mercedes engine
AT3 PE 206	DB 211.???		Caterpillar engine (10/95). TVM 430
AT3 PE 207	DB 211.???		Caterpillar engine (01/96). TVM 430
AT3 PE 208	DB 211.???		Caterpillar engine (1994)
AT3 PE 700	DB 211.289	1962	700 h.p. MWM Deutz engine

5.5. MECCOLI & VECCHIETTI

Two minor players in track maintenance contracts with SNCF which are based in the same depot just south of St. Pierre-des-Corps marshalling yard near Tours. The two companies have recently acquired a DB Class 211 each, both of them prepared for use by Sifel. Vecchietti has ex SNCF shunter Y 51228, built in 1958 although the loco no longer operates.

MECCOLI Fleet

Former No.	SNCF Approval No.
SNCF BB 66610	AT3 TR 176
SNCF BB 66611	AT3 TR 175
DB 211 110	AT3 PN 140
SNCF Y 6234	AT2 TR 038

VECCHIETTI Fleet

Former No.	SNCF Approval No.
SNCF BB 66606	AT3 TR 173
SNCF BB 66608	AT3 TR 174
DB 211 128	AT3 PN 141
SNCF Y 51228	AT3 PE 060

6. SNCF SELF-PROPELLED SNOWPLOUGHS

The SNCF has several rotary snowploughs. Brief details of those known are as follows:

No.	Type	Built	Location
CN 1	Beilhack type HB 600	1972	Chambéry
CN 2	Beilhack type HB 600	1972	Chambéry
CN 3	Beilhack/91	1981	Dijon
CN 4	Beilhack	198?	St. Gervais les Bains. (1000 mm)
CN 5	ex BB 4119	1928	Toulouse
CN 6	ex BB 4123	1928	Toulouse
CNS	ex BB 60021		Aurillac

Note: CNS has traction motors at one end only and must be pushed by a loco. Converted 1967. Equipped for push-pull with BB 66000.

▲ **Preserved Locomotives.** A1A-A1A 62036 on 5th September 1993 at Richelieu on the Train à Vapeur de Tourraine preserved line. **Les Nixon**

7. PRESERVED LOCOMOTIVES & RAILCARS

The current status of the motive power is indicated as follows:

M	Museum, on display (not active).
MA	Museum, active.
MR	Museum, under repair.
MS	Museum, stored.
P	Plinthed.
S	Stored.

7.1. STEAM LOCOMOTIVES

The French use a simple system to classify steam locomotives based on the number of axles. Thus, a French 141 is a 2-8-2 and so on. Most loco numbers begin with the axle arrangement, followed by a class letter then the serial number. If the class letter is preceded by a T, this denotes a tank engine. Confusingly, this is known in French as a "locomotive tender".

The system for describing steam locomotives used here is the one which is in general use in Germany. Firstly, letters and numbers are used to describe the wheel arrangement as follows:

Driven axles are denoted by letters where A=1, B=2, C=3 etc.

Non-driven axles are denoted by numbers.

This is then followed by 'h' for superheated locos (from the German "heizdampf"), or 'n' for saturated locos (from the German "nassdampf").

The number of cylinders follow, then codes for various features, i.e.:

v	compound.
z	rack locomotive with 1 pinion.
zz	rack locomotive with 2 pinions.
t	tank locomotive.

e.g.: 1D1h2t is a superheated 2-8-2 tank locomotive with 2 cylinders.

Number	Details	Built	Status	Location
5 "SÉZANNE"	1A1n2	1847	M	MCF Mulhouse (CF Montereau-Troyes).
6 "L'AIGLE"	1A1n2	1846	M	MCF Mulhouse (CF Avignon-Marseille).
33 "ST. PIERRE"	1A1n2	1843	M	MCF Mulhouse (CF Paris-Rouen).
80 "LE CONTINENT"	2An2	1852	M	MCF Mulhouse (CF Paris-Strasbourg).
NORD 701	2AAn4v	1885	M	MCF Mulhouse.
ÉTAT 2029 "PARTHENAY"	1Bn2	1882	MS	MCF Mulhouse (SNCF 120 A 36).
PO 340	1B1n2	1882	M	MCF Mulhouse (SNCF 121 A 340).
PLM C 145	2Bn4v	1902	M	MCF Mulhouse (SNCF 220 A 85).
NORD 2.670	2B1h4v	1903	M	MCF Mulhouse (SNCF 221 A 30).
PLM 1423	Cn2	1854	M	MCF Mulhouse (SNCF 030 A 1).
NORD 3486	Cn2	1890	MS	MCF Mulhouse.
030 C 815	Cn2	1878	MS	MCF Mulhouse.
030 C 841	Cn2	1883	M	Delson, Canada.
030 TA 628	Cn2t	1874	MS	MCF Mulhouse.
030 TB 2	Cn2t	1870	P	MCF Mulhouse.
030 TB 130	Cn2t	1900	MA	Volgelsheim. CFTR.
030 TB 134	Cn2t	1900	MA	Volgelsheim. CFTR.
030 TU 13	Cn2t	1943	P	Caen (USATC 6102).
030 TU 22	Cn2t	1943	M	Longueville (USATC 4383). AJECTA.
MIDI 312 "L`ADOUR"	C2n2t	1856	M	MCF Mulhouse (SNCF 032 TA 312).
130 B 348	1Ch2	1862	MA	Longueville AJECTA.
130 B 439	1Ch2	1882	P	Capdenac SNCF station.
130 B 476	1Ch2	1883	MA	Richelieu. TVT.
EST 32.031	1C1h2	1925	M	MCF Mulhouse (SNCF 131 TB 31).
MIDI 1314	2Cn4v	1902	M	MCF Mulhouse (SNCF 230 B 614).
230 B 114	2Ch4v	1908	M	MCF Mulhouse.
230 C 531	2Cn4v	1905	MS	Villeneuve St. Georges (MCF).

230 D 9	2Ch4v	1908	M	MCF Mulhouse.
230 D 116	2Ch4v	1911	MA	Nene Valley Railway, Wansford, GB.
230 G 352	2Ch4v	1922	MR	Richelieu. TVT.
230 G 353	2Ch2	1922	T	Paris La Villette depot. SNCF.
PO 4546	2C1n4v	1908	M	MCF Mulhouse (SNCF 231 A 546).
NORD 3.1192	2C1h4v	1936	M	MCF Mulhouse (SNCF 231 E 22).
231 C 78	2C1h4v	1930	MS	Oignies (MCF).
231 E 41	2C1h4v	1937	P	St. Pierre des Corps.
231 G 558	2C1h4v	1922	MA	Sotteville SNCF depot. PVC.
231 H 8	2C1h4v	1912	MS	MCF Mulhouse.
231 K 8	2C1h4v	1912	MA	Paris Sud Est SNCF depot. FACS.
231 K 22	2C1h4v	1914	M	Nördlingen, Germany.
231 K 82	2C1h4v	1920	M	St. Étienne. For future mining museum.
NORD 3.1102	2C2h4v	1911	M	MCF Mulhouse.
232 U 1	2C2h4v	1949	M	MCF Mulhouse.
PLM 4A51	Dn2	1878	M	Miramas. APPAF. (SNCF 040 A 51).
PLM 4B9	Dn4v	1892	M	Carnoules (SNCF 040 B 9).
NORD 4853	Dn2	1880	M	Longueville. AJECTA.
040 TA 137	Dn2t	1922	MA	Mortagne-sur-Sèvre. TVV.
040 TA 141	Dn2t	1923	MR	Vigy. CFVC.
140 A 259	1Dh2	1928	MS	MCF Mulhouse.
140 A 908	1Dh2	1892	MS	MCF Mulhouse.
140 C 22	1Dh2	1916	MS	Les Ifs. (No tender).
140 C 27	1Dh2	1916	MA	Conflans Jarny. CITEV.
140 C 38	1Dh2	1919	MR	Ambazac. TVML.
140 C 231	1Dh2	1916	MA	Longueville. AJECTA.
140 C 287	1Dh2	1917	MR	Sainte Foy l'Argentière. TVML.
140 C 313	1Dh2	1917	P	Reims SNCF station.
140 C 314	1Dh2	1917	MA	St. Quentin. FACS.
140 C 344	1Dh2	1917	M	MCF Mulhouse.
141 C 100	1D1h2	1922	MA	Richelieu. TVT.
141 F 282	1D1h4v	1925	M	MCF Mulhouse.
141 R 73	1D1h2	1945	M	Thionville. CITEV.
141 R 420	1D1h2	1946	MA	Clermont Ferrand SNCF depot.
141 R 568	1D1h2	1945	MA	Conflans Jarny. CITEV.
141 R 840	1D1h2	1946	MA	Cosne-sur-Loire. AAATV.
141 R 1108	1D1h2	1946	MR	Breil sur Roya. AAATV.
141 R 1126	1D1h2	1947	MA	Toulouse St. Jory. SNCF.
141 R 1187	1D1h2	1947	M	MCF Mulhouse.
141 R 1199	1D1h2	1947	M	Nantes SNCF depot.
141 R 1207	1D1h2	1947	MR	Winterthur (Switzerland).
141 R 1244	1D1h2	1947	MA	Brugg (Switzerland). Club Mikado.
141 R 1298	1D1h2	1947	M	Miramas. APPAF.
141 R 1332	1D1h2	1947	S	Thionville. CITEV.
PO 5452	1D1h2t	1922	M	MCF Mulhouse (SNCF 141 TA 452).
141 TB 407	1D1h2t	1913	M	Longueville. AJECTA.
141 TB 424	1D1h2t	1913	MA	Volgelsheim. CFTR.
141 TC 19	1D1h2t	1922	M	Longueville. AJECTA.
141 TC 51	1D1h2t	1935	M	Longueau SNCF depot. (MCF)
141 TD 740	1D1h3t	1931	MA	Limoges Puy Imbert. CFTLP.
241 A 1	2D1h4v	1925	M	MCF Mulhouse.
241 A 65	2D1h4v	1931	M	Neuchâtel (Switzerland).
241 P 9	2D1h4v	1947	P	Guîtres. AAATV.
241 P 16	2D1h4v	1947	M	MCF Mulhouse.
241 P 17	2D1h4v	1947	MR	Le Creusot Schneider works.
241 P 30	2D1h4v	1949	MS	Vallorbe station. (Switzerland).
242 AT 6	2D2h4v	1949	M	MCF Mulhouse (SNCF 242 TA 6).
150 A 065	1Eh4v	1912	MS	MCF Mulhouse.
150 P 13	1E1h4v	1940	M	MCF Mulhouse.

7.2. ELECTRIC LOCOMOTIVES

BB 36	BoBoe	1924	MS	MCF Mulhouse.
BB 824	BoBoe	1924	MR	Boissy St. Léger RATP depot.
BB 833	BoBoe	1924	MR	Boissy St. Léger RATP depot.
BB 1282	BoBoe	1900	M	MCF Mulhouse.
BB 1501	BoBoe	1922	MS	Nîmes (MCF).
BB 1632	BoBoe	1925	MS	Nîmes (MCF).
2CC2 3402	2CoCo2e	1929	MS	Montluçon (MCF).
1ABBA1 3603	1ABoBoA1e	1927	M	MCF Mulhouse.
BB 4110	BoBoe	1929	MR	Toulouse St. Jory.
BB 4175	BoBoe	1932	MS	Nîmes (MCF).
Midi E 4162	BoBoe	1932	M	Miramas, APPAF. (SNCF BB 4177).
2D2 5516	2Do2e	1934	M	MCF Mulhouse.
2D2 5525	2Do2e	1935	MA	Montrouge SNCF depot. COPEF.
CC 7108	CoCoe	1953	MS	Nîmes (MCF).
BB 8238	BoBoe	1954	P	Breil sur Roya. AAATV.
BB 9004	BoBoe	1954	M	MCF Mulhouse.
2D2 9134	2Do2e	1951	MR	St. Étienne.
2D2 9135	2Do2e	1951	MA	Paris Charolais SNCF depot.
BB 9411	BoBo e	1960	MS	Nîmes (MCF).
BB 12087	Bo-Bo e	1957	P	Nouvion-sur-Meuse
BB 12120	Bo-Bo e	1959	M	CFV3V, Treignes.
CC 14018	CoCoe	1959	M	MCF Mulhouse.
CC 14183	CoCo e	1956	M	Petite Rosselle. MMPR.
CC 20001	CoCoe	1958	MR	Sotteville works. (MCF).
CC 40109	CCe	1970	M	MCF Mulhouse
CC 40110	CCe	1970	MA	Paris La Chapelle SNCF depot. MFPN.

7.3. DIESEL LOCOMOTIVES AND SHUNTERS

BB 60032	BoBode	1938	M	MCF Mulhouse.
C 61002	Cde	1950	MA	St. Jean du Gard. TVC.
C 61103	Cde	1950	MA	St. Jean du Gard. TVC.
C 61032	Cde	1952	MA	Richelieu. TVT.
C 61035	C de	1952	MA	Anduze. TVC.
C 61041	Cde	1952	MA	St. Quentin. CFTV.
C 61042	Cde	1952	MA	Mortagne-sur-Sèvre. (030 DA 42). TVV.
C 61046	Cde	1953	MS	Le Havre Musée des Arts & Techniques.
TC 61101	Cde	1951	MS	St. Jean du Gard. TVC (spares).
TC 61107	Cde	1951	MS	Le Havre Musée des Arts & Techniques.
A1AA1A 62001	A1AA1Ade	1946	MR	CFTA. Gray
A1AA1A 62029	A1AA1Ade	1946	MA	Volgelsheim. CFTR.
A1AA1A 62032	A1AA1Ade	1946	MA	Richelieu. TVT.
A1AA1A 62036	A1AA1Ade	1947	MA	Richelieu. TVT.
A1AA1A 62062	A1AA1Ade	1947	MR	CFTA. Gray
A1AA1A 62073	A1AA1Ade	1947	MA	Les Hôpitaux Neufs. CFT
A1AA1A 62095	A1AA1Ade	1947	MA	entre de la Mine, Dignies.
BB 63013	BoBo de	1953	M	MCF Mulhouse.
BB 63121	BoBo de			CFV3V, Mariembourg, Belgium (CFTA)
BB 63123	BoBo de			CFV3V, Mariembourg, Belgium (SBB)
BB 63139	BoBo de	1954	MA	Wassy. CFBD.
BB 63149	BoBo de			CFV3V, Treignes, Belgium (SNCF)
CC 65001	CoCode	1956	MS	MCF Mulhouse.
CC 65005	CoCode	1956	MA	Courpière. AGRIVAP.
CC 65006	CoCode	1957	MA	Richelieu. TVT. On hire to CFTA.
BB 71010	BBdm	1965	MA	Le Bouveret, Switzerland.
BB 71017	BBdm	1965	MA	Saujon. CFTS.
CC 80001	CCde	-	M	Renault museum. Flins.
Y 2107	B dm	1952	MA	Noyelles. CFBS.
Y 2121	B dm	1953	MA	St. Amand-les-Eaux. AAMCS.

Y 2228	B dm	1956	MA	Saujon. CFTS.
Y 2291	B dm	1959	MA	MCF Mulhouse.
Y 2296	B dm	1959	MA	Caen. SNTC.
Y 2297	B dm	1959	MA	Musée des Trains Miniatures. Grasse.
Y 2402	B dm	1962	MA	Volgelsheim. CFTR.
Y 2406	B dm	1962	P	Varennes-Vauzelles, near Nevers.
Y 2423	B dm	1962	M	Ecomusée du Hauts Pays. Breil-sur-Roya.
Y 2475	B dm	1965	MA	L'Arbresle. TVML.
Y 2498 "OLIVIER'	B dm	1968	MA	St. Quentin. CFTV.
Y 5130 "FABIEN"	B dm	1961	MA	Treignes, Belgium. CFV3V.
Y 6013	B de	1953	M	Miramas. APPAF.
Y 6022	B de	1924	P	Chemin du Canal, Remiremont.
Y 6202	B de	1949	MA	Sabres. CFTLG.
Y 6424	B de	1955	MA	Bédarieux. TTLM.
Y 6482	B de	1954	MA	Annonay. Viaduc 07.
Y 6502	B de	1956	MA	CFV3V. Mariembourg, Belgium.
Y 6563 "CAROLE"	Bde	1957	MA	CFV3V. Mariembourg, Belgium.
Y 6574	Bde	1957	MA	Sainte Foy l'Argentière. TVML.
Y 11252	Bde	1956	MA	Pacy sur Eure. CFVE.
YBD 12004	Bdm	1932	MA	Sabres. CFLG.
YBE 15053	Bdm	1936	MA	L'Arbresle. TVML.
Y 50105	B dm	1943	M	Elbeuf Ville. CFTFL.
Y 51125	B dm	1954	MA	St. Denis près Martel. CFTHQ.
Y 51135	B dm	1954	MA	Saujon. CFTS.
Y 51147	B dm	1955	MA	Richelieu. TVT.
Y 51232	B dm	1955	MA	Les Hôpitaux Neufs. CFTPV.
Y SP 30 002				TRANSVAP. Connerpé

7.4. DIESEL RAILCARS

X 2402	BBdm	1951	MA	Vogelsheim. CFTR.
X 2403	BBdm	1951	MA	Nîmes. AAATV.
X 2419	BBdm	1952	MA	Thoré-La Rochette. TTVL.
X 2423	BBdm	1952	MA	Carhaix. CFTA.
X 2425	BBdm	1952	MA	Cahors. Quercyrail.
X 2426	BBdm	1952	MA	Pont Audemer. CFTP.
X 2431	BBdm	1952	MA	Boulogne Outreau yard.
X 2448	BBdm	1956	MA	St. Amand-les-Eaux. AAMCS.
X 2468	BBdm	1955	MA	Attigny. CFTALC.
X 2475	BB dm	1955	M	St. Étienne. For future mining museum.
XD 2511	BB dm	1937	MR	De Dietrich, Reichshoffen.
X 2709	B2dm	1954	MA	Cahors. Quercyrail.
XR 7716	22	1954	MA	Cahors. Quercyrail.
X 2716	B2dm	1955	MA	Toucy, AATY.
XR 7762	22	1955	MA	Toucy, AATY.
X 2719	B2dm	1955	MA	Dijon Perrigny. ABFC.
XR 7708	22	1955	MA	Dijon Perrigny. ABFC.
X 3601	B2dm	1948	MA	Pacy-sur-Eure. AJECTA.
X 3623	B2dm	1949	MA	St. Quentin. CFTV.
X 3710	1AA1dm	1949	MS	Aspach. CFTVD.
X 4203	Bo2de	1959	MS	Ambert. AGRIVAP.
X 4204	Bo2de	1959	MA	Renault museum. Flins.
X 4206	Bo2de	1959	MA	Anduze. TVC.
X 4208	Bo2de	1959	MA	Ambert. AGRIVAP.
X 4511 + XR 8515	B2 + 22	1964	MA	Cahors. Quercyrail.
X 5506	1A2dm	1949	MA	Pacy sur Eure. CFVE.
X 5509	1A2dm	1950	MA	Pacy sur Eure. CFVE.
X 58??	?	?	MA	Château-Chinon. TMMB.
X 5815	1A2dm	1953	MA	L' Arbresle. TVML.
X 5822	1A2dm	1953	MA	Sabres. CFLG.
X 5830	1A2dm	1954	MA	Wassy. CFBD.
X 5845	1A2dm	1954	MA	Miramas. APPAF. (AT3 MR 102)

CLASS X 3800 (PICASSO) DIESEL RAILCAR (B-2)

A classic SNCF diesel railcar with a strange driving cab on the roof to make room for the engine which is where the cab should be! These cheap units kept many a branch line open and unsurprisingly are the mainstay of tourist line operation.

Built: 1951–62.
Engine: Renault 517G (250 kW) or Saurer.
Weight: 32 tonnes.
Seats: –/62 (some 12/32).

Builder: ANF/De Dietrich.
Transmission: Mechanical.
Length: m.
Maximum Speed: 120 km/h.

X 3801 Elbeuf Ville. CFTFL
X 3810 Carnoules. CFTCV.
X 3814 Toucy, AATY.
X 3817 Arques. CFTVA.
X 3818 Esternay. CFTT.
X 3823 Elbeuf Ville. CFTFL.
X 3824 Le Cannet. Comité Cannes-Grasse.
X 3825 Capdenac. Quercyrail.
X 3834 Courpière. AGRIVAP.
X 3835 Mézy. Moulins.
X 3837 Vigy. CFVC.
X 3838 Attigny. CFTALC.
X 3846 Narbonne. ATM.
X 3847 MCF Mulhouse.
X 3850 Attigny. CFTALC
X 3853 Arques. CFTVA.
X 3858 Volgelsheim. CFTR.
X 3865 Aubenas. Viaduc 07.
X 3866 St. Quentin. CFTV.
X 3867 Carhaix. CFTA.
X 3871 Toucy. AATY.
X 3876 Clamecy. CFTA.
X 3886 Blainville. ABFC.
X 3889 Aubenas. Viaduc 07.
X 3890 Loudéac. CF du Centre Bretagne.
X 3897 Attigny. CFTALC.
X 3898 CFV3V. Mariembourg, Belgium.
X 3900 Narbonne. ATM.
X 3907 Caen. SNTF.
X 3926 Saujon. CFTS.
X 3934 Ambert, AGRIVAP.
X 3937 Pré-en-Pail. CFTO. (Spares)
X 3939 L'Arbresle. TVML.
X 3943 Dijon Perrigny. Amis de la Ligne Bourg-Cluse.
X 3944 Bédarieux. TTLM.
X 3953 Connerré. CFTS.
X 3959 Cahors. Quercyrail.
X 3968 Espalion. CFT Aveyronnais.
X 3976 Carnoules. CFTCV.
X 3989 Annonay. Modélistes et Amis du Rail Vivarois.
X 3998 CFV3V. Mariembourg, Belgium.
X 4001 St Étienne. Association de Sauvegarde Matériel Ancien.
X 4013 Sancerre. Discotheque!
X 4025 Besançon. ABFC. (Spares)
X 4028 Narbonne. ATM.
X 4039 Dijon Perrigny. ABFC. (AT3 DJ 043).
X 4042 Merlebach Nord. MMPR.
X 4046 Denain. CFT du Hainaut.
X 4051 Dijon Perrigny. ABFC.

X 5852	1A2dm	1954	MA	Sentheim. CFTVD.
X 9152	AAdm	19??	M	Miramas. APPAF.
PO ZZEty 23859	B2dm	1934	M	MCF Mulhouse (SNCF X 2211).
État ZZB2Ef 23901	A1pm	1921	M	MCF Mulhouse.
État ZZy 24091	B2dm	1937	M	MCF Mulhouse (SNCF X 3421).
État ZZy 24408		1935	M	MCF Mulhouse (SNCF XB 1008).
XABDP 52103	BoBode	1945	MR	MCF Mulhouse.
Est ZZABSC Ety 54005		1936	MS	MCF Mulhouse (SNCF XM 5005).
PLM LZZBE 39	Bdm	1928	MA	La Barque-Fuveau. Museum.

7.5. ELECTRIC MULTIPLE UNITS

Z 1208	A1AA1A	1914	M	MCF Mulhouse.
Z 1567	BoBo	1930	MS	Le Mans. MCF.
Z 1572	BoBo	1930	MS	PSL for St. Mandé Museum.
Z 3713	BoBoBo	1938	MA	Elbeuf Ville. CFTFL.
Z 3714	BoBoBo	1938	MS	MCF. Mulhouse.
Z 4156	BoBo		MS	MCF.
Z 4909	BoBo	1913	MS	Brive. MCF.
Z 4313	BoBo	1927	MS	MCF.
Z 5177	BoBo	1956	MS	Trappes. ASTR.
État ZABEyf 23001	Bo2	1902	MS	MCF Mulhouse.
Z 23156				MCF Mulhouse
Z 216	Boe	1908	M	La Mure.
Z 450	Boe	1908	M	La Mure (Snowplough).
Z 10003	Boe	1901	M	La Mure.
Z 10004	Boe	1902	M	La Mure.
Z 10212	Boe	1901	M	La Mure.
Z 10316	Boe	1908	M	La Mure.
Z 10422	Boe	1908	M	La Mure.

7.6. GAS TURBINE POWER CAR

T 2057		197?	M	MCF. Mulhouse.

8. MUSEUMS AND MUSEUM LINES

The number of rail museums and museum lines in France has mushroomed in recent years but this proliferation has spread resources a little thin and many have difficulty staying in service. Small outfits tend to disappear and new ones appear regularly. Many of the lines are in scenic areas with tourism potential. They range from the purely tourist/children's railway where in some cases narrow gauge diesel locomotives run disguised as steam locomotives, garden railways, to fully-fledged preserved branch lines.

This guide concentrates on the main centres and ignores garden railways and diesels disguised as steam. There are also preservation groups which own locomotives and run them over SNCF tracks. The main ones are 231 G 558 at Sotteville, 231 K 8 at Paris Sud Est, 141 R 420 at Clermont Ferrand and 141 R 1126 at Toulouse. SNCF should not be forgotten as it owns 230 G 353 based at Paris La Villette.

In this edition, we have decided to present the many operators in alphabetical order with an indication of which part of France to find it (N, S, E, W, for example – C = Centre) as well as the nearest SNCF station. "Summer" generally means the French school holidays in July and August. Sunday services usually also run on public holidays. In "summer" these are 14th July and 15th August. It is difficult to keep up with operating times and dates. Readers are recommended to consult the Internet web site for more and up-to-date details at http://www.trains-fr.org.

CFT stands for Chemin de Fer Touristique, CF Chemin de Fer, TT is Train Touristique.

Amicale Amandinoise de Modélisme ferroviaire et de CF Secondaires   AAMCS

An association with a 2.5 km 600 mm track along the river Scarpe from a point near St. Amand-les-Eaux (N) station. A branch of the association is specialising in preservation of postal vehicles. AAMCS has tried to run regular tourist services on the St. Amand–Maulde-Mortagne freight line but SNCF have not been very cooperative. A railcar and several shunters are kept safe in a local factory (Railtech) compound.

Standard gauge: diesel 3, diesel railcar 1. 600 mm gauge: 8 diesel.

Association des Autorails Touristique de l'Yonne   AATY

This association is just getting back on its feet after years of trying to win access to part of the Montargis–St. Sauveur line in the Yonne département between Paris and Dijon. Operations restarted tentatively from Toucy and it is hoped to reopen the line to St. Sauveur and even relay track to Étangs de Moutiers in future.

Autorails de Bourgogne–Franche-Comté   ABFC

Association operating tours over SNCF network with no network at present. ABFC has a project to operate trains on the Maron–Chaudeney line near Toul. Railcars are normally based at SNCF's Dijon Perrigny depot.

4 diesel railcars.

Train Touristique Livradois–Forez   AGRIVAP

Courpière–Sembadel (C). 85 km. Stock: Ambert. Nearest SNCF: Pont-de-Dore.

One of the longest tourist lines in France in a very wild and beautiful area, with potential to expand further – from Sembadel to Darsac SNCF station to the south and from Sembadel to Estivareilles to the east. AGRIVAP stands for Musée de la Machine Agricole et à Vapeur, a museum of agricultural and steam machinery at Ambert. Diesel loco CC 65005 is used for "short line" feeder freights to SNCF at Courpière. Operates diesel train Ambert to Sembadel some afternoons in July and August and Courpière to La Chaise-Dieu in Sunday and Wednesday mornings mid-July to mid-August. Steam operates Ambert–Olliergues Saturday afternoons mid-July to late August.

Steam 1, diesel 1, diesel railcars 2.

Association Provençale de Préservation Ferroviaire   APPAF
Miramas SNCF depot (SE).

An association with a large number of locos and DMUs in the old repair shop by Miramas station.

6 steam, 1 electric, 1 diesel, 5 diesel railcars.

Autorail Touristique du Minervois   ATM
Narbonne (Rue Paul Vieu)–Bize-Minervois (S). 20 km. Nearest SNCF: Narbonne (500 metres). Depot: Narbonne.

Operates Saturdays and Sundays in mid-July to mid-September.

2 diesel railcars.

CF de la Baie de Somme   CFBS
Le Crotoy–Noyelles-sur-Mer, Noyelles–St. Valéry-sur-Somme–Cayeux-sur-Mer (N). 27 km 1000 mm gauge. Nearest SNCF: Noyelles.

One of the best established preserved narrow gauge operations in France is only a short distance from the Channel ports. Steam operates daily in afternoons in July and August. Diesel to Cayeux on Saturday/Sunday mornings. Wednesdays, Saturdays, Sundays in September, Sundays to mid-October. Steam weekend at end of April.

9 steam, 5 diesel, 5 diesel railcars.

Chemin de Fer de Vendée   CFDV
Mortagne-sur-Sèvre–Les Epesses–Les Herbiers (W). 22 km. Depot: St. Laurent-sur-Sevre. Museum: Les Epesses. Nearest SNCF: Cholet.

Steam operates Friday to Sunday June to September plus Wednesdays in July and August.

Steam 2, diesel 2.

CF Forestier d'Abreschwiller   CFFA
Abreschwiller–Grand Soldat (E). 6 km 700 mm gauge. Nearest SNCF: Sarrebourg (bus).

This is a forest railway dating back to 1884 which closed in 1966. The beauty of the line was realised and a tourist service began in 1968. Operates daily on Sundays afternoons April to September, plus Saturday afternoons and Sunday mornings May to August and weekday afternoons in July and August.

4 steam, 1 diesel.

CF de Haute Auvergne   CFHA
Riom-les-Montagne–Lugarde-Marchastel (C). 16 km. Nearest SNCF: Neussargues. Stock: Riom-es-Montagne.

Part of the closed Neussargues–Bort-les-Orgues line. It is hoped that the line can reopen to Bort. Operates Thursdays, Saturdays and Sundays July, August and September.

2 diesel railcars.

CF du Lac d'Artouste   CFLA
La Sagette–Lac d'Artouste (SW). 9.5 km 500 mm gauge. Nearest SNCF: Lourdes.

Narrow gauge line with rack section to a lake, 2000 metres up in the Pyrénées. The journey to this outpost is well worthwhile. The Artouste dam dates back to the CF du Midi electrification schemes. The railway was originally built for moving construction supplies. Offers marvellous views if the weather is clear. Take warm clothing just in case! Operates daily July to September plus Saturday/Sunday in October.

14 diesel.

CF des Landes de Gascogne   CFLG
Sabres–Marquèze (SW). 4 km. Stock: Sabres. Nearest SNCF: Labouheyre.
Operates daily, serving an open air museum, June to end September. Steam on Sundays.
Steam 1, diesel 6, diesel railcar 1.

CF de St. Eutrope   CFSE
Parc de St. Eutrope (C). 2.5 km 600 mm. Nearest SNCF: Orangis Bois l'Épine.
Whilst garden railways are not documented here, this park railway is included as it has a good collection of stock and is in the Paris area. Operates Saturday and Sunday afternoons May to November. Steam on Sundays.
Steam 7, diesel 9, diesel railcars 1.

CFT Amagne-Lucquy–Challerange   CFTALC
Attigny–Challerange (N). 40.3 km. Nearest SNCF: Amagne-Lucquy. Depot: Attigny.
Operates Sundays and public holidays June-September.
4 diesel railcars.

CFT du Centre Var   CFTCV
Stock: Carnoules (SE).
This association hopes to operate on the Carnoules–Brignoles line and has acquired two "Picasso" railcars.

CFT de la Forêt de la Londe   CFTFL
Elbeuf Ville–Petit Couronne (NW). 8 km.
This operation has stopped. Stock was supposed to move to Les Ifs (TTEPC).

CFT du Haut Quercy   CFTHQ
Martel–St. Denis-près-Martel (SW). 7 km. Nearest SNCF: St. Denis-près-Martel.
Operates with diesels daily in July and August. Steam on Sundays. In September, operates only Sunday afternoon.
1 steam, 1 diesel.

CFT du Mont des Avaloirs   CFTMA
Alençon–Pré-en-Pail (W).
Operations suspended. Stock transferred to CFTA at Carhaix for sale.

CFT Mouzon–Stenay   CFTMS
Mouzon–Stenay (N). 22 km. Nearest SNCF: Sedan.
Operates Sundays and public holidays June-September.
Stock from CFTALC.

CFT de Pontarlier–Vallorbe   CFTPV

Les Hôpitaux Neufs–Fontaine Ronde (E). 7.5 km. Nearest SNCF: Pontarlier.

The first part of the projected reconstruction of the 23 km Pontarlier–Vallorbe (Switzerland) line. Operates Sundays June to September plus Wednesdays and Saturdays in July and August. Steam operation only occasional.

Steam 1, diesel 4, diesel railcar 1.

CFT du Rhin   CFTR

Volgelsheim–Sans Soucis (NE). 9 km. Nearest SNCF: Colmar.

Tourist operation over a freight line serving the Rhein port. Near the beautiful town of Colmar. Steam operates afternoons on Saturday/Sunday June to September.

Steam 3, diesel 6.

CFT de la Seudre   CFTS

Saujon (SNCF)–La Tremblade (W). 21 km.

Operates Wednesdays and Sundays in July and August plus Fridays in August and the first two Sundays in September.

1 steam, 1 diesel, 1 diesel railcar.

CFT du Tarn   CFTT

St. Lieux-lès-Lavaur–Les Martels (SW). 3.5 km 500 mm gauge. Nearest SNCF: St. Sulpice.

A small railway north-east of Toulouse. Operates Saturday and Sunday afternoons and Mondays from mid-July to the end of August then Sundays in September and October.

3 steam, 8 diesel.

CFT de la Traconne   CFTLT

Esternay–Sézanne (C). 15 km. Stock: Esternay. Nearest SNCF: La Ferté-Gaucher.

Tourist operations on freight line run by CFTA. Operates Sunday afternoons May to mid-October, plus mornings on first Sunday of each month..

2 diesel, 1 diesel railcar.

CFT du Vermandois   CFTV

St. Quentin (SNCF)–Origny–Ste.-Benoîte (N). 22.5 km. Depot: St. Quentin.

Operates steam and diesel trains on Sundays and public holidays in summer.

2 steam, 3 diesel railcars.

CFT de la Vallée de l'Aa   CFTVA

Arques–Lumbres (N). 15 km. Depot: Arques. Nearest SNCF: St. Omer.

A recent operation over the St. Omer–Lumbres freight line, otherwise used for SNCF cement traffic. Close to Calais with several other tourist attractions nearby, including V2 launch site! CFTVA has Polish 2-10-0 Ty52 6690 which it hopes to run in 2000. Operates Saturdays and Sundays July to September.

1 steam, 2 diesel railcars.

CFT de la Vallée de la Doller CFTVD

Cernay–Sentheim (E). 14 km. Nearest SNCF: Cernay. Depot: Burnhaupt.

Runs from Cernay St. André, not SNCF station. Operates Sundays June to September. Daily except Monday and Tuesday in July and August.

Steam 1, 4 diesel, 4 diesel railcars.

CF du Vivarais CFV

Tournon–Lamastre (SE). 33 km, metre gauge. Nearest SNCF: Tain l'Hermitage (across river Rhône). Depot: Lamastre.

Once part of a much larger system. Extremely scenic and now one of the best known, most active French operations. Operates Saturdays and Sundays mid-March to October, daily except Monday in May, June and September and daily July and August.

7 steam, 2 diesel, 4 diesel railcars.

CF de la Vallée de la Canner CFVC

Vigy–Hombourg–Budange (E). 12 km. Stock: Vigy. Nearest SNCF: Hombourg.

Operates on Sundays July to September from Vigy. Operation started in 1985 after the line closed to freight in 1976.

1 steam, 1 diesel, 1 diesel railcar.

CF de la Vallée de l'Eure CFVE

Pacy-sur-Eure–Breuilpont et Cocherel (N). 16 km. Nearest SNCF: Bueil. Depot: Pacy-sur-Eure.

Operates trains on Sunday afternoons from June to the end of October.

3 diesel, 1 diesel railcar.

CFT de la Vallée de l'Ouche CFVO

Bligny-sur-Ouche–Pont d'Ouche (SE). 5 km, 600 mm gauge. Nearest SNCF Beaune.

Operates Sundays mid-April to early October and daily in July and August.

2 steam, 4 diesel.

CF de la Provence CP

Puget-Théniers–Annot (SE). 20 km, metre gauge. Nearest SNCF: Nice. Depot: Puget-Théniers.

Steam trains, the "Train des Pignes" on this part of the Nice–Digne line on certain Sundays between May and October.

Musée Français du Chemin de Fer MCF

Nearest SNCF: Mulhouse Musée.

France's national rail museum is situated at Mulhouse, near the Swiss and German borders, and close to Basel. This is a superb collection of railwayana, including around 50 locomotives. Open daily except 25th/26th December and 1st January.

Steam 36, diesel 3, electric 7, EMU 9, DMU 6.

Musée des CF de Longueville
Longueville (C).

AJECTA has taken over the old SNCF roundhouse here for use as a museum and workshop. The biggest collection of steam in Franceoutside the Mulhouse museum. Open to public Monday-Friday in July and August. Operational steam to Provins over the weekend of "Historic Monuments" in mid-September. Other specials throughout the year, particularly with 140 C 231.

Steam 9, diesel 3, diesel railcars 1.

Musée de la Mine de Petite Rosselle   MMPR
Petite Rosselle–Puits Simon (E). 8 km. Nearest SNCF: Forbach.

A mining museum with a short line and some stock. Open daily in the afternoon July to mid-October.

2 steam, 20 diesel, 2 diesel railcars.

Musée des Transports de Pithiviers   MTP
Pithiviers–Bellébat (C). 4 km 600 mm gauge. Depot: Pithiviers. Nearest SNCF: Malesherbes.

This system was once part of a large sugar beet carrying network. The line is noteworthy for being the first preserved railway in France with operations starting in 1966. Operates with diesel Friday and Saturday afternoons plus steam on Sunday afternoons May to October. In September steam operates Thursday and Sunday afternoons. In October, Sunday afternoons only.

13 steam, 2 diesel, 2 diesel railcars.

Musée de Transports de la Vallée du Sausseron   MTVS
Valmondois–Butry. 1 km 1000 mm. Nearest SNCF: Valmondois.

A short line attached to a transport museum, operating Saturdays and Sundays May to November with steam on the first and third Sundays of each month.

Steam 7, diesel 4.

Petit Train de la Haute Somme   PTHS
Froissy–Cappy–Dompierre. 7 km 600 mm gauge. Nearest SNCF: Albert. Depot: Froissy.

The remains of a network serving the Front during WW1. The biggest collection of 600 mm gauge locos in France. Operates daily except Mondays and Thursdays in July and August. Sundays in September.

9 steam, 10 diesel.

Quercyrail
Cahors–Cahors–Capdenac (SW). 71 km. Stock: Cahors. Nearest SNCF: Cahors and Capdenac.

Operates charters along valley of river Lot in July and August, Sundays only in September and October.

1 diesel, 3 diesel railcars.

Rive Bleue Express
Evian-les-Bains–Le Bouveret (Switzerland). 20 km. Stock: Le Bouveret. Nearest SNCF: Evian

An international line along the southern shore of Lac Léman (lake Geneva). Diesel trains on Tuesday mornings and Saturdays; steam (Swiss loco) or diesel (SNCF BB 71010) on Sundays. Return can be made by boat.

Steam 1, diesel 1.

Tacot des Lacs

Bourron Port-au-Sable–La Plaine (C). 2.5 km 600 mm gauge. Nearest SNCF: Nemours.

A bit more than a garden railway. The line operates Saturday/Sunday afternoons, with steam on Sundays, June–November.

5 steam, 3 diesel.

CFT de la Sarthe   TRANSVAP

Connerré-Beillé–Bonnetable (C). 17.8 km. Nearest SNCF: Connerré.

Operates Sundays from July to August.

Steam 2, 1 diesel, 3 diesel railcars.

TT de l'Ardèche Méridionale   TTAM

Vogüé–St. Jean (SE). 14 km. Nearest SNCF: Montélimar.

The remains of the Le Teil–Aubenas line. Runs daily except Saturday in July and August and Sundays until the end of September.

1 diesel railcar.

TT du Cotentin   TTC

Carteret–Port Bail (W). 10 km. Nearest SNCF: Carentan.

Operates Thursdays and Sundays from Carteret and Tuesdays from Port Bail in July and August, Sundays to mid-September. The Carentan–Baupte section of this line has been abandoned.

1 diesel, 1 diesel railcar.

TT Etretat–Pays de Caux   TTEPC

Etretat–Les Loges (W). 6 km. Nearest SNCF: Les Ifs. Stock: Les Ifs.

A nascent operation in a very pleasant coastal area. Much stock recovered from abortive operations from Caen and Elbeuf. Les Ifs station also houses a future museum dedicated to Wagons Lits. Operates daily afternoons July to mid-September and Saturday/Sunday afternoons all year.

Diesel 1, diesel railcar 1.

TT Guîtres–Marcenais   TTGM

Guîtres–Marcenais (SW). 15 km. Depot: Guîtres. Nearest SNCF: Coutras (5 km).

Operates steam on Sunday afternoons May to October plus Saturdays mid July to mid August. Extra diesel workings take place on Tuesdays and Thursdays from mid July to mid August.

Steam 3, diesel 1, diesel railcars 2.

TT de Languedoc-Méditerranée   TTLM

Bédarieux–Hérépian (S). 7 km. Stock: Bédarieux. Nearest SNCF: Bédarieux.

This operation has been hampered by SNCF demanding a fortune for track access. The eventual aim is to operate from Bédarieux to Lamalou-les-Bains and Mons-la-Trivalle. It is hoped to operate on Saturdays and Sundays April to November, plus Fridays in June and September and daily except Mondays July and August.

1 diesel, 1 diesel railcar.

Train Touristique de la de Blaise et du Der   TTBD

Eclaron-Braucourt–Wassy–Doulevant-le-Château (E). 38 km. Stock: Wassy. Nearest SNCF: St. Dizier.

Tourist operation close to France's largest lake, the Lac du Der-Chantecoq. Railway also operates "short line" freight to St. Dizier. Operates on Sundays at 15.00 from Wassy in July and August, to Eclaron the first and second Sunday of the month, to Doulevant the other days.

2 diesels, 1 diesel railcar.

TT de la Vallée du Loir   TTVL

Thoré–La Rochette–Trôo (C). 18 km. Nearest SNCF: Vendôme.

Operates Saturday and Sunday afternoons in July and August plus Sunday mornings from mid July.

1 diesel railcar.

Train à Vapeur des Cévennes   TVC

Anduze–St. Jean du Gard (S). 13.2 km. Depot: Anduze.

Operates steam and diesel trains daily in July and August plus Tuesday to Thursdays, Saturdays and Sundays in September. Uses traction from CITEV. For steam, avoid Mondays and Saturdays! Buses run on weekdays from Alès and Nîmes. Close to the famous Pont du Gard.

1 steam, 1 diesel, 4 diesel railcars.

Train à Vapeur des Monts du Lyonnais   TVML

L'Arbresle–Sainte Foy l'Argentière (SE). 20 km. Depot. Sainte Foy. Nearest SNCF: L'Arbresle.

Steam operation every Sunday July to September. Uses an SNCF branch serving a quarry at Sainte Foy.

Steam 1, diesel 3.

Train à Vapeur de Touraine   TVT

Chinon–Richelieu (C). 20 km. Depot: Richelieu. Nearest SNCF: Chinon.

Operates daily mid-May to late-September.

2 steam, 1 diesel.

Voies Ferrées du Velay   VFV

Tence–Dunières Ville (SE). 17 km 1000 mm gauge. Nearest SNCF: Firminy.

Part of the old Vivarais system (see CFV) whose operation had been suspended for several years. Hopefully the line will reopen to St. Agrève (37 km) some day and steam traction will be restored. Operates from Tence Wednesdays, Saturdays and Sundays in July and August plus Sundays from Dunières in September.

2 diesels, 1 diesel railcar.

ADDITIONAL ABBREVIATIONS

AAATV Amicale des Amis et Anciens de la Traction Vapeur.
AJECTA Association des Jeunes pour l'Exploitation et la Conservation des Trains d'Autrefois.
CFV3V Chemin de Fer à Vapeur des Trois Vallées, Mariembourg, Belgium.
CFTLP CFT Limousin Perigord (141 TD 740 runs only on SNCF lines)
CITEV Compagnie Internationale des Trains Express à Vapeur.
FACS Fédération des Amis des Chemins de Fer Secondaires.
MCF Musée National du Chemin de Fer.
TMMB Train Musée Morvan Bazois.

BUILDERS

The following builder codes are used in this publication:
(All are in France unless stated otherwise).

Adtranz	ABB/Daimler Benz Transport, Zürich and Berlin.
ANF	Ateliers du Nord de la France, Blanc Misseron. Now Bombardier.
Alsthom	Société Générale de Constructions Electriques et Mécaniques Alsthom.
Alstom	Alstom, Belfort and Aytré, France.
Arbel Fauvet Rail	Arbel Fauvet Rail, Lille.
Baldwin	Baldwin Locomotive Works, Philadelphia, Pennsylvania, USA.
BDR	Etablissements Baudet-Donon-Roussel.
Billard	Anciens Établissements Billard & Cie., Tours.
Brissonneau & Lotz	SA des Établissements Brissonneau & Lotz, Aytré. Also known as B&L.
Brown Boveri	Brown Boveri, Baden, Switzerland.
CAFL	Compagnie des Ateliers et Forges de la Loire, St. Chamond. Later Creusot-Loire.
CEM	Compagnie Electro-Mécanique, Le Havre, Le Bourget & Nancy.
CFD	(Compagnie de) Chemins de Fer Départementaux.
CGC	Compagnie Générale de Constructions Batignolles, Paris, Châtillon & Nantes.
CIMT	Compagnie Industrielle de Matériel de Transport, Marly les Valenciennes. Now Alstom.
Carde & Cie	Carde & Compagnie, Bordeaux.
Carel & Fouché	Établissements Carel & Fouché SA, Le Mans.
Creusot-Loire	Formerly SFAC and CAFL.
De Dietrich	De Dietrich & Cie., Reichshoffen. Now Alstom.
De Dion	Société des Automobiles De Dion, Puteaux, Paris.
Decauville	Société Nouvelle Decauville-Aîné, Corbeil.
Études	Société d'Études pour l'Electrification des Chemins de Fer.
Fauvet Girel	Établissements Fauvet-Girel, Suresnes, Arras & Lille.
Fives-Lille	Compagnie de Fives-Lille pour Constructions Mécaniques et Entreprises, Fives, Lille.
Franco-Belge	Société Franco-Belge de Matériel de Chemin de Fer, Raismes. Now Alstom.
Francorail-MTE	Consortium of Carel et Fouché, Creusot-Loire, De Dietrich, Jeumont-Schneider and MTE.
GEC-Alsthom	GEC-Alsthom, Belfort and Aytré, France. Now Alstom.
Henschel	Henschel Werke AG, Kassel, Germany.
Jeumont	Société des Forges et Ateliers de Constructions Électriques de Jeumont.
LHB	Linke-Hoffmann-Busch, Salzgitter, Germany. Now Alstom.
Lilloise	Société Lilloise de Matériel de Chemins de Fer, Aulnay-sous-Bois.
MTE	Le Matériel de Traction Électrique. Formed from SFAC, Jeumont and SW.
Moyse	Établissements Gaston Moyse, La Courneuve.
Oerlikon	Société Oerlikon, Switzerland.
Renault	Regie Nationale des Usines Renault, Billancourt.
SACM	Société Alsacienne de Constructions Mécaniques, Mulhouse.
SEMT	Société d'Études de Moteurs Thermiques-Pielstick, St. Denis. Now Alstom.
SLM	Schweizerische Lokomotiv- und Maschinenfabrik, Winterthur, Switzerland.
Saurer	Adolf Saurer, Arbon, Switzerland.
Schneider	Société des Forges et Ateliers du Creusot, Usines Schneider, Le Creusot.
SFAC	As Schneider, renamed in 1949.
Siemens	Siemens AG, Berlin, Nürnberg & Erlangen, Germany.
Socofer	Société de Construction Ferroviare, Tours.
Soulé	Soulé Fer et Froide, Bagnères de Bigorre. Now CFD.
Sprague-Thomson	Société Parisienne de Matériel Roulant, Paris.
Sécheron	SA des Ateliers de Sécheron, Genève, Switzerland.
SW	Schneider-Westinghouse.
SWS	Schweizerische Wagons und Aufzügefabrik AG, Schlieren.
TCO	Société Traction CEM-Oerlikon.
Vevey	Ateliers de Constructions Mécaniques SA, Vevey, Switzerland.

ROVER TICKETS

The Eurodomino (ED) Pass was revamped from 1st April 1999. The 3-, 5- and 10-day passes have been replaced by a basic 3 day pass with an option to purchase up to 5 additional days travel (all over a period of one month) at a set incremental price increase. This system is being applied in continental Europe but in the UK Rail Europe has priced all passes from £19 with £10 increments. Additional days can cost *nothing at all*, £10 or £20!! The strong pound means it may be cheaper to buy ED outside the UK.

The ED pass is valid for unlimited rail travel on services operated by SNCF. Youth passes are not available for first class travel. Child fares cost 50% of the appropriate adult fare rounded up to the nearest pound. Tickets may be used on overnight journeys commencing after 19.00 on the day before first day of validity. Nationals cannot purchase tickets for use in their own country, except where they are normally resident abroad (and have been so for a minimum of 6 months).

Prices which are **higher** than a local equivalent ticket are shown in bold. Readers should note this situation may change if Sterling falls significantly in value. TGV, Talgo and EC supplements are all included in the pass price. Seat reservations, sleeper and couchette berths are not included.

Type	Adult 1st	Adult 2nd	Youth 2nd
3 days in a month	**£179**	£119	£99
8 days in a month	**£339**	**£239**	**£189**

France Vacances Pass. Unlimited travel on the whole of the SNCF network plus discounts on car hire, accommodation and tourist attractions. Reservations not included. Tickets are available only at the following SNCF stations: Marseille St. Charles (Billets Internationaux), Nice (Bureau Information), Roissy and Orly Airports, Paris Gare du Nord (Bureau Information), Paris Gare St. Lazare (Bureau Information), Paris Gare du Lyon (Guichets Internationaux). (NB: The same stations are also the only outlets for Eurodomino in France).

Prices: 1st Class 4/15 – FRF 1504; 2nd Class 4/15 – FRF 1312; 1st Class 9/M – FRF 2464; 2nd Class 9/M – FRF 2272.

Paris Visite. Unlimited 2nd Class travel on SNCF trains, RATP metros, buses & trams, RER , and APTR & ADATRIF buses within multiple zones of the Greater Paris region. Also discounts at 14 tourist attractions. Children (4-11) 50% reduction.

Prices (in FRF):	1 day	2 days	3 days	5 days
Zones 1–3	55	90	120	175
Zones 1–5	110	175	245	300
Zones 1–8	155	225	280	350

Mobilis. One day unlimited 2nd Class travel within eight zones. Maximum area as listed above for *Paris Visite*. Not valid to Charles-de-Gaulle Airport. Card number must be written on magnetic strip ticket and name on card. Prices range from Zones 1–2 – FRF 30, to Zones 1–8 – FRF 110.

Regional Passes

SNCF and regional governments have expanded the range of passes, most of which are only available at weekends in the summer months. Valid in 2nd Class on TER, TGR and Grandes lignes rail services and buses. Not valid on TGV. See local leaflets for information.

Aquitaine Temps Libre. 48 hours unlimited travel for groups of 2–5 persons around Bordeaux as far as Hendaye, Pau, Mont-de-Marsan, Arcachon, St. Nicolas-St. Romain, Sarlat, Brive, Bussière-Galant, Angoulême, St. Mariens-St. Yzan and Le Verdon. Validity now runs all year – from 00.01 Saturday to 23.59 Sunday – but is available on any two consecutive days in July and August. Price: FRF 200.

Bourgogne Liberté. Unlimited 2nd Class travel 00.01 Saturday–18.00 Sunday in an area centred upon Dijon, Macon and Nevers, extending to Villeneuve-la-Guyard, Is-sur-Tille, Auxonne, Dommartin-les-Cuiseaux, Romanèche-Thorins, Chauffailles, Moulins-sur-Allier, Chantenay-St. Imbert, Saincaize, Cosne and Neuvy-sur-Loire. Available throughout the year. This ticket may be extended to 3 or 4 days validity in May if the 1st and 8th May public holidays fall on Friday or Monday, from Ascension Thursday to Sunday and from Saturday to Whit Monday. Price (1998): FRF 100 .

Pass Bretagne. One day unlimited travel on Saturdays in July and August in the area west of St. Malo, Dol, Fougères, Vitré, Rennes, Châteaubriant, Redon and Vannes. Price: FRF 50.

Carte Isabella. Unlimited travel in July, August and September for 24 hours over the SNCF lines Théoule-sur-Mer–Ventimiglia (Italy) and Nice–Tende. Price: FRF 60.

Pass Lorraine. One day unlimited travel travel in an area centred on Metz and Nancy, extending to Montmédy, Longwy, Thionville, Apach, Forbach, Sarreguemines, Lutzelbourg, Saales, Remiremont, Bains-les-Bains, Damblain, Neufchâteau, Revigny and Clermont-en-Argonne. Available Saturdays, Sundays & public holidays in July, August and December only. Price: FRF 50.

Passbask. One day unlimited travel (plus until 14.00 on the following day) on the SNCF line from Bayonne to Hendaye and ET/FV metre gauge line from Hendaye to Donostia-San Sebastian. Available daily late May to late September. Price: FRF 60/ESP 1500.

Note: All prices shown are as at 1999. For regular news about tickets and prices see "Today's Railways".